Ethics for Zombies

The Predigested Brains of History's Great Moral Thinkers

Dr. Ryan M. Lozano

Table of Contents

Chapter 1: Why?

Why Study Ethics?

Why take an Ethics class? Well, generally because you're required to by someone higher on your particular academic food chain. If you didn't have to, let's face it – you probably wouldn't, and likewise probably wouldn't feel one iota academically poorer for its omission in your already too-busy schedule.

Why write an Ethics text? That's a bit trickier. There's certainly no shortage of Ethics textbooks out there – some good, many bad, almost all dry as the Mojave. So in my case, I'm writing a book the same way I approach teaching my class – I teach as I'd want to be taught, and will write as I'd want to read. This isn't to say my attempt will be entirely without faults, but it will certainly be somewhat shorter on boredom and a bit longer on practical, real-life explanation and application.

This text is a bit different because I'm not going to be including primary source documents. We won't be reading Plato, Kant, Rawls, or any of the rest, but we'll discuss them all in detail – skipping to "the good parts" as often and as best we can, and getting to the meat of what each of them felt compelled to convey to us, as directly and painlessly as possible. In my experience teaching, I think we very often lose something when we try to read the original texts. This is certainly not to say that they're without value – far from it! But when we need to understand Ethics sooner rather than later, whether in the course of a short semester, before the big meeting, or whatever the situation may be or may call for, then it simply won't do to try to read all the "classics" and puzzle through their meaning(s). It is my hope that reading this book will encourage you to read those books – later, when you have time to really read them closely and carefully, ideally in context, with plenty of reference materials close at hand to understand them as they were intended. Don't give up on the old philosophers entirely – just adjust how you approach them.

I'm going to begin as I begin my classes, with an explanation of what Philosophy isn't (and only then what it is), followed by the sorts of questions philosophers ask, attempt to address where Ethics and Moral Philosophy (interchangeable terms for our purposes) fit in, and then finally answer the burning question – how, exactly, will you apply Ethics to your real life, i.e., your degree, your job, your life outside this funny little environment we call the classroom, or in this case, the text.

Actually, that's not entirely true; if I waited to tell you how you'll use this, you'd never make it that far. We're simply not interested in learning what we know perfectly well we'll probably never use, and rightly so. At the time I'm writing this, I'm in my mid-thirties, have a handful of graduate degrees under my belt, teach full-time on the faculty of an American college, and I have never had to call into use half of the things I was taught in college. I have never once, for instance, used college algebra in my professional life (and not in my personal life, either, that I can recall); I still have no idea why my English professor thought I needed to read *Beowulf*. Don't get me wrong – I enjoyed it immensely (yes – I'm one of *those* people), but I still have no earthly idea how having read it prepared me for a life lived in the real world.[1]

So back to the BIG question (the first of a handful we'll encounter) – **WHY SHOULD EVERYONE STUDY ETHICS?** It's quite simple – Ethics is the one thing just about every conscious, semi-socialized adult can't possibly avoid encountering on a daily basis. You will be faced with ethical challenges every single day, possibly every hour or more if you work in certain fields - healthcare and law enforcement come quickly to mind; I'd say business and politics too, but we all already know there's no Ethics needed or wanted there. Seriously though, while you may be able to avoid all that yucky math you had crammed down your academic throat, along with the characters and their attendant motivations and plot points that you learned for the Literature exam then promptly forgot, you simply can't avoid Ethics – even if you try.

But wait – are you saying that I need to study Ethics so I can be (or become) an ethical person? No – not at all. Chances are, you're already an ethical person – when faced with an ethical quandary of some sort or other, you probably (hopefully?) already do the right thing. Ethics isn't designed or intended to turn unethical people around;[2] it's designed to help us understand and articulate intelligently WHY we do the right thing already. Stay with me – a short quiz will follow when we get to questions of value in a few pages...

---

[1] (*spoiler alert*) Although come on – how many of us, reading Beowulf, didn't reach the denouement and say (if only to ourselves), "Holy @#$%, you mean to tell me that Hrothgar was Grendel's father?! Whoa!" But I digress...

[2] Though we're sending copies of this text to congress and major media organizations, just in case.

Chapter 2: What is this Philosophy of which you speak?

Philosophy – What it is, and what it isn't.

Getting back to Philosophy in general, many (too many) never experience it at all, or have a lousy experience of it, and then shy away from it. Many students I've asked over the years, when they're asked to think about "Philosophy," actually have a notion closer to a parody of the real thing, and it's no wonder they're either intimidated by it or would choose to avoid it all together.

Philosophers have a tendency, just like professionals in any other field, to speak in jargon, assume you've read what they've read (or at least skimmed it for the high points), are up on the latest developments in the many fields that comprise the discipline, or have simply fallen lost sight of real life from the dizzying heights of their particular ivory tower. Because of these, we sometimes come across as pretentious, and our work as pretentiously obscure. What we say, write, etc., can seem unintelligible to the uninitiated, and sometimes, even our best efforts to parse philosophical concepts in layman's terms can seem cryptic at best. We're not trying to be difficult; we're just dealing with "heavy" stuff on a daily basis, and sometimes forget that not everyone else does too.

In fact, Philosophy *can* be a very practical matter, regardless of how "deep" some aspects of it may seem at first glance. Don't get me wrong – some parts of what we're going to cover are, in their original form, as dry and dusty as one could possibly hope to avoid. Others, on quite the other hand, you could sit down with a glass of your favorite whatever, and practically read (and even enjoy!) as literature. I consider it my job not to "dumb it down" for my students or my readers, but rather, to open up the texts in such a way that we're able to look at the arguments in their most direct form.

The other potential pitfall lurks on the opposite extreme – simplifying Philosophy to the point where it is no longer thought-provoking, but merely cute or witty; aphoristic bumper sticker, t-shirt, and fortune cookie slogans that may make us smile, but rarely make us think.[3] Social media may be partially to blame for this time, and certainly this is where most of the offenses take place today, but it's certainly easily corrected by taking a look at what real Philosophy (including Ethics – we haven't lost track of that) is commonly mistaken for, versus what it actually is, or rather, what it ought to be if we hope to benefit from it.

I find the best way to approach figuring out what Philosophy is (for our purposes, at any rate) is to identify precisely what it is most certainly not, and work backwards from there. Contrary to what daytime television and television news media, Philosophy (as we intend it) is neither our motivated personal mission statement-based outlook on life, nor our generalized worldview (or, if you want to be trendy, "zeitgeist."). It's also not the meaning

---

[3] With the possible exception of, "Did Adam and Eve have belly buttons?" That one could very quickly take you down a number of assorted-sized rabbit holes, theological, philosophical, physiological, and otherwise…

of life,[4] nor the search for the meaning of life, though our time would perhaps be more profitably spent reading Douglas Adams or watching Monty Python than pondering this option as an outlet for our inquiry.

Philosophy isn't just skepticism, either, though it's easy to see how it is often viewed that way. My son (at the time of this writing) is three years old and has already been a philosopher for about 18 months now. In fact, everyone in the world becomes a philosopher at around the same age, when they learn that fundamental question; "why?" Those of us who choose to pursue it professionally simply never grow out of it. For philosophical purposes, skepticism means doubt of a radical sort, and has a grand tradition associated with it, going all the way back to Socrates, and his battles in Plato's dialogues to defeat it, alongside sophistry. The version most of us are more familiar with though is that of Descartes.

You know Descartes; whether or not you realize you do or not, you do. He's the "I think, therefore I am" guy. Or, in modern parlance, and as more commonly seen, again, on bumper stickers, t-shirts, and in "tweets," "I _____, therefore, I am," with your choice of golf, fish, BBQ, etc. to fill in the blank you feel best defines your personal raison d'etre. Anyway, here's how he arrived at that (briefly). Descartes starts out with a position of radical doubt – specifically, he doubts that anything at all exists, even himself. But wait a moment; doubting is a sort of thinking. And for there to be thinking taking place, there must be a thing that thinks. He seems to be that thinking thing, so he reasons that he thinks, therefore he exists, or, as we're more accustomed to seeing it, "I think, therefore I am."[5] Isn't that nifty?

Back to what Philosophy is not, it's not a collection of beliefs, no matter how systematic. For instance, a religion, particularly Eastern religions may represent a philosophy of sorts, but does not encompass Philosophy in its entirety. Philosophy is likewise no longer an inquiry in general, as it was in the bygone days when a chemist might refer to himself with no small amount of boasting, as being a "natural philosopher."[6] Likewise, Philosophy isn't simply a history of great ideas, though I admittedly approach it that way in teaching my introductory course. So, if we've exhausted some of the more prevalent and burdensome possibilities for what Philosophy decidedly is not, then how should we approach what it is? I'm not going to answer that – not directly, anyway. Instead, I'd like to go over a few questions – these are the questions that everyone asks, but philosophers ask them in some rather unique ways, and add an extra level of questioning that isn't frequently seen anywhere else. As we go along, thing of each of these categories of questioning as a rung on a ladder – we're climbing as we go, going from fairly basic to reasonably complex. Or, if you prefer, from the level of questioning we have access to as fairly young children to the level

---

[4] 42.

[5] In the arguably more impressive original Latin, "Cogito, ergo sum" – hence, this is sometimes referred to simply (or snootily) as "the cogito."

[6] At least until 1861 or so, when Hegel (a philosopher) finally irritated von Helmholtz (a chemist) sufficiently to make the rest of the scientific community abandon us forever – even in their appellations!

of questioning that we are unlikely to encounter (or have cause to encounter) reflectively prior to our undergraduate education, or sometimes even later or never at all…

Questions Philosophers Ask.

We start asking factual questions at a really young age – *really* young – toddler young. "Why?" and it's best known conspirators, "who," "where," and "what" are asked early and often; "how" will come a bit later, since I know you're wondering. We are, for all intents and purposes, fact-gathering machines of the highest order – we have constantly got factual data streaming into our heads, from all our senses, and our brains then conveniently package it, not only in terms of what is the case in the world, but, perhaps more importantly, what is our particular relation to what is the case in the world. The example I most frequently give in my classes is that of the cheetah. We've all seen them on TV, or in books, or at the zoo, and most folks, from a very young age, well into adulthood, know that they're the fastest animal. What's more, we know that they're faster than *you*. If the cheetah and I find ourselves out on the savannah, and it's hungry, I'm simply not going home that day, because I don't run unless there's a buffet. I have just established 1) a fact about the world in which I live, and 2) the importance of that fact in my life, with regard to my relation to it.

Frequently, these facts are operating entirely independent of our awareness or ignorance of them – for instance, gravity. We may know, on some unconscious level, that when we fall, we do so at the rate of thirty-two feet per second per second, but we're not constantly aware of it, absent an obsessive fixation with such things (which I can't recommend). More frequently encountered in our day-to-day lives are the "facts" (though we may not identify them as such) of our schedule or our interpersonal commitments. As before, these function the same in all instances – we establish what is or is not the case, we determine its relevance to us, and we act accordingly, without ever giving it a second thought. And it's no wonder – we've been doing it non-stop since we were barely over a year old!

To our continual fact collecting we then introduce valuation in the form of on-the-spot or sometimes ongoing appraisal and evaluation of what to do in a given situation, given the facts that we've established, and, in many cases by extension, how we feel others ought to act in the same or a similar situation. Sometimes this occurs reflectively, and sometimes, predictively, or, what should we do in light of what *has* occurred, and what should we do in light of what *may* occur. Beyond this, questions of value help us determine things on a wide gradation – from a species level, to a national level, to a corporate level, to a personal level. Sometimes it may involve setting a national policy (think any and every contentious[7] issue ever discussed by political parties), or it could simply be a discussion carried on with ourselves, concerning, for instance, whether or not we should tell the truth or a lie in a given situation when it might be to our cost or advantage to do one or the other.

---

[7] To borrow a bit from the late George Carlin, a contentious issue is anything that people are generally "bored with, tired of, or pissed at," in other words, anything that can be argued about could be considered contentious to one or more parties.

Questions of value are also where we tend to get angriest when discussing (or debating) Ethics. It is here that we find the most variation on personal opinion, belief, education, and stance on issues that are unavoidably the bailiwick of the ethicist, and in turn, give us the most to argue about. In other words, it is practically impossible to discuss questions of value on some level without someone's feelings getting hurt, their moral outrage triggered, or their religious beliefs questioned, not to mention any of the hundred or more other things that could potentially upset them. To illustrate this, I generally point to the issue of abortion, and for our purposes, I will take the extreme positions of the issue as most illustrative of how quickly and easily people can be offended, realizing, of course, that most people fall somewhere in the middle, and very few on either end of the spectrum with regard to this particularly divisive issue.

Abortion is technically defined, in the practice of medicine, as the premature exit of the products of conception (the fetus, fetal membranes, and placenta) from the uterus. It is the loss of a pregnancy and does not refer to why that pregnancy was lost, which, for purposes of ethically discussing a contentious issue, we will quite obviously assume was not spontaneous (i.e., a miscarriage), but the result of direct medical intervention with the intention of causing the loss of that pregnancy. Now, how ought we to look at this in order to form an ethical opinion of 1) the moral consequence (if any) of what has been done to this point in time, and 2) what ideally ought to be done moving forward. On the one hand, abortion is seen by some as being inherently evil, a violation of God's creation, and wrong regardless of circumstances. On the other, it is quite simply the surgical excision of unwanted tissue, not unlike having a mole removed or a wart burned off. See what just happened there? Everyone who applauded the first explanation was appalled by the second, and quite possibly vice-versa. It's little wonder then that the ethical outcry associated with establishing national (let alone personal) policies based in Ethics is not only so difficult at the outset, but further, difficult to validate without upsetting and alienating at least one person, and much more often, several people.

How can we know for sure that you're already ethical, except perhaps for not (yet) having an academic explanation for your ethical behavior? Well, let's administer a quick pop quiz and see where you fall:

You're walking on your way to class, already late, and right in front of you, a little old lady with a walker falls right over into the path of oncoming traffic. You are on the scene right away, and undeniably in a position to help. So, do you:

A) Help her up, dust her off, and get her on her way – maybe even walking her to her destination to assure her safety.
B) Step gingerly over her, and continue on your way, maybe even a bit perturbed that you were momentarily delayed.
C) Step gingerly over her, then turn, snatch her walker, and make your way to the nearest pawn shop, perhaps to buy your text for class.

Now, unless you're a sociopath or a jerk, you probably chose "A," even though it might momentarily inconvenience you. The question to then be addressed is, "Why?" You may have never encountered this situation, or even one substantively like it, ever before, so how did you know how to behave? That's precisely what we're going to aim to find out as we make our way through the centuries and the theories of work in Ethics. Again – we're already (hopefully) all ethical, but explaining the why can be difficult to articulate, especially to others, without quite a bit of background in the history, development, and rationale behind ethical thinking. Our work in asking and responding to questions of value will assist us greatly in figuring this out.

Backing away a safe distance from contention, we encounter the third level of questioning, and for many people, the final destination on their analysis of their world – questions of explanation. Once we have identified the facts of the matter, our proper relationship to them, and evaluated them appropriately, we can connect these prerequisite steps into coherent bundles in an attempt to understand them at a deeper level – either causal,[8] functional, or teleological. We'll be working quite a bit with both causality and teleological (goal-oriented) thought when we get to Aristotle, but for now, suffice to say that this is the level of thinking and questioning when and where we begin to put the pieces together in a manner in which we not only understand, but we can also explain to others.

For instance, when I leave my office or classroom, and need to go downstairs but feel too lazy to take the stairs to get there, I can travel by elevator, but how? When I press the little button, is the little troll who lives in the wall by extension pressed into service and inclined to scurry up the cables and pull me to my destination, or might there be some sort of hydraulic system in place? Obviously, this is an over-simplified take on things, but it illustrates our though process fairly accurately with regard to how we package information, and, perhaps more importantly, how we explain it to others, both to demonstrate our understanding and instruct them.

The final sort of questions we ask in Philosophy, those which are more or less exclusive to the discipline, are not really questions in the same sense as before, but rather lines of inquiry unto themselves. These are the so-called "meta-questions." Meta is simply the Greek prefix that implies something is after, adjacent to, or transcends the concept that it precedes; so in this case, a meta question is quite literally a question about the question itself. We won't be encountering this directly until we discuss Nietzsche several chapters from now, but this level of questioning will be lurking in the background or implied in nearly every philosopher we encounter. This will be the level of questioning through which we're able to trace our understanding of the words we employ when asking questions involving the three preceding, lower orders, and also the means by which we attempt to assess our own conceptual equipment and its adequacy for understanding concepts.

In Ethics, the most frequent encounters with meta-questions involve the meanings of descriptive words we employ to assess and make assertions about moral behavior, such as good, bad, better, worse, evil, and the like. Without giving spoilers for too much of our discussion of Nietzsche, consider for a moment the following hypothetical example. A

---

[8] Note this is "causal," *not* "casual." As in causal Friday, since I think we should have at least one day a week when everything happens for a reason ☺

spaceship lands, an alien visitor steps out, and you have been tasked with explaining some basic ethical concepts to him, working under the reasonable assumption that he already understands basic English, and has a working vocabulary similar to your own (a stretch, I know, but bear with me here); how would you explain the word, "bad" to him? If one of the first things that comes to your mind is the temptation to define "bad" as "not good," then you're not alone. This is a particularly tricky enterprise for us, as we almost all know (on some level) exactly what it means, can be reasonably assured that everyone else has at least a similar if not the exact same understanding of what it means, and yet we find it difficult if not impossible to clearly and coherently articulate exactly what we mean when we describe something as being "bad" in such a way that all ambiguity can be removed.

We encounter similar problems when thinking of and talking about emotive descriptors. I have been in love before. Depending on your age and level of socialization as you read this, you have very likely been in love before also.[9] Beyond even our individual experiences, there is certainly no shortage of examples of love in popular culture – music, movies, literature, and the like. So how can we know that we're all experiencing the same emotion that we are content to describe as love? Maybe one of us really means something closer to lust, or, on the rather more innocent end of the spectrum, maybe we really intend something closer to "caring," but how can we ever be assured? Meta-questions (boldly) tackle questions like this, demand that we look carefully at just what we're saying, and hold us to equally careful definitions, which are absolutely vital in Ethics, if for no other reason than for the sake of clarity and (relative) ease of understanding.

A major part of Philosophy, and one that we'll be encountering incidentally along the way, but especially so in handling meta-questions is the philosophical process of analysis and synthesis. Briefly, analysis is the process by which we take complex arguments or lines of reasoning and break them down into manageable chunks; synthesis is the putting back together of these chunks once the work of analysis is completed, ideally in a more easily understandable format than it was when we began. The first step of analysis is locating presuppositions, implications, and the logical structure of the sets of ideas or argument we're examining. Secondly, we need to determine where knowledge is possible, explore the relevance of what we're being presented with, and then finally, show the relationships between the various parts of our intellectual map of the problem, and act accordingly.

The first part of analysis, the identification of presuppositions, requires a bit of work on our part, not because it's difficult, but because we're not used to thinking like this. Take, for instance, the Ethics class or text itself; what can be reasonably presupposed, based on the fact that there are such things and/or that they continue to be required? Now we go down the rabbit hole a bit. The fact that they're required implies that significant numbers of people in a position to require them find value in their being on offer for the rest of us, or at the very least, they view the benefit of having them as outweighing substantively the cost of producing and offering them. This tells us that the world must in some way be in need of them, and we can reasonably ask ourselves and one another what the implications of this might be. One certainly is that absent structured studies of ethics the world would be at

---

[9] If not, put this book down momentarily and sign up for online dating.

least less ethical, as it would depend entirely on individuals finding their ethics for themselves rather than being instructed, by whatever means, in it. This may not get us as far along as we'd ideally like, but it certainly provides a baseline for further study and productive questioning.

To help us wrap our minds around this, and think of it in technological terms, a computer analogy may be in order. We all have (more or less) the same hardware – that is, we are equipped with minds reasonably capable of rational and abstract thought, and, with a few exceptions, we're all moderately intelligent enough to take in sensory data, assess what it might mean in general as well as to ourselves, and then act accordingly. This means, because we're (hopefully) all already ethical individuals, that, as mentioned above, when faced with an ethical quandary, we probably (again – hopefully) already do the right thing. Where we differ, carrying forward the computer analogy, is in our different operating systems. Each of the ethical theories we'll be discussing can be thought of as a slightly different operating system, that, while it might compute the same data into the same result, may do so in a different way. In other words, while we all see the same thing in terms of problems to be discussed and dealt with by Ethics, we approach the solution uniquely, depending on our we understand ethics on a personal basis. Some of us may be Virtue ethicists, others existentialists, still others consequentialists or deontologists[10] – which we are, is in the end, not nearly so important as what we do.

---

[10] If any of these terms seem frightening right now, have no fear! They'll become very familiar to you as we go along, and none of them are nearly so daunting or difficult as they may sound at our first exposure to them.

Chapter 3: What is Ethics?

Moral Philosophy.

We've now got a pretty solid idea of what Philosophy is, and so our focus turns to what Ethics is.[11] While there are myriad definitions from which to choose, we'll go with the simplest, most straightforward definition; Ethics is a rational inquiry into how one ought to act and how one ought to lead one's life. Because it's an inquiry, we know right off the bat that it's going to involve asking a number of questions. Because it's a rational inquiry, we know that the focus and tone of our inquiry will attempt to avoid emotional or impassioned approaches in favor of those that can be reasoned with and through. At this level, we are able to examine not only our own moral behavior, but that of other individuals and groups – so which groups' behavior are we then concerned with, primarily?

Ethics (as we will be doing it) is exclusively concerned with the voluntary conduct of people who have a reasoned control over their actions. The voluntary aspect of this statement implies that the action being judged on moral grounds flows from their will, their volition, their conscious choice to behave in the manner being questioned or affirmed. That they have a reasoned control over these actions implies not only the use of the will, but also the conscious considerations of alternatives to the chosen action. By definition then, this excludes (at a minimum) four groups of individuals who cannot be said to possess this reasoned control over their voluntary conduct, and hence, can't be profitably judged on any ethical basis. These groups are the very young (i.e., the infantile), the very old (i.e., the senile), the profoundly mentally disabled, and the insane. We're walking a rather fine line here, and one that tends to blur between the realm of Ethics and the realm of Law (more on that shortly), but in general, this is a solid guide.

Ethics is a *normative* enterprise, which means more or less what it sounds like – it establishes norms[12] for an individual, or more often, a group of individuals, as to what sorts of behaviors are considered acceptable; it is not, however, a *descriptive* enterprise. The hard sciences (physics, chemistry, and the like) engage in descriptive work when they describe the reaction between chemicals, for instance. The chemist is unlikely though to append any normative statement onto his already sufficient descriptive one, e.g., Sodium and chloride combine to form NaCl... and it's "good." The so-called "soft" sciences (anthropology, psychology, sociology, etc.) do more or less the same thing when describing the behavior of people, e.g., this tribe venerates its ancestors by consuming their deceased bodies, something we very likely *would* append a normative statement onto!

---

[11] For our purposes, *Ethics* and *Moral Philosophy* are completely interchangeable, since Ethics is the branch of Philosophy specifically concerned with morality.

[12] For Cheers fans, "Norm!"

This is not to say that Ethics has cornered the market on normative efforts though – we are in the questionably good company of other studies such as law, religion, and etiquette, all of which have some degree of overlap, but nonetheless, have intentions quite separate from what we're interested in here. To that end, it's important to recall that we want to think of Ethics as a verb – an action word, something done. Specifically, it does so in three main steps. First and foremost, Moral Philosophy **attempts** to come up with a principled account of how we ought to act. Notice we say "attempt" and not "guarantee," because there is no guarantee that our project will be successful – at least not initially, but this gives us a jumping-off point. If and when we are able to develop this account, we are then tasked with **examining** exactly what goes into choosing and living well. Finally, we are adequately prepared to **proceed** on the assumption[13] that there are indeed some right and wrong answers to the ethical questions raised, and that some of these answers can be rationally supported, while others cannot.

Ethics and the Law.

The first normative enterprise Ethics shares some overlap with is Law, mainly because both of them function to a certain extent to provide guidance to our conduct and help us live together in reasonable peace, despite a multitude of conflicting goals. But the law is, for the most part, much more formalized than our ethics typically are, not least because we have come to feel that it has to be. For instance, if you were to enter my lecture hall and see, emblazoned on my chalkboard in foot-tall, bright red, bold letters, "PLEASE DO NOT SPIT ON DR. LOZANO," you could make a few reasonable deductions – someone, at some point, spit on me in the seminar.[14] Laws function that way – reactively, as a quick perusal of "weird laws" books of websites will tell you. Someone did something that was considered dangerous, beyond the pale, or otherwise harmful to the community within which they found themselves, and a law was enacted to prevent it from happening again, or at least penalize any future offenders. Ethics isn't nearly so codified; we have Ethics texts that run to several hundred pages, but they're nothing compared to the hundreds of volumes of legal codes in print.

Likewise, there are typically stiffer penalties for violations of laws – including fines, imprisonment, even death, depending on the crime.[15] Ethics has no such formalized punishments; sure, I might feel a pang of conscience if I really transgress some agreed-upon ethical guideline, or you might thereafter disapprove of me in some way socially,[16] but I'm unlikely to be penalized in any legally recognizable way unless my transgression was both immoral *and* illegal. There are, of course, some actions that are both illegal and immoral – murder and theft come quickly to mind. This is because many of our legal rights have at least a distant basis in our morality – we seek to protect certain basic rights by

---

[13] Which the great American philosopher Samuel L. Jackson reminds us in *The Long Kiss Goodnight*, "makes an ass out of you, and umption!"

[14] And I killed 'em – but we're here more interested in was I *justified* in doing so?

[15] Especially here in Texas – we're more than happy to kill you for just about anything we can, and in the most creative ways possible!

[16] I have, in fact, taken candy from babies, as my toddler would tearfully attest.

making their violation illegal, since they are already considered ~~my most if not all~~ to be moral prerogatives. At the same time, though, it is neither the function nor the intent of the law to enforce morality – you can be a perfectly law-abiding jerk for instance, and there seems to be no shortage of folks ready and willing to illustrate this truth for us on a regular basis.

Of course, not all illegal acts are immoral. It would be, for example, a federal crime to not pay your taxes, but on the face of it, it's hardly an immoral action on your part to not pay them. One could certainly make a rather convoluted argument that the tax revenues go to support programs for widows, orphans, and the like, and that by avoiding paying them you are thus depriving those individuals of support they're perhaps due, but by direct argument, there's not really any immorality taking place.[17] Perhaps appropriately for reasons of balance, not all immoral acts are illegal. Adultery is the example most commonly offered by my students, and they're quite correct – in only a few instances[18] is this immoral behavior also illegal. Finally, laws themselves can be unjust or immoral – an area of regular contentious debate, primarily as concerns issues of discrimination, particularly for reasons of race, sex, sexual orientation, age, and so on, but these are becoming less frequent.

Ethics and Religion.

What about Religion? I can't think of a single religion that doesn't have at least an implied moral code, and most of them have a minimal (and sometimes quite extensive) list or scriptural discussion of explicit moral directives to be followed by faithful adherents. This can be a sticky point for some people, because very often (though certainly not always, and less frequently these days) our first exposure to morality is when it is given within the context of a religion, and we are sometimes inclined to think that because of this, that it must always be. This is not necessarily so, as we'll see when we take a look at Socrates' assertions in *Euthyphro*. The primary reason is this – religions are able to contain both divine revelation, that is, God or the gods literally revealing moral guidelines to someone, who then shares them with the people of that faith and human reason. While the latter is part of our working definition of Ethics, the former is tricky, not least because on this account, God has seemingly given different people different (and sometimes conflicting) messages as to what He[19] expects from us.

And additional difficulty we encounter in the overlap between Ethics and Religion is this – very often, we couch our religious understanding of moral duties in terms of our relationship (or lack thereof, as the case may be) to God. This impacts not only how we regard God (or the gods, etc.), but what we feel or believe God expects from us, behavior-wise, toward Him, toward others, even toward ourselves. Obviously then this will tend to

---

[17] Best of luck to you if you decide to attempt to convince the IRS of this.

[18] The *Uniform Code of Military Justice*, for one, and a few states, as of this writing.

[19] For simplicity's and consistency's sake, whenever I refer to God in this text I'll be using the personal pronoun "he;" you are of course welcome to think of Him (there I go again) as any, all, or none of "he, she, it, they, etc." – it doesn't really matter for our purposes, though I know people have strong opinions on this, so suit yourself.

muddy the waters significantly if we introduce a system of Ethics, derived from our religion, that is in any way contingent upon a shared belief. What if, for instance, we simply don't share that belief or set of beliefs? Are we then outside the scope of Ethics? Must we simply look elsewhere, and if so, where? And so on. Best, for our purposes, to simply avoid religiously-predicated Ethics all together, though we will be taking a look at both St. Augustine of Hippo and St. Thomas Aquinas a little later on – not to examine their religiosity per se, but to see where it takes them with regard to their specific understanding of the basis of our moral duties.

Ethics and Etiquette.

I will here confess to having never read *Emily Post*; I regularly mix up my salad and dinner forks; and yet, I've been deemed competent to teach Ethics to others. How could this be so? Well, while both aim generally at how we ought to behave among and around others, these are two very different senses of "ought." Ought, as we all know, functions very similarly in English, and is frequently considered to be interchangeable with, should – this is generally not the case in Ethics, however. What's the difference? Allow me to illustrate: "You should have your car's oil changed about every four to five thousand miles of driving." As opposed to: "You really ought to get those brakes looked at before you go out on the road again." This illustrates well (I hope) the certain additional weight that an ought statement carries with it – there's a sense of urgency, of warning, an imperative or directive that probably ought not be ignored.

Likewise, I can flagrantly and even theatrically violate the guidelines of etiquette while still well within the confines of relative moral innocence. I can, for instance, begin giggling at an otherwise somber memorial service, or break wind rather noisily during a lull in a worship service, both in relative moral innocence, until I lie by blaming it on the kid seated behind me.[20] Just as with law, behavior that is reasonably innocent in terms of morality can be exceedingly contrary to the rules of acceptable social decorum.

Defining Good and Bad.

At a minimum, at some point along the way in each of the philosophers' theories we'll be taking a look at, we're going to have to define just what we (or rather, they) mean when referring to actions (or even attitudes and approaches) as good or bad, right or wrong. Addressing these questions will not only provide us with the basis of our particular normative theory, but will also give us an insight into the sorts of goods that the theory in question views as worth seeking, as well as illuminate the basic principles according to which we ought to be governing our actions. As part of this, though, we have to be vigilant, on a better than average basis, as to whose perspective we're viewing our answers from – are my actions available for judgment by me alone,[21] by the society in which I live, by a higher intelligence, and so on.

---

[20] I'd like to state for the record that I haven't personally done either of these things, lest you think I'm a horrible person, but I have seen both of them done, and yes – it amused me. Mea culpa.

[21] Highly unlikely, except perhaps for Robinson Crusoe, and even he had Friday to impress.

Through all of this, what Ethics is really attempting to do is not to help us decide what to do – as already discussed, most of us, when faced with an ethical decision, already do "the right thing" most of the time, provided we're fully aware of the situation. Our effort isn't to decide what to do, but rather how to articulate why we've done what it is we decide to do. That seems to be what most of us have the most trouble with – explaining to others the grounding reasons behind our moral actions, and it's tricky, because we're more or less back to the spaceship example; we're not satisfied with defining "bad" as "not good," but we're often hard-pressed to come up with anything more solid, especially when pressured to do so. However, if and when we are brought to a point where we're able to articulate a few basic principles intelligently, and we can justify how we've differentiated right from wrong, we're on the road to being able to not only determine our moral duties and obligations for our own use, but also to explain to and instruct others in how to do so.

So how do we know what we are reasonably safe in referring to as "good," i.e., how will we identify something as good on a fairly reliable basis that we can impart to others? Good things are divided into two distinct classes, and it's vital that we understand the distinction between them; all goods are either *final* or *instrumental*. This has to do with the end[22] we intend.[23] By extension, ends are also either final or instrumental – final if they are good in and of themselves, what we might also refer to as "inherently" good; instrumental if they are only (or partially) seen as good because they enable something beyond themselves. Philosophy, and by extension, Moral Philosophy, is only concerned with final ends, and so we generally define good as that which is truly desirable or worth having for its own sake, on its own merits, and makes no reference or appeal to, nor is it contingent upon anything beyond itself.

The BIG Question.

Here's the really BIG, seriously huge, massively overarching question, with which all moral philosophers are obsessed and/or concerned (say it aloud, all in one breath, to impress your friends): **Given the likelihood of conflicts between our ethical demands and our own self-interest, what reason(s) do we have to act justly or morally – especially in situations where we're required to refrain from actions that would directly contribute to our own happiness or where we could more easily profit from acting unjustly?** In other words, why are we so concerned with trying to be good, when it's usually easier, and very often more fun, to simply be bad? We go to a great deal of trouble to learn about Ethics and then to "be" ethical; why? Seriously – why do we bother with all of this instead of simply living our lives however we see fit, consequences be damned? I regret to inform you that I would be answering this question in any sort of final or settled way, at least not in the scope of this text. The reason being that this is the question that has perplexed ethicists since there have been such creatures.

---

[22] When you see this in Philosophy, think of the Greek word *telos* – end, plan, goal, aim, design, etc. – whatever we're working toward through our action(s).

[23] Was that a haiku?

It's not to say that answers haven't been proffered with some regularity over the millennia – plenty of people have put forth answers that were to them satisfactory, and they in turn must have thought would satisfy the rest of us, but we keep returning to this same question (in various forms) over and over again. The most enduring answers, the ones to which we'll devote the lion's share of our attention here, were offered by a bunch of old, dead, White guys. Plato will tell us that only the just are truly happy, which isn't a great deal of help because we're then tasked not only with defining happiness, but also figuring out how to tell who's just, as well as arriving at a definition of justice we can all agree upon and live with. Aristotle will then tell us that we must act virtuously, though he'll neglect to tell us which virtues we'll have to seek and maintain in order to do so. Hobbes (for whom the cartoon tiger was named) seems to think that we're just self-interested enough, on a species level, that our selfishness will align, like the dawning of the Age of Aquarius, with other peoples' selfishness, and we'll just sort of work it out. Hume will try to convince us that we're more sympathetic than we might believe we are, and we act accordingly, even when it's not reasonable to do so. And finally, to provide a foil to Hume and just generally be a troll, Kant will tell us that we must always appeal to our reason, even when it seems to trump our instincts and inclinations.

Almost all of these will fit broadly into three main theories, which we'll encounter more or less chronologically as we work our way through the ages. Some of them fit in nicely, with plenty of room to spare – the ethical equivalent of your favorite jeans/ sneakers/ sweater combination; others will have to be somewhat awkwardly shoehorned into the category, but will be made to fit – sort of. The categories are the Virtue theories, the Consequentialist theories, and the Deontological theories. Virtue theories are exactly what you might expect, telling us that when we form or possess virtuous character traits, we are led to the highest good. Consequentialist theories, as the name would tend to imply, are primarily concerned with the consequences of our ethical action, and because of their concern with the end (aim, plan, goal, design, etc.) are also called Teleological theories. Deontological theories, from the Greek *deon*, duty or obligation, are, you guessed it – interested in performing those actions to which we can be said to have a duty or an obligation.

Normative versus Meta-Ethics

Normative ethics is what we'll be focusing on for most of our time together, with a little bit of meta-ethics incidentally encountered, with the exception of Nietzsche, who will focus almost exclusively on a project that's mostly meta. Normative ethics are, like our project in general, attempting to do something – in a general sense what they're trying to do is develop an account of good and bad, the basic principles that direct our understanding of right and wrong, virtues, and so on, all in a way that is both practical and substantive. It's a practical in the sense that it's not purely theoretical and we can actually take it and do something with it – specifically, we can apply it to contentious issues in such a way as to resolve them, or at least make the core issue intelligible and render it open for moral debate. It's substantive in that it doesn't apply Mom's old standby, "because I said so, that's why!" but rather gives us a bit of substance, a bit of meat, on which to base our understanding, more forward through ever more complex combinations of theory and application, and again – to do something with the Ethics so it's not simply dead words on a page.

Meta-Ethics moves beyond these substantive issues because the subject matter with which it is concerned is normative ethics itself – it is the means through which we understand the meaning of the terms we have to contend with in the various normative theories we wade our way through – think of it as our life preserver amidst a sea of otherwise confusing vocabulary. This is also where we make the all-important distinction between fact and value claims, undoubtedly the place where ethical discussions seem to find the most cause for contention, especially as people misunderstand the difference between them. As an example, the claim "X is wrong," is a value claim; it does not become contentious until it is misunderstood as being a factual claim. The key to telling the difference, not only between fact and value claims, but more importantly, between normative and meta-ethical notions is that Meta-Ethics does not develop any specific account of the right, the good, the ethical, but only informs the account(s) generated by the normative theories.

The primary problem of Meta-Ethics, or at any rate, what renders it frustrating to students of Moral Philosophy, is that if (and it may in fact be a BIG "if") terms like the "right" and the "good" can even be defined, we're left with the difficulty of then doing so. After all, questions like, "what does the good smell like?" and "what does the ethical sound like?" don't compute for us – these are concepts that are simply not reducible to empirical descriptions of the sort we're usually so content to remain dependent upon, e.g., I'll believe it when I SEE it, and so on. This may be initially frustrating to us, but with a little guidance, there's no reason for it to remain a roadblock to our understanding, either of the terms, or the theories themselves.

Interlude: A Note on the Historical Eras of Ethics

As with any topic discussed chronologically, it makes the most sense to break the study up into eras in order to better organize things, draw special attention to unique opportunities for comparison and contrast, and overall provide a more coherent picture of the evolution of a particular discipline, and Ethics is no different in this regard. I'm afraid that here I'll be going according to the general view, breaking our time together, as well as our philosophers into three rather broad categories; the classical/medieval, the early modern, and the contemporary. It's important for me to approach things this way for a few reasons; firstly, it allows us to look at the theoretical development of Ethics from more or less the start of the study to the most recent scholarship, watching along the way which themes prevailed despite the years, and which were ever so gently shoved aside here and there to make way for newer (though not necessarily always better) theories. Secondly, this gives us a better understanding for why the philosophers wrote in the first place, for fairly early on, every philosopher is going to be, in a certain sense, replying to those who came before him, either immediately or by way of a distant sort of spiritual legacy that links them. So, I certainly hope you will bear with me. Besides, placing these guys (yes – they're all guys) in their historical context gives us a better insight into their motivation as well as their work, than we might otherwise have.

Chapter 4: Introducing The Classical & Medieval Era

While the classical era could conceivably go back as far as Homer (circa 8th century, B.C.[24]) if not somewhat before that, for our purposes, I will begin with Socrates, who, as near as we can tell, was born circa 469 B.C. The classical era alone (not to include the medieval) will include our discussions of Socrates, Plato, Aristotle, and, barely making it in under the wire, time-wise, St. Augustine of Hippo, who dies just prior to the end of the 5th century A.D.[25] The medieval era, sometimes also called the middle ages, or, lamentably (because they were anything but) the "dark" ages, are generally agreed to have begun around 500 A.D., if only because it's easier to round up from the Fall of the Roman Empire,[26] and are said to have ended around 1500 A.D., because again, it's easier to round up from Columbus' "discovery" of the "new world." Some historians stop it short a bit earlier, around the time of the Italian Renaissance of the 14th century, and our final philosopher of this era, St. Thomas Aquinas will come in well under even that timeline, but it's easiest to work with nice, millennia-long chunks, so our classical and medieval periods will be roughly two sequential thousand year chunks.

We're going to be moving, in rather quick succession, through the work and thought of these five men, and it may seem at first glance that little time passes between them, but don't be fooled – there are sixteen centuries separating Socrates and Aquinas, and there are HUGE factors, cultural, religious, and linguistic, not to mention philosophical separating them. Our first three subjects will go quite quickly; Socrates taught Plato, who then taught Aristotle, who then taught Alexander the Great, making possible the process of Hellenization that directly enables Aquinas to think and work in the way that he does as the inheritor (albeit not directly) of the Greek philosophical tradition. Along with the way we'll witness a shift in the cultural center of the then known world, from Athens to Rome and beyond into Northwestern Europe, and the more influential shift in the religious character of the Philosophy being done from Greek polytheism[27] to Roman Catholic Christianity,[28] both of which will effect profound changes in the approach to and character of Ethics.

---

[24] I'll be using this, "Before Christ," as opposed to the newer, and possibly more palatable to some, "Before the Common Era." Why? Because this is how I was taught, and I'm too old and far too set in my ways to change now. Deal with it.

[25] *Anno Domini*, i.e., "the Year of Our Lord." Please, NEVER say the ludicrous and ignorant "after death" as it is sometimes supposed to be, and for whatever reason or failure on history teachers' part, persists to the great irritation of the rest of us.

[26] Officially, Rome falls, or rather succumbs fatally to the Visigoths and others in 476 A.D.; realistically, it had been in the process of "falling" for a long time leading up to that. As it turns out, the "barbarians" who took it over ended up becoming nearly as Roman as the Romans had been, but again – I digress.

[27] Technically the Greeks held to a henotheistic pantheon, with Zeus as the high god, but why split hairs?

[28] The Roman Catholic Church left the (Eastern) Orthodox Church in 1054; the protestant reformation(s) wouldn't occur until several centuries later.

Along the way, we're going to see some HUGE shifts in the way our philosophers (and everyone influenced by them) think about the connection and interdependence between religious beliefs and ethical theories. This is a theme that will more or less ebb and flow throughout the whole text, but within the Classical-Medieval era we're going to see things turn a 180 in pretty short order (remembering again though that it will actually take nearly two millennia to do so). We'll begin with Socrates' Euthyphro, in which we're told that we don't need to appeal to the gods (note the plural) in order to know the proper course of moral action; by the time we get to St. Thomas Aquinas, we will be told that we absolutely must appeal to God (note the singular), but this revolution will be a drawn-out evolution in real-time, and will be based in reason, but the reason itself varies, so warrants a look at it...

Both the Greeks and our medievalists will be insistent upon the use of reason in arriving at their ethical theories, but the basis of their reason is coming from a completely different place. For the Greeks, particularly for Aristotle, our reason is what truly differentiates us from the rest of animate nature – we are the rational animals, and that reason doesn't depend on any influences above and beyond ourselves. Medieval Moral Philosophy will be likewise dependent on reason, but finally, all reason will demand religious faith, and all Ethics and meaning will be found *only* within a religious context. By extension, this means that all human value will be determined by religious values, and what those values ought to be directed and limited by a strongly religious approach, accompanied by religious boundaries.

Another point of contrast between the Greeks and our saints deals with their fundamentally different understand of our (human) place in the world. The Greeks viewed themselves, and by extension, us, as just another part of the natural world. Birds, bees, rocks, trees, us – all here as the products of natural forces,[29] responsive to natural forces, and understandable through natural means, and in natural terms. Basically, man[30] can be studied in the same way as the rest of animate nature because we're just another part of it, albeit a slightly more complex aspect of it.

In sharp contrast, the Christian view of man, informed and differentiated by the broader Judeo-Christian understanding of man's place in the world and in the hierarchy of living things, is understandably quite a bit different. From their perspective, everything that exists (still including the birds, the bees, the rocks, the trees, and us) is part of God's creation; at this point, there's no real conflict with the view of the Greeks. Here's where the conflict enters: man, being made in God's own image,[31] is absolutely and fundamentally different from everything else in that creation. Specifically, we have something everything else doesn't have – a soul. Now, as a point of clarification, the Greeks had a concept of soul, but when they used the term, they mean something closer to what we mean when we say

---

[29] Please see your parents if you have not yet had the "birds and the bees" talk.

[30] Ladies, lest you be offended or feel left out, when our thinkers (especially prior to the contemporary era) refer to "man," they mean it in the sense of *anthropos* – men, women, humans, people, us – __*all*__ of us, regardless of gender.

[31] We generally understand this to mean with regard to our spiritual make-up, not necessarily in terms of physicality and the like.

"mind" – that is, our capacity for rational and abstract thought; our concept of soul as something that floats up and sits on a cloud, playing the harp after our earthly life, is something of a uniquely Christian notion. Our soul, besides just making us distinguishable from the rest of creation, is what makes us God's children, and what tasks us with certain duties, behaviors, and the like that are moral in nature. Because this component is "above" The empirically evidenced sorts of things we can easily pick out in the natural world as we experience it daily, we call it *super*natural.

Back to the Greeks, since we're natural sorts of creatures, right along the other natural creatures with whom we share the planet, then whatever good we are capable of being, finding, *doing* (remember – Ethics is a verb!) must be not only in this world, but will need to be found and done in this life. Think of this as James Dean's Ethics – live fast, die young, and leave a good looking corpse, but with Ethics – get whatever good you're going to do done fast, because your time is limited, and when you're done, you're done for good.[32] This is why we have the legacy of things like the famous (or infamous?) Roman orgy. The orgy was a feast and drinking party... that ended up spilling over to the physically amorous sorts of stuff that we now associate it with, and which got the Malcolm McDowell star-vehicle "Caligula" into some serious hot water with the film ratings folks.[33] Why? Simple, really – because whatever good we're going to seek in this world, regardless of where we might be inclined to find it, was going to be gained in a natural way, during the present life.

Again, the Christian medievalists give us a sharp contrast to examine, because it was decidedly not any of the goods of this world, but the insurmountable good that would be found in a world beyond this one – in heaven. This is why, or rather, how, we can explain medieval Christian monastics living in the comparably rough conditions of the monastery, getting little sleep, eating poorly,[34] wearing hair shirts and the like, and devoting their entire lives to worship activities. This present life was essentially thought of as a boot camp to train for the life beyond the grave, or even as a hurdle to be cleared in order to be promoted to the life beyond this one, but the "goods" to be found here actually have no value which would make them worthy of being sought after – especially not for their own sake. Life here really only serves to prepare us for the hereafter wherein our soul will enjoy the only real good, in the presence of God.

Obviously with differences like these, finding common ground according to which we can group these in any way other than chronologically seems like quite a stretch. However, despite their diametrically opposed notions of where we fit in the world and where we can find, and be, and *do* good in the world, but there is some overlap – not in their goals, but in the fact that they have goals at all. Here's what we mean by that – both of them are what we refer to as *teleologically*-oriented[35] in their approach to Ethics, that is, they have a goal (end, aim, plan, design, etc.) that they're attempting to achieve in their identification and

---

[32] Pun intended.

[33] Seriously – look it up – it was the first mainstream movie to "earn" the now infamous X rating we tend to associate with, ah... more "adult" features.

[34] Not always (or even often) the case, but it does serve to illustrate my point.

[35] Also from the Greek word, *telos*, like we discussed earlier; see also "teleological."

achievement of the good. Regardless of their religious views (or lack thereof), both our Greeks and our medieval philosophers are ultimately concerned with the goal toward which all of our rational conduct can and should be directed and worked toward. The goal will likewise determine our standard, against which we'll measure actions and character for their goodness, dependent entirely on to how great an extent they contribute to helping us realize the final end (aim, goal, design, plan) being questioned.

So here's a brief roadmap of where we're going in this era. We'll be starting out with Socrates, who will set our baseline, both with regard to the role (or lack thereof) of religion in Ethics, as well as establish the direction in which we'll be going. Next up will be Plato, where we'll be redirected somewhat, as he introduces his famous theory of Forms, specifically the Form of the Good, and who will begin a theme that will stretch throughout the whole text – justice. Aristotle will give us our most direct discussion of teleology, as he examines the nature of human good, which he identifies as happiness. Finally, our two saints, Augustine of Hippo and Thomas Aquinas, will carry forward Plato and Aristotle, respectively, in telling us that the only goal worth seeking will come to us in the afterlife, and until then, we should act virtuously because God has commanded us to find true happiness until we go to be with Him.

Chapter 5: Socrates

First, a bit of a confession: Socrates didn't actually right the work that we're looking at as illustrative of his ethical thought. In fact, he didn't write anything that we have; everything we know about him comes from Plato, Xenophon, and Aristophanes, and there's a bit of difficulty there because we're tasked with trying to pick out the "true" Socrates. But that's not what concerns us here, and we really just want to get to the bottom of his ethical thought, which doesn't come through anywhere more clearly or more famously than it does in *Euthyphro*. Here's a quick crash course in the Platonic[36] dialogues: Socrates is always going to be the protagonist and primary speaker, and they're almost always going to be called by the name of whomever is being argued with by Socrates. In the case of *Euthyphro*, he's arguing with a guy named, you guessed it – Euthyphro. No don't worry – you won't have to read the dialogue to do this; in fact, you're not going to be reading any of the primary source texts that we'll be discussing. It's my hope that you will want to read them, at your leisure, later, but for now, we'll be examining the high points of each, the key concepts to be mined from them, and what they can tell us in terms how we ought to conduct our lives. So, without any delay, let's jump straight into *Euthyphro*!

Socrates bumps into Euthyphro outside the Athenian courts, ironically, while awaiting his own trial for impiety. Euthyphro, whose name means something like "sincere" is there, bringing his own father up on charges of murder, for having caused the death of one of their bond workers, who was himself (again with the irony) a murderer. So right from the get-go, we have two senses of piety – that which is toward the gods of Athens, whom Socrates stood accused of not respecting, and filial piety – that which one owes to their parents. The entire dialogue attempts to settle on an understanding of what is pious versus what is impious. Euthyphro considers himself quite the religious expert, so Socrates seems to have come to the right man to get his answers. For our purposes though, what this is really getting at by asking what makes an action pious is the same as asking what makes an action right, or good, or ethical, or moral, or so on.

We should take just a minute and talk about Socrates' method. Not the Socratic method like you learned in school (although you called it the "scientific" method), or like we see in courtroom drama television series, but his actual modus operandi – how he went about involving himself in these discussions in the first place. Socrates seems to have spent the bulk of his time hanging out in the agora,[37] the marketplace of Athens, where people would sell their wares and services, where business deals would be struck, and so on. So, Socrates would walk around the agora, approaching people known to be (or who considered themselves to be) subject matter experts, and he would then question them relentlessly. We only know a little bit about Socrates' wife, Xanthippe, and most of it comes from stories

---

[36] This does *NOT* mean that they're just friends, but without "benefits" – it means it was written by Plato.

[37] Just a great big, wide-open space, like a flea market; if you know someone who's <u>agora</u>phobic, who has a fear of wide-open spaces, this is where that comes from.

rather than hard facts. That aside, I always imagine her standing there, looking a little bit embarrasses, as Socrates approaches yet another poor sap in the marketplace, to their cost, if much to our benefit.

The overarching question of this dialogue is, "What makes an action right?" It's actually, "What makes an action pious?" but we're less interested in that than we are with the direct impact on Ethics, so from here on out, we'll be substituting that appropriately. So, is an action right because it pleases the gods (remember, this is ancient Greece, so it's going to be plural), or is it pleasing to the gods because it is a right action to begin with? Obviously, the real question here concerns the connection between morality and religion, and, more importantly, the assumptions inherent that will *force* morality to be *dependent on* or *independent of* religion. Let's take a look at both and see what it results in.

If an action is right because God[38] wills it to be right, then it forces all morality to be dependent on a religious foundation, and by extension, we can only know the morally right course of action within a religious context. Take a minute to think about what that means – it means, basically, that the only source of moral authority and teaching you have available to you are the scriptures of a given religious tradition, a clear prophetic edict from a religious authority figure, or a direct revelation from God, ala burning bushes, pillars of fire, and the like. This is problematic on the face of things because it categorically denies the possibility of an atheist, or even an agnostic, of being ethical, which doesn't seem to hold up to our experience in and of the world. Additionally, and even more problematically, if the rightness of a given action is based on the will of God, then the question becomes, could God have made (or still make) any action right, simply by willing and declaring it to be so. Imagine for a moment God deciding to knock off a few of the Commandments (as in "The" 10); suddenly, murder is alright; would that make it ethically allowable? Again, probably not.

What if the opposite were the case? If God wills that we do certain things because they're right, then rightness is independent of God, and He's only reflecting a higher standard of morality than Himself, and morality would exist without Him. In this way, Ethics is independent of religious belief and practice, but more importantly, this means we're capable of determining our own moral course of action, using our reason alone. Here's the potential problem with this one: there's not only no mention of God, but it we can rely on our own rationality without recourse to religious belief, religious authority, or a direct revelation. This isn't a big problem for Socrates, except as Xenophon portrays him, a reverential and deeply religious man, but it's going to be a big problem for Saints Augustine and Aquinas. But for the time-being, that's where we're at, and that's the overarching idea Socrates wants us to understand – we make no appeals to the gods in order to be ethical.

Leaving religion to one side for a bit, are actions right because we approve of them, or do we approve of them because something about them is inherently right? Or, since we are

---

[38] It's just going to be easier for everyone to refer to God in the singular here; if you like, for continuity's sake, you may certainly continue to think plural, ala polytheism – same net result, just a bit clearer this way, especially since most folks reading this are unlikely to be polytheists, but I digress… (yet again)

thinking in teleological terms here, is an outcome good because it's desirable, or does something about it speak to us in such a way that we desire it because it's good? If the first is true, then our sense of rightness depends on what we personally believe, desire, and feel; we are in a very real sense forcing actions or situations to be good based on the attitude we hold. If the second is true instead, then rightness, goodness, and the rest aren't answerable to what we want, what we think, or how we feel. The contrast is between our subjectivity and our attempts (most of them feeble) at objectivity. We're subjective sorts of creatures, and we bring a lot of baggage with us to everything we examine; Socrates seems to be challenging us here to leave a lot that behind, and base our evaluative attitudes as rationally as well possibly can.

As a final thought on Socrates, before we move on to Plato, we're left with an interesting observation; the question of whether or not we can do wrong and then deny that we ought to be punished for our wrongdoing. Now realistically, we seem on the face of things, to do this on a regular basis, but do we really? Say for example that we're stopped by a police officer for speeding; we might very well acknowledge our fault in having sped through the school zone, but argue that our knowledge of having done so is punishment enough in itself, and we ought to be let off with a warning. But is that really what's going on here? Socrates seems inclined to say no, despite how we might interpret it for ourselves. Instead of arguing that we've done wrong but ought not to be punished, we argue that what we've done isn't wrong in the first place. It's a tough sell on the face of things, but that's essentially what we're doing in these situations – defending the rightness or morality of our actions at the outset. This may seem like an odd place to essentially leave us handing, but Socrates is setting us up nicely for a theme we'll see beginning in Plato that will show up all along the way, right up to our last moral thinker, John Rawls, and that theme is justice.

Chapter 6: Plato

Ideally, I would have liked to split Plato into two parts, and hey – it's *my* book, so I suppose I very well could, but we'll just have a bit longer time together here instead. Specifically, the two parts I would be inclined to split his thought into would be that which we see in the dialogue *Protagoras*, and that which we see in his famous (infamous?) *Republic*. Both carry through the overarching theme of virtue, and so, with a few pauses here and there for clarification, we can jumble them together without a whole lot lost in terms of clarity. Both will likewise serve to establish his approach to matters ethical, at least in terms of how other philosophers will be responding to his work from here to the end of the text. The primary theme of *Protagoras* is the question of whether or not virtue is the sort of thing that can be taught (and by extension, learned), and in *Republic* we move to a much more abstract understand of virtue as that which helps us perform our characteristic function of rationality, as well as we ought or are able to.

Protagoras

A brief play-by-play of Protagoras goes something like this: Socrates asks the Sophist Protagoras how and with whom his young friend Hippocrates[39] ought to be educated. Protagoras tells him that if he wants him to be a fine sculptor, he should study with Phidias, to be an expert physician, he should attend the Aesculapian school. Socrates then asks what he might learn if he were to study with Protagoras himself, and the answer given is "virtue." The dialogue then goes on to explore what virtue is, and whether or not it's the sort of thing that can be taught in the first place. The specific Greek word they use is *arête*, which, although most commonly translated as "virtue," can also mean "(moral) excellence" or "goodness."

If something is intended to be taught competently it's certainly helpful to know what the subject matter is, and the first question that arises is whether virtue is one thing, or separate things that have all been subsumed under the general heading together. This may seem like a bit of gratuitous hair-splitting, but it's an important distinction to make, because if they are separate, then it should be possible for a person to be an exemplar of one virtue, but the antithesis of another. Protagoras' answer that the various qualities of characters which we often call virtues are really just *parts* of virtue is likewise problematical, because if for instance one virtue is separate from and not in any way like another virtue, then one could match up easily with the opposite of another, which doesn't seem at all likely. If your head hurts at this point, don't feel at all bad – mine does as well, just from trying to explicate this for you.

Socrates then pursues the question or whether virtue can be taught, because there seems to be something about it that doesn't fit nicely into our other academic exercises, but at the

---

[39] Not necessarily the guy we associate with medicine, but perhaps another Hippocrates.

same time, there is something about us that reflects, generates, and expresses virtue, or at least the merits of the concept on its own. In this way, I suppose you could say virtue is a bit like art – we may have a tough time articulating exactly how it ought to be best defined, but we "know it when we see it." Furthermore, the virtuous person seems to be guided, no matter which of the particular virtues they exhibit or exemplify, but something that is both unified but also universally applicable. Virtue as expressed in our actions and attitudes also seems to presuppose a bit of knowledge on our part. We're not courageous, for instance, if we have no idea what awaits us on the other side of the hill and we charge it blindly; we're courageous precisely because we know what awaits us and we face it with a certain mindset.

In this way, virtue seems to in some way regulate our moral conduct, but it does so in a rather broad way that while easily perceived and even understood and described by us, eludes our senses, and so can't be described empirically as we might other things in our experience. Our senses can only pick up on particular instances of universal principles at work, and we seem to know the universal more on an intuitive than on a sensate level.[40] So if virtue can't be understood or learned by experience, how can it possibly be taught? In most contexts, such as learning the vocabulary of a foreign language, we are content to point to the items themselves, because they are particulars; because virtue is a universal though, it can't be pointed to, only particular instances of it in action, from which we are left to deduce (hopefully) the universal principle at work "behind the scenes" of what we've witnessed.

In order to benefit, and by extension, to learn, when instances of virtue are pointed out to us, our minds have to be prepared and sufficiently mature and experienced to be able to internalize what we're seeing. So we may not be able to be taught virtue in the same way as we're taught a skill or a vocabulary, but we are able to be taught how to best pursue the sort of knowledge at which philosophical reflection aims, presuming we're able to enter into a sort of sympathetic relationship with the examples that present themselves and that are pointed out to us as exemplary. What we have here is a sort of "members only"[41] approach to the life of virtue – Plato seems to be telling us that it's not available to just anyone and everyone, but only to those who have been conditioned in such a way as to be receptive to lessons of this sort. Skinnerian psychological overtones notwithstanding, we do seem to be brought up this way – conditioned through praise to behave in a way that seems in keeping with the many virtues we praise in society, and penalized for transgressions that we generally associate with their reciprocal vices. At the end of the day, we're left with the notion that if virtue is seen as the principle behind the many attributes of character we label "virtues," then this is only because it is right universally – something that will be important to several of the ethical systems we'll be examining later on.[42]

---

[40] More on this when we discuss David Hume, several chapters hence.

[41] Pause here to shudder at the remembrance of when *Members Only* jackets were all the rage in what we were deluded enough to call "fashion" back in the 1980's.

[42] Especially that of Immanuel Kant, with regard to his categorical imperative.

Republic

We here pause for a brief (and lamentably unpaid) commercial, in which I admonish you in the strongest possible terms to add Plato's *Republic* to your proverbial "bucket list" – read this book before you die – you'll be better for having done so. I would not do so were this not most of the most important books in Western civilization – perhaps *the* most important book, major religious texts apart. The reason for this is the incredible influence this book has had – intellectually, historically, and the rest, on just about every aspect of our academic lives certainly, but also our personal lives, because in this one book we find the origin of many of our most pressing questions about all of these things. It is sometimes simply filed under "political science," and it is indeed inclusive of that, but is so much more. Plato believed that society could not be saved by political means, but rather, that it would require the sort of wisdom Philosophy provides. Obviously, a few rather biting criticisms are implied here, not least of which is that society is in need of saving in the first place; I think we can all agree that it is. Second, considering that politics doesn't seem to have settled matters in terms of saving society since the time he wrote this (and in all fairness, neither has Philosophy), we probably owe any attempt a fair hearing, because really – what could it possibly hurt?

Carrying forward our discussion and growing understanding of virtue as Plato sees it, we come to our first definition of the term as something we can work with. Virtue for Plato is the trait that enables an object, a skill, or, for our purposes, a human being, to perform its (or their) characteristic function well. This is easiest to think about in the simplest terms of an object – specifically a tool used for a particular activity. Think for a moment of a hammer. Now, think of the attributes an object must be in possession of for us to identify it accurately as a hammer. Perhaps you're tempted, as my students often are, to say that it must have a handle, a head, and be capable of pounding in nails, all of which are accurate to some extent, but allow for the use of a broom, a puppy, and a rock, respectively, to also be used as hammers, none of which strike me as particularly preferable in this instance. We also have the difficulty of which hammer we're defining – claw hammers, ball-peen hammers, roofing hammers, jack hammers, sledgehammers, rubber or wooden mallets, etc. All of these, though quite different in intended use, and perhaps even in appearance, have some unifying trait running through them – the "hammerness" of the hammer – that which enables them to perform their characteristic function well. Whatever that elusive trait is, is the hammers' virtue; our virtue as human beings, is our rationality – it is what allows us to perform our characteristic function, rational thought, well.

The next term Plato wants to be sure we understand, and one that just about every subsequent philosopher will have their own (different) definition for, is the good. It would be too simple to have just a straight definition of the good, so Plato instead gives us three distinct categories of good things, from which we will have to choose and into which he will be asking us to categorize concepts, specifically Justice. First, there are those things which are good because they are desired for their own sake, without any reference to any further good to come from them, and not dependent on anything else for their inherent and intrinsic goodness – harmless pleasures and enjoyable activities would fall into this category. Second, there are things that may be desirable for their own sake, but also for the consequences arising from them. Things like knowledge and health are counted in this category, as its arguably good to have both, but each can also beget further benefits that render it even better. Finally, there are those things which are not particularly desirable in and of themselves, but are only sought for their beneficial consequences. Most medical treatments probably fall into this category – no one seeks out things like colonoscopies and root canals for the enjoyment to be found through them, but because they want good digestive and dental health, respectively.[43] Plato then wishes for us to decide which of these categories Justice ought to be placed into and thought of as a part of, but more on this momentarily.[44]

Plato also wants us to begin thinking about the parts of roles of our souls. Now, when the Greeks refer to "soul," they're not thinking of an ethereal bit of us that floats up following our earthly demise and takes up harp playing; their thinking of the mind – the capacity for rational and abstract thought, and the word they use is familiar to us, at least in its derivative senses, *psyche*. Because Plato will be likening each of us as individuals to the polis,[45] our minds are likewise divided as the constituent bodies found within the polis. Our reason and rational capacity, that by which we're about to judge actions, attitudes, and the like, is the ruling class, which gives us good insight into which aspect of our mind Plato wants our emphasis and efforts placed. Our emotions, which he terms "spirit," is the soldier class of our mental life – it is emotional, but can be shaped and directed by our rationality. Our passions and desires, the appetitive aspect of our human natures, Plato likens to the working class, as this is where we seek to satisfy our most basic needs (*vide* Maslow), and, when we can, to seek pleasure as well. The polis as well as the individual's mind will be divided in this way.

The first character who appears on the scene to (attempt to) match wits with Socrates is the Sophist "philosopher" Thrasymachus. A bit of background on the Sophists is in order; they were a school of rhetoricians who prided themselves on their eloquence and persuasion – even if the truth had to be sacrificed in order to enable the other two. Right away we're plunged into a discussion of what justice is. For our purposes at this point, we can more or less interchange "justice" and good, right, moral ethical, etc., like we did with "piety" in our examination of *Euthyphro*. Thrasymachus asks Socrates to give him a definition of justice, but then qualifies his statement by adding, "don't tell me that it's the <u>right</u>, the <u>beneficial</u>, the <u>profitable</u>, the <u>gainful</u>, or the <u>advantageous</u>, but tell me clearly and exactly what you mean; for I won't accept such nonsense from you." Socrates responds by saying that's like asking for a number, but disallowing any of the multipliers that can be used to arrive at that number, or, in other words, all the underlined terms can't be disallowed because all of them are pretty good synonyms, or at least descriptors, of justice or what it ought to be.

---

[43] I haven't had either of these procedures, so it's not personally anecdotal on my part, but from what I understand, neither is particularly pleasant.

[44] In the book, it's Glaucon who attempts to get Socrates to categorize it into one of these three, but for our purposes, it's just as well to say Plato is asking us to.

[45] *Not* Sting's backup band, but rather, the Greek city-state, e.g., Athens, Sparta, etc.

Back to our discussion of the good as mentioned above, Glaucon has a good question – which category does justice properly belong in? The answer he gives is a bit of a frustrating one, because he has Socrates placing justice in the highest category, where things are desired for their intrinsic value, not for their consequences. Why does he do this? As near as I can tell, just to be a pain in the ass. Here's why: If he places justice in the second category, where things are desired for their own sake as well as for the consequences they bring, then the debate is essentially over – we can probably all agree, with perhaps a little pushing and shoving, that justice in and of itself is good, but also results in good outcomes. We could likewise also argue, albeit with a little bit more pushing and shoving, that justice isn't particularly good on its own merits, but very often results in positive outcomes. So not only does Socrates do this to be a pain, but he also forces the debate to be continued, because now the burden of proof is on him to show Glaucon (and the rest of us) that justice is something desirable for its own sake.

If we are going to say that justice is desirable for its own sake, and that "good" is more or less substitutable for "just" for our purposes, then what is it that makes a person good? Is it like art, will we simply "know it when we see it," or can it be made more specific? Furthermore, who could be said to exemplify goodness in this world (recall that Plato thinks, and we agree, is in need of saving), especially when so many of us are otherwise content to lust after power and wealth? It's a tricky thing to come up with a list of genuinely good people,[46] and most of them that come to mind are probably dead – all the good ones usually are. If we inverse this though, we seem to have little trouble thinking of people who are anything but good; why is that? Well, for starters, the bad get a lot more media coverage, and more often than not the egregious nature of their actions brings them to our attention more noticeably than the "everyday saints" who are walking around doing good we might be loath to take notice of.

The Ring of Gyges

The question then arises, or ought to, what is it that *really* makes us good? Glaucon is quick to remind Socrates that many people seem good/just, but what really determines our conduct aren't the virtues,[47] but the fear of punishment and the expectation of reward. It's awful to admit it, and certainly cynical as hell, but he's got a point. Think about it for a minute – do you or do you not have a list of people still walking the earth *only* because it would be a criminal offense to shuffle them loose this mortal coil? If not, you're probably young, but have no fear – the list will grow as you grow a bit older. To be perfectly honest, I tend to avoid doing most bad things I might otherwise be inclined to do for no higher moral purpose than not wanting to get in trouble for them – don't you? I also tend to do more good when folks are around to see and appreciate it. But is that all there is? Is Ethics really so simple as simply wanting to avoid punishment and get rewarded?

---

[46] And no, your mom, no matter how good she may be, doesn't count.

[47] And there's certainly no shortage of virtues whose virtues are extolled to choose from! Aristotle and others will give us a whole laundry list of them, but that's hardly helpful or instructive if we're left with the task of choosing from among them...

To make his point abundantly clear, Glaucon reminds Socrates of the Ring of Gyges. Gyges had been a shepherd in Lydia (modern-day Turkey), and one day, while out doing his shepherding, a chasm opened in the earth, into which our eponymous hero, being an inquisitive guy, decided to venture. Inside he saw a great bronze horse, with a window in the side of it, through which he saw a man with a ring on. Taking the ring, he climbed back out of the rent in the ground, and went on his merry way. Attending a meeting of the local shepherds' guild, and fiddling with the ring, he found that if he turned it just so, he would be made invisible, and by turning it back again, reappear.[48] Glaucon says that if we were to give a just (read: good) and unjust (read: bad) man this same sort of ring and observe their conduct,[49] in time, their behavior would be the same – the good man could no longer expect reward for his behavior, and the bad man would no longer fear any punishment, and so each would pursue their own desires, completely free from consequence or retribution.

Socrates takes on Glaucon's assertion by tracing out their lives, but, to better account for the vagaries of individual character (i.e., some people are better or worse, better able to resist or give in to corruption than others to begin with), he wants to make the question as large as possible, so we can examine it more clearly. Thus, the question is transformed into one regarding the good state (or polis), because in important respects, the person and the polis are reflections of each other. We are, each of us on an individual level, a microcosmic representation of the macrocosmic reality of the city-state within which we live. When we work to make our city better, we are in turn made better, and we are indirectly enabling others to be made better as well. The important point of including the story is not to examine what people would do if they were able to make themselves invisible;[50] the point of this, as well as the rest of Ethics is to determine not how we *do* behave, but rather, how we *ought* to behave.

The Allegory of the Cave

The next famous story included in Republic is that of Plato's Cave (as it's often called). In the cave, men are shackled and can only see a wall in front of them on which shadows are projected – they take these shadows to be reality. Before we go any further, no – we don't know how they got there, how they go to the bathroom, or any of that; it doesn't matter – it's just an allegory – a story to be interpreted to reveal a hidden meaning, usually a moral one, as in this case. **SPOILER ALERT** Anyway, one of these shackled guys breaks free (somehow), climbs to the light, sees reality as he had never before seen it, then returns to the cave to inform his friends what they've been missing while stuck in the cave.

Because it's an allegory, everything has an additional layer of meaning we need to understand in order to benefit from the story. Being shackled is the same as saying we're tied to body – we only experience things from our own point of view, for the simple reason that that's all we have access to directly. The shadows are taken for reality, just as we tend

---

[48] This should sound hauntingly familiar to Tolkien fans, as it's the inspiration from which old J.R.R. drew his account of Bilbo – sometimes it pays to be a geek.

[49] I know; "how are you going to *observe* an invisible man?" Suspend disbelief, smart guy.

[50] One word: VEGAS.

to take our own passions and points of view as the only real truth (as Protagoras had argued). Think of how many times you've thought, "this world would be so much better if only everyone thought the way I do!" This thought usually occurs to me when I'm driving. The prisoner who breaks his chains and climbs to the light, seeing what he's never before seen, is beginning to realize that everything he had taken as true was really just a shadowy illusion.

When the freed prisoner returns to the cave to inform his fellow captives about his experience outside, they don't believe him, and accuse him of having been "blinded by the light."[51] The light is the guidance of Philosophy to the universal truths to be found within Ethics. What we are intended to begin to realize here is that our search for ethical truths is going to be a search for those ethical truths that are universal in their application, and that will be based in relationships; specifically, how do we relate to the polis, how do we related to God (or the gods), how do we relate to our neighbors, and finally, how do we relate to ourselves, something that won't really be taken up again until we get to Kant several chapters from now. What *Republic* offers us is an unflinchingly rigorous behavioristic approach to Ethics – we become ethical by having our good behavior rewarded, our bad behavior punished, and through it all we learn to become ethical ourselves within a disciplined system.

Presaging the Utilitarians

As a final thought on Plato and his *Republic*, before we move on to his student, Aristotle, we see an early indication of an approach to Ethics that we won't see in its fullest expression for another two thousand years. Socrates notes that we are corporeal (embodied) beings, and we're inclined by pleasure and pain – we tend to seek pleasure, and avoid pain (unless you're into that sort of thing). This will be something we'll see again when we get to Bentham and Mill, but for now we're given the image of a charioteer, being pulled by both a good horse (reason) and a bad horse (passion/emotion). Because we can never fully put aside our passionate aspect, we instead have to develop a will capable of resolving itself to follow the right (moral) course of action. This will can't determine the correct course of action on its own, and our passions and desires know only how to satisfy themselves, so where does this leave us? The answer Plato gives is that we rely on the supremacy of our reason to guide us through life – an answer that will be picked up next by Aristotle.

---

[51] Cue the song by Manfred Mann's Earth Band, and you're welcome for the ear-worm.

Chapter 7: Aristotle

Like the other writers on Ethics of the Classical Era, Aristotle defines the good as that which we desire for its own sake, but adds to this that the good is also what does, or at least what ought to serve as the aim (remember – *telos*) of all our actions and choices. Whereas in Socrates and Plato this good was never precisely specified, Aristotle tells us right away that the good is happiness. The word he uses here is *eudaimonia*, and "happiness" is how it is most often translated, though it could also be rendered just as accurately as "flourishing," "satisfaction," "perfection," or "completion." Happiness itself is then defined as being an activity of the soul (remember – when the Greeks say, "soul," they really mean "mind") in accordance with excellence (the Greek word for which is *arête* – "(moral) excellence," "goodness," or, most commonly, "virtue"). So essentially, happiness is a mental activity that is guided by and exercises the human virtues.

Aristotle's definition of virtue builds on Plato's, but restricts it somewhat; it's still a characteristic that enables something to perform its characteristic function well, but instead of the "hammerness" of the hammer, Aristotle is only interested in humans; tools, artifacts, and objects need not apply. Okay, so what is our characteristic human function? For Aristotle, our defining characteristic, that which separates us from my golden retriever (along with a lot of other things, I hope) is our rationality. We are animals, Aristotle tells us, but we are the *rational* animals. So our virtues, whatever they may be (and have no fear – he'll provide us with a whole laundry list of them), are best thought of as dispositions of the mind in accordance with reason.

Plato's approach had been to tell us a story, or rather, a series of stories, and allow us to find our way through to the nuggets of ethical truth to be found therein; Aristotle is much more direct than that. Rather than lead us through allegory in an attempt to reveal ethical truths, Aristotle defines his subject matter right off the bat in Book I of the *Nichomachean Ethics*, and then proceeds to justify the method by which he selects both his subject matter and his definitions. Let's here take a brief aside for a dual confession. First off, Aristotle didn't write the book – it's (as near as we can tell) a compilation of lecture notes taken by one of his students at the Lyseum, so it's not necessarily indicative of his writing style or ability, but it is very direct, as you might expect notes or an outline to be, which definitely works to our advantage. Second, it reads like stereo instructions – certainly not something you'd want to read as literature, though if it doesn't sour you on Aristotle entirely, I would highly recommend you pick up a copy of his Politics and/or Poetics (they're usually bound/published together anyway), which are masterfully written and interesting whether or not you have any particular interest in either subject.

Our Aims

As part of his attempt to define our subject matter and justify his approach, Aristotle considers the opinions commonly encountered, but also specifically those of poets and philosophers – why would he do this? Poets, perhaps being a bit more passionate than the rest of us, give us a point of reference, if perhaps, an extreme one. Philosophers, ideally the exemplars of rational thought and action, give us a reciprocal point against which to gauge our position, which, as the common people, is probably somewhere between the two. Here he is giving us a bit of a preview of how his notion of virtue will be presented – as a point between extremes. This will also allow him to make an assertion that will guide our understanding from this point forward: all doing, making, investigating (to include any interrogative activity), all deliberate actions and choices made (no matter how innocuous they may appear), *all* aim at some good to be achieved through these activities, and are directed by and to them in this way.

Aristotle points out that many of the aims we have are really only intermediate aims, and we desire them not because they're good or truly desirable and in and of themselves, but only because they're the means by which our higher aims are made possible or attainable. The good is that "at which all things aim," but there's a difference in the *ends* at which all things aim. In some cases, the activity itself is the end; in others, the end is some product beyond the activity. Allow me to give you a rather vulgar example, with my apologies, since it's the best one I can think of to illustrate the point. The former instance is sex for *re*creation – you're just there to have a good time, and that's it, and that's all; the latter is sex for *pro*creation – you're there to perpetuate our species, create a life (or lives,) etc. In every case where the end is something to be attained beyond the action, the product is considered superior to the activity that resulted in it. As before, we're interested here in the furthest end we can achieve, because our approach is fundamentally teleological.

Politics

When we think of Ethics, Politics is probably not the first thing that it occurs to us to associate with it. Aristotle describes politics as the "master science of the good," and more than anything, this probably surprises us, takes us aback, but it makes sense, if only we consider where he's coming from. Politics, as Aristotle thinks of it, contains all that the "most honored capacities" of strategy, household management, oratory, and so on – skills we use not just in what we now think of as politics, but in every interaction, moral, romantic, and otherwise, with everyone around us – in other words, politics is the means by which we inform and practice our ethics. While we might do well to remind our government officials of this, let's not get ahead of ourselves just yet. The end of politics, as Aristotle sees it, is the good of mankind, and the reason he gives is this: to do something good for one person (even yourself) is a source of satisfaction, but to do something good for an entire nation and for states is nobler and more divine. Aristotle has chosen his words here carefully, and he means it is indeed divine, godlike, to do good for others. Hence, we can say, despite evidence to the contrary, that politics and ethics are indeed connected intimately, so much so that one informs the other, and vice versa.

Happiness as the Good

The primary problem with identifying happiness as the good is the burden we then have of sorting through everyone's personal definition of what leads to happiness, and what makes either or both actually good. People have a different notion of happiness as the good depending on their circumstances; if we're starving, we're much more likely to eat that McDonald's burger, even if we know perfectly well there's no real "meat" to be found anywhere in it. If we're stuck outside in the freezing cold, suddenly Uncle Eddie's ugly holdover jacket appears much more fashionable to us. Aristotle reminds us that arguments which proceed from fundamental principles are different from the arguments that lead up to them; we have to start from what is known, but here again we encounter some potential problems. We have those things that are known to us – our collected facts about the way the world is and our relationship to and within it; but we also have what is known pure and simple – these are closer to the universal truths Plato had been looking for. For our purposes, we'll proceed under the assumption that the general guidelines Aristotle sets forth for us are sufficiently adaptable to our individual circumstances so as to be reliable.

The most notable kinds of life (and yes – there are certainly others) are, according to Aristotle, the following three. The most accessible to us is the sort of life that conforms to what we just mentioned – it takes its cues from our circumstances, which vary of course, and tends to pursue pleasure first and foremost. This is probably the way that most of us, without any prompting, think of happiness – as the satisfaction of basic needs, depending on our circumstances. Then there's the political life we mentioned earlier, which aims at honor and the creation of happiness for as many as possible, which we recall is thought of as "nobler and more divine" than creating happiness for ourselves alone. Finally, there's the contemplative life, but more on that later...

If the good varies depending on our lifestyle and our circumstances, then the good will necessarily be something different in different actions and in each situation. But if we have to limit ourselves to what we consider as the good, or if there is some one end of *all* that we do, Aristotle tells us that the good we're looking for will be the one attainable by action. In other words, the good must be something that we can identify, work toward or for, and ultimately, achieve. But what if there appears to be several ends – how do we know which one to seek? The end we're after will be the *most* final and perfect of the goods we have to choose from. We have some additional help in selecting by remembering that the good will need to be pursued as an end in itself, because this will be more final than something we pursue as a means to something else. Whatever we always choose as an end in itself and never as means to something else is called final in an unqualified sense – there's no need for us to justify or support our choice, because it's readily apparent to everyone.

Happiness seems to be the best fit for this kind of good, and for a very good reason – it applies better, or at least more closely, to happiness than to anything else, for the simple reason that we *always* choose happiness as an end in itself and *never* as a means to something else. For example, we like to be liked by other people, we like to feel pleasures (physical, emotional, *and* intellectual), and we choose which virtues we exhibit, all partly for themselves – we would choose them even if we didn't stand to get any further advantages from them. But we also choose them partly for the sake of happiness because all of these things, in addition to their own merits, make us happy. No one chooses happiness because it will then make us be liked by others, because it will bring us pleasure, or because it will lead us to virtue; in other words, we don't choose happiness as a means to anything at all. Finally, Aristotle tells us that the final and perfect good must additionally be entirely self-sufficient – whatever will make like something desirable and lacking nothing. Happiness is something final, and self-sufficient, and is the end of our actions, but Aristotle's not ready to call it the *highest* good yet – something further awaits us.

Rationality

Aristotle was the world's first biologist, zoologist, taxonomist, and that really shines through in several places here; he wants to put us into our proper category, specifically with regard to what separates us from the rest of animate nature. We are animals, he tells us, but we are differentiated, from my golden retriever[52] for instance, as the *rational* animals. Within our lives the rational element works specifically in that we are able to obey the rules of reason, but we are also capable of possessing and conceiving of rational rules when and if they're needed. What we mean by this is that our lives are determined by the activity of rational thought, as opposed to merely possessing the rational element. Because activity leads to goods, and goods are sought for their own sake as the ends of all our actions, activity has a pretty good claim to being the function of mankind. Our proper function then will be an activity of the mind (he actually says, "soul," but we know he means "mind") in conformity with a rational principle.

Based on this, we now are able to make a few (incidentally rational) claims about what we ought to be doing, how we ought to be living, and so on. Our proper function is a certain kind of life, which is an activity of the mind, and consists in actions performed in conjunction with the rational element that defines us as a species. If someone of high standards performs these actions well and properly, in accordance with the excellence (remember: *arête*/virtue) appropriate to it, we reach a further conclusion: The good of mankind is an activity of the mind in conformity with virtue, and if there are several virtues (as there very often are), in conformity with the best and most complete... in a complete life. This last part is contentious because "complete" could mean two rather different things depending on context. Complete could mean that your life is lacking nothing, that you are completely satisfied (fulfilled, perfected, etc., i.e., *eudaimonia*); but it could also mean that it's completed as in over – you're dead.[53] If the former is true, we have a solid basis on which to claim status as ethical individuals; if the latter is true, we can still do this, but only retrospectively.

As to the types of things that can be good, we divide them into three classes: external goods, goods of the soul (mind), and goods of the body. External goods are fairly straightforward – that's your stuff – your car, your house, your clothes, your other possessions, and so on; they are external because they are external to you, and, aside from your ownership of or other tacit connection to them, they're not automatically part of your reality from the get-go. Goods of the mind actually refers to the mind's actions and

---

[52] I have a very old, but very sweet, golden retriever named Bear, who, while he's undeniably good natured and has the best of intentions, is also dumb as a sack of hammers and still thinks he's a puppy who doesn't weigh 80 pounds.

[53] Or, depending on your situation, married.

activities – anything you do to keep it busy, engage it rationally or imaginatively, or employ any mental activity. Goods of the body are just what you'd think they are – good food, good sex, good exercise, good sleep, etc. Because the mind can operate (somewhat) independently of the body,[54] and because we're defining the end correctly as consisting of actions and activities, the end is necessarily included among the goods of the mind and *not* among external goods or goods of the body.

Are what we're describing here best thought of as characteristics or activities? Characteristics may exist within us without producing any good result – we may have them without ever publicly exhibiting them; an activity, on quite the other hand, *must* produce a result. Actions that are performed in conformity with virtue are themselves pleasant, and obviously, virtuous. Actions which conform to virtue are naturally pleasant in themselves, and are viewed as such by rational individuals who love virtue. Someone who doesn't enjoy performing noble (read: good/virtuous) actions, or who does so, but only grudgingly, is, with a good margin of probability, not a good person at all.

How exactly does Aristotle think we're ever going to be capable something like this, and is it even accessible by everyone? Plato gave us that fashionably-unfortunate "members only" approach; does that extend to his most famous student? Thankfully, no. If happiness depends on *arête* (excellence – virtue), it will be shared by, or at least accessibly to *all* rational people. Provided we don't fit into one of the previously discussed four categories, and our capacity to be ethical, and by extension, virtuous is thereby unimpaired, then study and effort will make happiness directly accessible to us. But as you might suspect, this doesn't come without a bit of effort. Think of it like this; most of us have probably, at one time or other, found a bit of money on the street – maybe only a penny, maybe a few bucks, sometimes several dollars. As ubiquitous as this experience may be (i.e., very few people have never found any money, ever), it probably wouldn't be a sound approach on which to establish our plans for retirement; it just wouldn't be a sufficiently reliable income stream, unless we're just exorbitantly lucky. It stands to reason then, that money is probably best not acquired purely through chance, but rather through some conscious effort on our part. Virtue and happiness work exactly the same, and as Aristotle reasons, if it is better that happiness be acquired in this way rather than by chance, it is reasonable on our part to assume that this is the way in which it is or ought to be acquired.

Virtues: Psychological Foundations, Intellectual, and Moral

The mind behaves in precisely the same way as the paralyzed limbs of the body, which is to say that it cannot act without some specific, given stimulus, and depends on our undertaking some action to make its characteristics known to anyone other than ourselves. You can see from across the street whether someone is short or tall, fat or thin, and so on,

---

[54] There's really no need to delve too deeply here into what's called the mind-body problem, but basically, it's this: how can the immaterial mind cause the body to act, and how can the body cause the mind to think. See Rene Descartes for more on this.

but you can't readily tell whether they're a virtuous or vicious[55] person until you quite literally "see them in action." There is something in our minds, however, in addition to the rational element which Aristotle says defines us, that opposes it and reacts against it – the passionate and/or emotional aspect. The mind participates in and accepts the leadership of reason, and, Aristotle informs us, even the irrational (passionate) aspects of the mind must bend to this reason.[56]

Virtues are divided in the same way as the mind; some are "intellectual" virtues, others are "moral" virtues, both of which, forming our character, can be described as a means (to some end). The moral virtues, which obviously we're more interested in for our purposes, also called the ethical virtues, pertain more to the irrational aspects of our minds, but are directed by and can take part in our reason. Our intellectual virtues, the so-called "virtues of thinking" simply require sound teaching received, experience gained, and time spent, and they are what we engage in throughout most of our academic lives spent in classrooms, seminars, and the like. Virtues of character, our moral virtues, come about as a direct consequence of following the right habits – we become habituated to acting virtuously. According to Aristotle, the *potential* to acquire these moral virtues is in us by nature as a function of our rationality, but whether or not we actually come to develop them is wholly dependent on the efforts we're willing to make, and is not *determined* by human nature.

We can reason from this that while virtues aren't implanted in us by nature (sorry, Plato), they are also not contrary to our nature; that is, there's nothing about our humanity, generally speaking, that either automatically makes one virtuous nor prevents them from becoming virtuous if the appropriate steps are taken. We have been equipped by nature with the ability to receive them, and forming the proper habits will bring that ability to completion and fulfillment.[57] So first we have the capacity to be virtuous, and we display the activity through our behavior only secondarily. Think of this as the opposite of your five senses; unless you're otherwise impaired in some way, you receive them at birth as part of the "human equipment package," and when you open your eyes for the first time, taste for the first time, etc., they're used. Virtues don't work like this – you don't possess them right out of the gate, and it's very likely that you won't ever possess a great many of them; virtues are acquired (on Aristotle's account) by having put them into action at some point along the way. What this means is that we can't claim the virtue of generosity for instance until we've undertaken and engaged in some generous action; we aren't courageous until we do something that requires courage on our part.

Because of this, it's of vital importance just what sorts of things we allow ourselves to become habituate to do, because the same causes and means that produce virtue in us can also destroy it, or worse, produce vices – we can become habituated to viciousness every bit as easily, if not a bit more so, because it's often the path of less resistance. We know that virtues will be acquired, or rather, will begin the process of being acquired once we first

---

[55] The suffix "ous" implies that the subject being described is "filled with" or "full of" something; the virtuous person is therefore "full of virtue," while the vicious individual can be said to be "full of vice" (and probably other things as well).

[56] Though David Hume will beg to differ, a few chapters from now…

[57] Note again two of our definitions of *eudaimonia* – sneaky, Aristotle – I see what you did there.

put them into our actions, and if we develop the habit of acting virtuously, we will (in time) become virtuous. Is Aristotle telling us to simply "fake it until we make it?" Not exactly – instead he seems to be telling us to act in manner that is obviously in accordance with the given virtue(s), and in time, when we've become habituated to acting this way, we can be said to be virtuous. There's no set time frame for this, and for obvious reasons it will vary between individuals, but he reminds us to make sure our activities are of a certain kind, because variations (for better or for worse) will be reflected in our characteristics and our perceivable characters. It's important therefore which habits we're instructed in from childhood on, a bit of a gloss on Plato's behaviorist approach to becoming ethical beings.

How Pleasure & Pain Play In

We can safely say that moral excellence is concerned in some way with pleasure and pain. Our love of pleasure can make us do "base" actions, and pain prevents us from doing noble actions. "Base" isn't really used all that often in our spoken language anymore (outside the sociology lab, at any rate), but think of it as being synonymous with "primitive" or "animal;" you take what you want by whatever means you feel are necessary, with little thought given to whether your approach is ethical or virtuous, or not. When we say that pain can prevent us from doing noble things, we're extending that beyond just physical pain, to include emotional and intellectual pains as well – even the point of inconvenience. It might, for instance, occur to me that to stop what I'm doing in order to help you, I may be late for an appointment, or otherwise distracted from the task at hand, and so I simply decide that I can't be bothered; pain has prevented me from behaving virtuously.

Pleasure and pain can't really be avoided in ethical discussions, and as we'll see, the primary differentiation between theories has less to do with what's causing one or the other than with the importance that they're assigned by the theory being discussed. Without giving too much of Hume, Bentham, and Mill away before we get to them, we can safely say that Aristotle is presaging some of the conclusions they'll reach by his discussion of pleasures and pains. Since virtues have to do with our actions and emotions, and since pleasure or pain are consequences of every emotion we feel and every action we undertake, virtue *must* have something to do with pleasure and pain – unavoidably.

Why is the influence of pleasure and pain on our virtues and vices so inescapable? Well, we'd have to go a really long way back to try to train ourselves out of it – our love of pleasure has been ingrained in us since infancy, reinforced regularly since then, and there's the whole "nature versus nurture" issue to contend with. Further, no one had to teach us in any way to appreciate it – it's just how we're naturally inclined toward it. In short, we'd better just accept the fact that pleasures and pains resonate deeply with us, in a way that we'd be hard-pressed to ignore or avoid, and so it's safe to say that virtue makes us act in the best way in matters that will result in pleasure or pain for ourselves and others (and remember – that's *all* of them), and vice will do just the opposite. It's harder for us to fight against our desire for pleasure than against any of our emotions, including anger, and so we have to watch very carefully our attitudes and approaches to it. If we have a right attitude toward pleasure and pain, we will be good; if a wrong attitude, we will be bad. This will very likely involve the realization that sometimes doing what is morally right may require us to forego a few pleasures, and possibly, endure a few pains – even if they're only minor inconveniences and the like. As Aristotle puts it most simply, it comes ultimately down to a matter of what we choose versus what we avoid; when we choose the noble, we avoid the base; when we choose the beneficial, we avoid the harmful; and when we choose the pleasurable, we avoid the painful. Remember to watch out for that last one though, as the right attitude will make or break the result.

What Makes An Action "Virtuous?"

So, as long as I do things most people would observe and then describe as virtuous, I'm good, right? Not exactly – Aristotle's not going to let us off quite that easily. For Aristotle, an act isn't automatically virtuous simply because we perform it justly or with self-control. The performing agent must also have certain characteristics or satisfy certain criteria as he performs it: First, you must *consciously* know what you are doing. Say for instance you open a door to exit a room and someone coming in thanks you for holding it open for them and enters; you didn't open it for them – in fact, you might well be justified in asking them to go back out! Second, you must choose to act the way you do it, and you must choose it for its own sake. Here we have two important aspects, the emphasis on our volitional, our active choice in the matter, as well as choosing something for its own sake, which is equivalent to saying it's desirable for its own sake or on its own merits, both of which meet our definition for calling something "good." Third and finally, the act must spring from a firm and unchangeable character that has been habituated to acting virtuously. In other words, you can't behave virtuously only when it benefits you, or when someone is watching;[58] you have to behave that way consistently, regardless of the circumstances.

Aristotle tells us that acts are called virtuous when they're the sort of acts that a virtuous person would perform. Okay, so far, so good, except perhaps that we're left in suspense as to how we're expected to know what that might look like. He doesn't help a whole lot when he goes on to inform us that the virtuous person is not only someone who performs these acts, but the person who also performs them in the way virtuous people do. Gee, thanks, Aristotle, that just clears everything right up. I don't believe I'm too far off his mark here when I liken this to art; we may not be able to easily or fully articulate our personal definition of art and what qualifies for the title, but, in a way that would make Potter Stewart[59] proud, we "know it when we see it." This rather irritatingly vague and imprecise guideline could be a good thing or a bad thing, depending on how we approach it. It's bad in that it doesn't provide us a whole lot of direction other than to go with our instincts as to what connotes a virtuous person and how we ought to best judge their actions accordingly. At the same time, it's good for precisely the same reason, because it allows us to readily adapt and cast a bit wider net in terms of what we can and ought to be looking for in judging another's (or our own) moral character.

---

[58] Aristotle expresses no opinions as to whether or not we ought to "dance like nobody's watching," though it is safe to assume he would approve.

[59] Late Supreme Court justice; see *Jacobellis v. Ohio* (1964) to get the joke.

Defining Virtue

As I mentioned earlier, Aristotle is an (perhaps *the*) early biologist/taxonomist, and he just can't seem to resist letting a bit of that natural science approach slip into his Ethics by attempting to classify virtue in much the same way as we might classify organisms of various sorts. Today we have the Kingdom, Phylum, Class, Order, Family, Genus, Species arrangement; Aristotle starts at a pretty close level of specificity with Genus, and he really wants for us to focus on what exactly virtues are, how we ought best to identify, categorize, arrange, and think about them, so we can be as precise in our approach as possible. To that end, we'll work through his Genus-level reasoning to describe fairly specifically what virtues are, and then proceed to get as specific as possible in our understanding of what they are – the better we understand what they are, the better our chances will be of participating in them consistently and effectively.

As to the Genus appropriate to virtues, Aristotle begins by telling us that they can't be emotions, because we are not called good or bad or praised or blamed for our emotions (but on the basis of our particular virtues and vices). The key reason here is that choice is not involved in our emotions, but choosing to act virtuously involves choice.[60] Our emotions are more or less spontaneous, and we are "moved" by and with the emotions we experience, but our virtues and vices don't work like this. We may be "disposed" in a certain way stemming from our virtues and vices, that is, we have a particular outlook[61] or approach to things depending on them, but we're not really moved in the same way as when we're happy or we're sad. So the virtues can't be counted as being in any way part of our emotional capacities.

Still trying to nail down precisely what virtues are on the Genus level, we can safely say that they're not, and can't be, capacities either, because we're not praised or blamed for the sorts of things we're capable of. Physically, I suppose I'm probably capable of viciously murdering the next several people I encounter in my day. I'm not likely to, nor am I particularly inclined to, but nonetheless, I'm capable – so is everyone else who is not physically impeded from doing so in some way. Intellectually, I'm capable of learning Swahili or quantum physics; I have no plans to pursue a study of either, but theoretically, I'm not excluded from doing either for lack of capacity to do so (more from lack of interest in them, if anything). Our capacities, both physical and intellectual (mental) are given us by nature, but nature doesn't develop us into good or bad people – our habits do. Now, we could probably dwell on this a bit and come up with a few more colorful alternatives, but in the interest of moving right along, we'll proceed in our reasoning as Aristotle does; if the virtues aren't emotions, and if they're not capacities, the only alternative that remains to us is that they must be characteristics.

Aristotle moves next to what we would call the Species level, but which he labels "differentia," and appropriately so, for it's at this level that we are able to differentiate our subject matter in order to better (or best) understand it. It's insufficient for our purposes to

---

[60] Duh.

[61] The glass is actually always full, though the air to water ratio varies.

define virtue in very general terms as a characteristic; we need to specify just what sort of a characteristic it is. Thinking back to his definitions of virtue we recall that every virtue (or excellence, *arête*) "renders good the thing itself of which it is the excellence," a needlessly convoluted way of saying that it makes something what it is on a fundamental and essential level. This would be the "hammerness" of the hammer, except now we're limiting ourselves to humanity, to the exclusion of objects, artifacts, tools, etc., but retaining the notion that our virtues cause us to perform our characteristic function, whatever it may be, well. From this, Aristotle gathers that the virtue of man will be a characteristic that makes him a good man, and which causes him to perform his own function well.[62] Because we are described by him as the rational animal, it stands to reason that what defines us on a specific level will be some sort of rational activity.

Virtue as the Mean

We've encountered the mean before, probably accompanied by the median and the mode, in our mathematics classes, and it means much the same thing here, with a few very slight variations in application. What we're shooting for in finding the mean is that "equal" part that is the median point between excess and deficiency, but it's important to distinguish between two differences senses in which "mean" can be used. The median of an entity, sometimes called the arithmetic mean, is a point equidistant from both extremes, and is the same for everyone. An example of this would be a number line between two and ten; the mean arithmetic will assist you in arriving at, no matter who taught you, or when or where you're looking at the problem, will always be six, entirely without exception. The other sort of mean, and the one we're interested in for our present purposes, is the mean relative to us, which is exactly what it sounds like, and is as a result, never (or rarely) the same for everybody. Here's the big secret to understanding Aristotle's Ethics;[63] it all comes down to Goldilocks and the Three Bears. Remember your fairy tales fairly well? It goes something like this: just as the ideal porridge was not too hot, not too cold, but just right, so ought our ethics to be, on Aristotle's account. Who knew it could be so easy?!

Virtue is best thought of in this way as the balance point between vices on either side, one of which is marked by excess, and the other by deficiency. This departs significantly from Plato's account, wherein virtue seems to be a point distant from vice on a sort of linear continuum. The important thing to understand is that this varies from individual to individual. Case-in-point, let's say that Bill Gates and I are walking down the street together (I don't know why – suspend disbelief!), and a homeless person solicits the pair of us for money. I give him a twenty dollar bill and Bill gives him the exact same thing; what makes me relatively generous and makes Bill a bit of a tightwad? Well, for starters, Bill made more money in the time it just took you to read that imagined vignette than I, working full-time as a professional philosopher, will make this fiscal year – probably a lot more. In this sense, what would have been extravagant for me might well have been stingy for him, and so

---

[62] The whole "he or she," "him or her" thing bugs me to no end when I encounter it in texts, so I'm just going to avoid it entirely. Ladies, when you encounter "he" and "him," feel perfectly free to substitute "she" or "her" – the context will be unaffected.

[63] Shh... don't tell anybody!

there's really no "one size fits all (or even most)" answer to how much should be given – it depends on the individual.

Think of it as a teeter-totter or see-saw; remember those, back on the playground in elementary school and at the city park? Alright, on one side you've got the fat kid[64] – he'll represent the vice of excess for us; on the other side, probably up in the air somewhat, is our skinny kid – he'll represent the vice of deficiency for us. The balance point in the middle, literal in this case, as well as figurative, is the point at which our virtue is found. Why relate this to a piece of playground equipment? Well, it keeps it on my mental level for one – I don't have to bear in mind any complex ethical definitions or recall specific moral rules, and I can visualize it nicely and easily. Furthermore, we know, most if not all of us from firsthand experience, exactly how this is going to work – the excess is going to pull down while the deficiency will be in turn lifted up, and in any case, a balance point will be reached between the two.

Aristotle gives us a handful of "real life" examples of the mean in the *Nichomachean Ethics*, and it's worth a few minutes of our time to review them in order to hammer home the idea. He tells us that in feelings of fear and confidence, courage is the mean, and therefore, the virtue; concerning the excess, we might call the vice recklessness, and the deficiency is obviously cowardice. In regard to pleasures and pains – not all of them, and to a lesser degree in the case of pain, the virtue (mean) is self-control, and the excess is self-indulgence; there isn't a word really for someone who is viciously deficient in regard to pleasure, and that's the case for several of these – sometimes we simply don't have a word available to describe it, and have to satisfy ourselves that the reciprocal vice is still a vice, though perhaps a nameless one. In the giving and taking of money, the mean is generosity, and the excess and deficiency are, respectively, extravagance and stinginess.

So we have three kinds of dispositions we can adopt as our outlook on things, which fall into two subcategories: we can be vicious in our approach, either excessively or deficiently, or we may be virtuous. Each of these is opposed to both the others; the vices which represent the extremes on either side are more opposed to one another than each of them is to the virtue, which is the mean, but the extremes (vices) are (obviously) opposed to the mean (virtue) as well. So if we're looking at this in terms of how to apply it to our behavior, and as before, if that's *not* what we're doing then why are we bothering at all, then how do we proceed, and what do we do? When one of the extremes is closer and more similar to the mean, we don't treat it, but rather the other extreme as the opposite of the mean, so the more we're naturally attracted to anything, the more opposed to the mean does the thing appear to us to be. So, for your chocoholics, you're going to want to shoot for the deficient end of the mean – which, depending on how bad your addiction is, might mean a single square instead of the whole Hershey bar, and so we described as more opposed to the mean those things to which our personal tendency is stronger.

---

[64] This isn't meant at all to be hurtful; I can poke gentle fun at him, since I usually *was* him back in grade school!

We've established so far that moral virtue is a mean, in what specific sense it's a mean, that it is a mean between two vices, one of which is marked by excess, and the other by deficiency, and that it aims at the median point in our actions and emotions. This is why it's so hard to be good – it's tough to find the mean, and difficult to maintain it. Back to the teeter-totter/see-saw example, the reason certain people seem exceptionally good, noteworthy and noble, and praiseworthy is that they're better at balancing, or rather, at maintaining their balance at the virtue point than the rest of us are. If you recall for a moment your days as a youngster at recess, it was downright tough to get that contraption perfectly level and hold it there without a fair amount of wobbling to either side. The Ghandis, Mother Theresas, Lincolns, and other exemplars of virtues are simply better at balancing than the rest of us vicious miscreants. This isn't to say the rest of us should give up,[65] but rather that we should first concern ourselves with aiming for the mean point of virtue, second avoid the extreme most opposed to it, and realize that occasionally we must settle for the lesser of two evils because in our attempt to stay at the virtue point, we're necessarily going to bounce back and forth between vices of excess and deficiency. Rather than this spoiling the whole thing as hopeless, Aristotle tells us that this is the way we'll most easily and most often cross the balance point and hit the mean – which is the point of excellence and virtue.

Pleasure

Pleasure is discussed throughout the whole work, but is given a carefully focused handling in Book X of the Nichomachean Ethics, in which Aristotle questions the seemingly accepted viewpoint of his day that pleasure should be avoided all together, not because it is all inherently bad, but certainly lest we get ourselves into some sort of carnal trouble. His argument is that peoples' actions would seem to indicate this isn't really what they believe, for despite claims to the contrary, we're pretty into pleasure, and that interest runs deeply in us at a species level. He reviews a few of his contemporaries' and earlier philosophers' arguments and arrives at a point where he is willing to tell us that while pleasure is undeniably a good in that it's pursued for its own sake, it's not *the* Good, or that which *all* good things have in common – the characteristic virtue of goodness, as it were. I only point this out because it will be important as a reference point with which to contrast our Utilitarian philosophers, who will suggest quite the opposite.

What then would meet and satisfy Aristotle's definition of *the* Good, that is, something which lacks nothing, so is complete, and is self-sufficient, not being dependent on anything else? He arrives, again, at happiness as absolutely meeting the criteria he established, because activities that result in happiness are important parts of a life lived in conformity with virtue's dictates. It is a life that involves study and effort on our part, not one that is spent purely seeking pleasure and amusement – another potential pitfall of the Utilitarian approach as we'll first encounter it. Now, we are unlikely, as 21st century readers to associate "happiness" and "study" with one another, especially as study probably brings to mind cramming for the big exam until the small hours of the morning, trying to consume

---

[65] Or "take our ball and go home," if we're continuing the playground analogy…

just enough coffee to keep you awake without bringing about a coronary. He doesn't mean *that* kind of studying.

Intelligence, Study, and Wisdom

You'll recall that Aristotle as the proto-biologist/anthropologist defined humans as being the rational animals, and it's this rational, or rather, intelligent/intellectual activity that he's thinking of here, as the highest possession and defining characteristic of us on a species level. With intelligence being our highest possession, the objects of our intelligence, that is, the things which occupy our thoughts, are the highest objects of knowledge, but are also the most continuous, in that we're able to study continuously more than to perform any other kind of action. Now obviously this doesn't mean we can study in the sense of cramming for the exam continuously, without (several) breaks, but we can absolutely do things that engage our minds much longer than we can, for instance, run, do jumping jacks, etc. We can, for example, lose ourselves in a good book until the small hours of the morning, realizing we have to be up in just a few hours, and still wanting to "just finish one more chapter." We can spend hours listening to our favorite music, watching our favorite movies, in conversation with our dearest friends, playing our favorite board and card games, and so on. This is the sort of "study" he's referring to, and it certainly sounds preferable to me compared to the sort we usually think of!

Aristotle reasons from this that the complete happiness of mankind is the activity of our intelligence, provided it is over a complete lifespan, because nothing connected with happiness can, on his account, be incomplete. So a life guided by intelligence is the best and most pleasant for us, if for no other reason than that intelligence, more than anything else, *is* us, and this kind of life will be the happiest! Recalling that virtue has both a moral purpose and an action, Aristotle wonders which is the decisive element, and it's not initially clear, because virtue and the concept of completeness depend on both. The activity that surpasses all others though must be a contemplative activity, and that activity will be the most conducive to our happiness – happiness being a kind of study or contemplation. But what kind of study or contemplation? The Greeks had plenty of terms that we might translate equally well for this; *episteme* for scientific sorts of knowledge, *phronesis* for the sort displayed by skillful politicians, and *sophia* as the sort practiced and held by those searching for the deeper meanings of life. It's this last one with which *philo-sophia*, the love of wisdom, is concerned. Someone whose activity is guided by intelligence, who cultivates their intelligence, seems to be the happiest, and so a wise man will attain and maintain a more happiness than anyone else. In other words, the happiest person in the world is, for Aristotle, the philosopher, and I'm inclined to agree, but then – I'm biased.

Interlude: A Note on the Inclusion of Christian Philosophers

Why have I included two Christian philosophers; am I trying to be purposively divisive, force-feed you religion, or make some sort of a statement? No. Well, maybe that last one. My intention in including these two is to show what was going on with Plato's and Aristotle's philosophies several centuries after their lives, and that takes us well into the Christian era, and that requires that we look at some Christian philosophers. Now, that having been said, it really does matter what you think about religion in general, Christianity in particular, or even Catholicism (when we get to Aquinas, especially), because we're not looking at these undeniably religious texts for religious reasons; rather, we want to read them to see what sort(s) of Moral Philosophy we can pull out of them, and then examine whether or not it is likewise applicable outside the scope of religious belief. So suspend judgment, at least momentarily, and we'll see what we can glean from these guys…

Chapter 8: St. Augustine of Hippo

Aurelius Augustinius Hipponensis, known to us more commonly at St. Augustine of Hippo lived roughly eight hundred years after Plato, whose ethical thinking inspired and influenced his own. He was a Roman citizen in what had been Carthage, so a bit of a history lesson/refresher is probably in order. Phoenician traders from what is modern-day Lebanon founded Carthage on the north coast of Africa sometime around the ninth century B.C.; they very quickly became the rivals of the Romans, some highlights of which were the Punic Wars,[66] the third of which Rome won, so by the time Augustine shows up, Carthage is a thoroughly Romanized territory. As a Roman, Augustine grew up a pagan polytheist, though his mother, St. Monica, was a Christian, and his father converted on his deathbed. Following his conversion, St. Augustine's religious and philosophical writings would come to form the foundation of (almost) all subsequent Western Christian theology and philosophy – especially for Roman Catholics and protestants. This is hardly surprising, considering that during his lifetime he wrote some fifty million words (suddenly that 2,500 word term paper doesn't seem so daunting, does it), and because his religious beliefs would greatly influence his philosophical thought.

Augustine was the last of the group of guys we commonly call the Early Church Fathers, many of whom, though certainly not all, are graced with the title of "saint," who wrote roughly from the time of the last New Testament text until Augustine's death in 430 A.D. These patristic writers (from the Latin *pater*, father) commented on and clarified the books that today comprise the New Testament canon, as well as a few of the extra-canonical books, and helped to shape the traditions that would influence the development of the Church from their time to our own. Augustine is particularly unique in that he's one of the few figures who is revered as a saint by Eastern Orthodoxy, Roman Catholicism, and, though many of them don't acknowledge saints per se, by protestant denominations. It is in Augustine that we find the first systematic development of the doctrine of original sin, an idea that would come to greatly influence Western Christianity, particularly in its protestant varieties – more on that shortly.

Forty-six years after the death of Augustine, 476 A.D., is the date typically given by historians for the Fall of the Roman Empire. To be fair, it had actually been in the process of "falling" for quite some time before that, but this is the date generally agreed upon as the Fall, for that date marks the victory of the Visigoths, led by Alaric, over what remained of the Roman military might, which wasn't much by then. This places Augustine at the very end of the Classical era; the Medieval era is generally considered to have been 500 A.D. (rounding up from the Fall of Rome) to about 1500 A.D. (rounding up from Columbus' voyages), though there are arguments made that it ended sooner, around the time of the

---

[66] If you're unfamiliar with these, they make for fascinating reading – better than fiction; especially the exploits of the Carthaginian general Hannibal (*not* Lecter), who famously led an army of elephants over the Alps into Rome...

Italian Renaissance. For our purposes, it really doesn't matter – Augustine is a great exemplar of Plato's philosophy at the end of the Classical and beginning of the Medieval, just as Aquinas is a great exemplar of Aristotle's philosophy during the "high Middle Ages." Both of them illustrate something that we'll see repeated with some regularity from this point forward – the contrast of Platonists, as the name implies, those whose though echoes Plato, and Aristotelians, those whose thought echoes Aristotle.

Good and Evil

Like Plato and Aristotle, Augustine is interested first and foremost in providing us with a working definition of the good, which up to this point you will recall has been defined first as that which is desirable for its own sake (Plato), and as that at which all things aim (Aristotle). Augustine will move forward without stating this directly, though assuming both definitions, to tell us that following God is the "chief good," and that happiness (recall *eudaimonia*) will consist in loving and enjoying that good. The other side of the coin, evil, is not thought of as an active force, but instead, simply as the absence of good. Think of your high school Physics class, and the definition you learned there for "cold;" there really is no such thing, only the absence of heat. In this way, on an Augustinian account, as we move further from the source of goodness (God) we are likely to become more evil, in just the same way as when an object is removed from the source of heat it will grow colder. This is one of the indicators that allows us to label him as a Platonist, since it's in keeping with Plato's understanding of virtue and vice as being on a linear continuum – the further we remove ourselves from one, the closer we are to the other.

Confessions

Augustine's *Confessions* is a masterfully-written book, the Western world's first true autobiography, and it deserves a spot on your bucket list (alongside Plato's *Republic*, remember) of books to read before you die – you'll be a better person for having done so, regardless of your views on faith. In it, Augustine tells us that he had been a sinner since the day he was born, and that in fact, all humans are born with a radical selfishness, and this causes us to sin.[67] Despite the fact that we're inherently selfish, and despite all the myriad sins we commit during our lives, we have been created to praise God, and we can't find peace in our lives until we do, as this is the "meaning of life," according to Augustine. Once we realize and come to terms with our sinful natures, we are ready to turn away from ourselves and toward God. To aid us in this, we need to be educated from childhood and corrected along the way, in order to have a right attitude toward sin, as soon as we are able to profit from correction. This should sound familiar, and Platonic, since it echoes Plato's behavioral approach to developing moral reasoning.

Beginning like Aristotle, Augustine wants to know what the highest good of human life, what we ordinarily call "happiness" really is, and more importantly, where it can be found

---

[67] Keep this thought tucked away for when we discuss Thomas Hobbes, following Thomas Aquinas – he's going to take this idea and run with it, arguing that we're *so* selfish that our ethical decisions can actually be based on our radical selfishness!

and how it can be attained. He rejects the physical body as the basis of this good, arguing that it must be an attribute of the soul. Now, here we have to take a brief aside; up this point, when we've encountered the word "soul" in the Greek philosophers, it's meant *psyche*, mind. Augustine still seems to mean that – some of the time, but we're also starting to see the transition to the Christian understanding of the term, that is *anima*, soul as we probably ordinarily think of it today. Sometimes it's hard to catch this in Augustine, as it's entirely contextual, but certainly something to be aware of and keep in mind. The good, whatever it is, will be a virtue (remember *arête*) that the soul obtains by seeking and following God. Before we can start on that project though, Augustine has to address a rather big problem.

The Problem of Evil

The proverbial elephant in the room, for Augustine as well as for any modern religious thinker, is what is commonly called the Problem of Evil – basically, why does a good God allow evil to exist in the world? There have been as many answers to this as there have been philosophers to posit them; Augustine's answer in unique, but is it also convincing? First, a little background and a few definitions are needed. Ethical monotheists, such as Jews, Christians, Muslims, and Sikhs, are those religions who state the claim that there is only one God, and that God is essentially good (that's the "ethical" part, in a slightly different context than we're accustomed to seeing it), tend to ascribe to God the following attributes, in no particular order of importance: God is omnipotent,[68] able to do absolutely anything; omnipresent, able to be present everywhere[69] simultaneously; omniscient, knowing everything that can be known; and omnibenevolent (sometimes styled as "omniperfect"), possessing infinite goodness. Here's where the problem comes in – you can think of God as having the first three attributes and still account for evil in the world fairly easily.

It's not until you ascribe to God that final attribute of "perfect or infinite goodness" that evil becomes truly problematical. Why would a God from whom only good things can come allow little kids to get cancer, villages to be decimated by hurricanes, and *Jersey Shore* to get six seasons while *Firefly*[70] only got one? Polytheistic religions can account for this easily, by blaming it on the "bad" god(s) of their particular belief system – Hades did it. Zoroastrianism has a particularly novel approach to this, in their bitheistic/dualistic theology, wherein the bad god does bad things, and the good god does good things. In later Christian thinking the Devil will fit this role nicely, but for now, Augustine has to (attempt to) address this problem and account for it before we can move on profitably.

Augustine begins to address the problem of evil by asserting that God made all things, and more to the point, made them all good. Evil then must be thought of not as a positive force, but as the corruption of a thing that began as good, for example a shirt that develops a hole,

---

[68] The prefix "omni" simply means "all," as in this case – all powerful.

[69] Even in Detroit.

[70] If you're already a fan, "go Browncoats!" If you're not already a fan, you're missing out on a really great show!

a body that develops disease, or a tree that develops rot. As support for this, he notes that our concepts of ordered relational comparisons, like better and worse, nobler and inferior, etc., all contribute to the overall good of things, and because of this are not ultimately evil. Evil must the come from our free will, as instances we seem inclined to call evil required the conscious decision of someone, the "evildoer" to commit an act or series of acts that we then describe as having been evil. If this is the case, then the will would seem to be completely free to act as it chooses to, and thus we're propelled into a discussion of what exactly free will must be.

Free Will, Original Sin, and Grace

Our will is nothing more than the volitional power of our mind – the ability to choose between options and alternatives available to us. For Augustine, every one of these acts we undertake is an act of love seeking to be united with some good. Sin, however, is a perversity of the will, and this is what causes it, and by extension, us, to turn away from God. For the will to be free, he argues, it must be free from external coercion – we cannot be compelled, intimidated, or in any other way pressured to act as we do. This is not, however, freedom from God, who represents and is the source of all our good as well as our potential to be good and do good. Just like Plato (and St. Paul), true freedom expressly implies the freedom we have to love that which will make us completely happy. So sin, and the evil that results from it is a kind of oppression, not true freedom, even if in sinning we believe we're acting the way that we have chosen to act.

Sin stems ultimately from a defect in our free will, just as sickness manifests from a disease in the body, and like sickness, it can only be treated and not necessarily irradiated, if for no other reason than that in the case of original sin, we are born with it already in place. Because of Adam's sin, we are born with a pre-corrupted nature, one which renders sin irresistible to us, and which makes it impossible for us not to sin. Think of it in terms of genetics – we might be predisposed, given our genetic code to develop Lou Gehrig's Disease or cystic fibrosis, but in the case of original sin, there's no element of chance involved – we've definitely got it and will suffer from it, simply as a matter of course, being Adam's descendants.[71] Not only that, but in addition to suffering guild for Adam's sin, we're also of course guilty of our own actual sins. This all seems fairly damning and certainly unavoidable, so how will Augustine account for our ability to resist sin from time to time? Grace. Grace connects us to Christ in the same way as our original sin connects us to Adam, and grace is what heals the will that has been corrupted by sin. It's irresistible, but not coercive – it moves our will inwardly toward that which is good. Grace is unmerited, cannot be bought, but can only be prayed for, because its effects will determine the choices we make from now until our physical death.

---

[71] Now obviously, if your reading of the *Genesis* account is not a literal one, there are going to be some issues with this, but continue to suspend judgment – the "hole in the otherwise good shirt" model still holds, regardless of your views on creation.

Of the Morals of the Catholic Church

Think back to that really ugly break-up you had. You know – the one where not only was this person out of your life, but you then proceeded to develop a real hatred and pity for them, probably expressed to one or more people, maybe even loudly and publicly. Augustine "broke up" with Manichaeism, and it wasn't pretty. Found by Mani, this was a variation on the still extant Persian (now Iranian) faith, Zoroastrianism, and it included elements of that belief system, along with Judaism, Buddhism, and Christianity. It was the original salad bar faith – Mani had taken beliefs he liked, left the rest, and apparently it was a pretty compelling conglomeration, because Augustine tells us in *Confessions* that he hung around them for nearly a decade before converting to Christianity in 387 A.D. It was a timely conversion, as Theodosius I, the first Christian Roman emperor,[72] had declared death to Manicheans in 382. Following his break-up, er, conversion, Augustine became an outspoken opponent of Manichaeism, though we can see a few of their ideas in his philosophy, especially the dual nature of good and evil, the idea of hell (as we now think of it), enmity toward "fleshly" sins, and so on. The main reason seems to have been his meeting of Faustus, a key Manichean, who was reputed to be wise but proved to be a dullard when Augustine questioned him. It can't have helped that Manichaeism was of the Gnostic[73] school of thought, which basically stated that knowledge of a certain sort can lead to salvation, a view that was too passive for Augustine, who sees a need for us to actively seek, find, and follow God.

Augustine's first assertion in *Of the Morals* is that happiness is in the enjoyment of man's chief good, and he places two criteria on just what that chief good can be. First, nothing can be better than it, and second, it cannot be lost against the will. He's going to proceed from this point to build his argument, arguing step-by-step through a logical progression in an attempt not only to inform us, but to convince us. But how will we know what to look for in order to satisfy our desire for our chief good? He tells us that if we seek what we can't obtain, we suffer torture – that crush you had on the object of your affections who was simply out of your league; it wasn't going to happen, but you wanted them nonetheless, and your desire tortured you.[74] If we have what isn't desirable, we've been cheated; he's probably thinking here of the Manicheans themselves, who, while they have an impressive sales presentation, at the end of the day, are selling an empty and worthless product. And finally, one who doesn't seek what is worth seeking is diseased – as in mentally; probably no need for further explanation there. Whatever this good is, he assures us, no one can be happy who doesn't enjoy it, and everyone who enjoys it is happy. Well, that's not particularly helpful; let's see where he goes from here...

---

[72] Okay, so technically Constantine was the first Roman emperor to become a Christian, but he converted on his deathbed, so it really doesn't count.

[73] From the Greek word *gnosis*, knowledge; these guys held that some people have a "divine spark" within them that allows them to reach levels of knowledge and salvation that are otherwise hidden from and unavailable to the rest of us.

[74] Put the book down and call them up – you might have a shot after all.

The Chief Good of Man

Regarding the two criteria Augustine placed on the chief good of man, if it can't be anything inferior to us, what remains? If we're able to find something that is both superior to us, and can be possessed by us if we love it, then we're clearly looking for something better than the being who makes the endeavor; in other words, my chief good can't be anything that I can create myself. The chief good also can't be lost against my will, because if I don't have confidence that I can continue to enjoy the good, how can I be happy if I'm preoccupied with my fear of losing it? I think here about middle school romances, wherein the participants are so into assuring themselves and each other, after all, you didn't write just anyone's name several hundred times on your notebook and binder, but their name, no doubt with little hearts around it, that when you broke up the next week (time to get a new binder) you had scarcely gotten to enjoy the relationship (such as it was) before it was over.

To find out what is better than us, it stands to read that we find have to find out what we are (duh). Are we body *and* soul? Are we just bodies? Are we just soul, and by soul, do we mean that we are just minds? Whatever is the chief good of either or both the body and soul, or of the soul only, will be our chief good. Augustine then gives us a list of the things that the chief good of the body is not: bodily pleasure (again – we'll revisit and challenge this with the Utilitarians), absence of pain (the Epicureans would have disagreed), strength, beauty (collective sigh of relief), swiftness, or whatever else is usually considered among the goods of the body. The chief good of the body is the soul, but the soul is not the chief good of man. Remember, the chief good of the body is necessarily *better than* the body, and the soul certainly meets this criterion. The body guided by a virtuous soul is in the greatest perfection available to it, and therefore, whatever gives perfection to the soul will be man's chief good, even if we call the body "man."

The question is here transformed from what is the body, i.e., is it body and soul, soul only, etc., but what gives perfection to the soul. When this thing is obtained, Augustine tells us, one of two options will result: either we will be made perfect, which is unlikely as Augustine would no doubt argue that only Christ is perfect, or at least we'll be much better off than we were without the thing in question – bingo. Virtue (*arête* again – excellence) gives perfection to the soul, and the soul obtains virtue by following God, which is therefore the happy life. The question then arises as to whether or not this virtue can exist by itself, or only within the soul – we trust that God will assist us in finding virtue, but how? Whether it can exist by itself without the soul, or only in the soul, it seems clear either way that in the pursuit of virtue the soul follows after something, which must either be the soul itself, or something outside of it, but what is it?

Here we can safely dispense with a few possibilities as unlikely or ridiculous; either the soul doesn't desire to reach what it's searching for (which is ridiculous), or, as Augustine says, in following after itself while foolish, it reaches the folly it flees from. So the soul is not seeking after itself, and the "something else" our soul becomes virtuous in following after must either be a wise man or God Himself. Remember though, that a wise man can be taken from us despite our protestations – Augustine is here probably thinking of Plato having lost

Socrates very much against his will, so it can't be a wise man that the soul is seeking. God is the only remaining alternative, in following after whom we live well, and in reaching whom we live both well and happily. This is how Augustine is able to argue that following God is the chief good, and happiness consists in loving and enjoying this good.

Enchiridion

Enchiridion means "handbook" or "guidebook;" think, "rules" or "instructions" – you know, those things you don't bother to read until you're three-quarters of the way through the project anyway, past the point of no return. Essentially, this book is a catechism; no, not that tediously boring catechism class you had to sit through as a middle school kid, but a model of Christian instruction, organized around the three theological (or "Pauline") virtues of faith, hope, and love (or charity). Just in case you're curious, under faith, Augustine discusses the Apostles' Creed as the means by which we teach Christian doctrine and refute heresies. For more on how this works, get a copy of the Creed in question and read it backwards, no – not like you'd play an Ozzie Osbourne record backwards to hear the hidden message, but rather, read it and see what it's refuting; "I believe in ONE God" was specifically necessary because there were other, early Christianities (note the plural) that had more than one God, sometimes several, and so on – all the way through the Creed. It's actually pretty neat, but I digress. Under hope, the Lord's Prayer, i.e., the "Our Father" is explained as the ideal model of Christian prayer. Finally, the part we're interested in, the section on love specifically deals with Christian charity or love – *caring* love (as opposed to romantic or erotic love).

The Trinity

The Supremely Good Creator (God) made all things good. Augustine's reasoning works as follows: The Trinity, i.e., Father, Son, and Holy Spirit, is supremely, equally, and unalterably good. The different facets of God (parts of the Trinity) are good even considered separately, but considered as a whole, i.e., as the Trinity, they are *very* good. They are (grammar Nazis, prepare to cringe), more gooder – the most goodest. Therefore, all good things must come from God. Evil then, when understood as sin, regulated, and put in the proper context, can enhance our appreciation of the good from a comparative basis. Vices in the soul, those which we call sins, are privations of the natural good approved of by God, that is, the good God provided has been taken away from us, or pushed away by us. If and when they are overcome and "cured," they aren't transferred to someone else; when they cease to exist in the healthy soul, they can't exist anywhere else, either, so they're best thought of as a disease to be treated/cured, rather than as a parasite that can jump from host to host.

Good Things, Corrupted

All beings were made good by God,[75] and, seeing that the Creator is supremely good, are themselves inclined to be good, but because they're not perfectly good like the Trinity, they're liable to corruption, i.e., their good can be diminished and increased. When our

---

[75] You want to correct this to "made well," don't you? But it's not a typo; read on.

good is diminished (by sin and its effects), it is an evil, but Augustine maintains that because we are made to be good, some good must remain, no matter how corrupted we become, to constitute our being, for no matter how small a creation of God may be, the good which makes it a being can't be destroyed without destroying the being itself. I call this the Hitler's pinkie toe argument because Augustine is essentially saying that no matter how bad we perceive something or someone to be, there's still at least a modicum of goodness in them somewhere – even if just their pinkie toe, that makes them partially good, otherwise they would quite literally cease to exist, on Augustine's account.

Augustine reasons that so long as a being is in the process of corruption there is in us some good of which we're being deprived, and if a part of us remains that can't be corrupted, then we're at heart incorruptible beings, and the process of corruption itself will result in the great good being manifested in us. If we don't cease to be corrupted, then we also can't cease to possess the good of which corruption is trying to deprive us. If we're ever thoroughly and completely consumed with sin and corruption then there will be no good left, since there will be no us within which goodness resides. In other words, corruption can only consume the good (us) by consuming our entire being, which Augustine doesn't seem to view as all together likely, if possible. So he reasons that every being is good – a great good if it can't be corrupted, a little good if it can be – most of us probably fall into the latter category, but hopefully not too deeply. If we're ever wholly consumed by corruption then corruption itself will cease to exist too, because there will be no being left in which it can dwell. This might sound vaguely familiar – think Star Wars and Lord of the Rings; you've got Senator Palpatine, a nice enough, kindly old guy, until the evil of the Sith overcomes him entirely as the Emperor/Darth Sidious, but at that point, he's thrown down a shaft into the main reactor of the death start. What about Smeagol? Just out for a nice afternoon fishing trip until he finds the one ring, the process of corruption overtakes him as he becomes Gollum, and he end winds up falling into the volcanic lava of Mount Doom. Both of them, once they are entirely consumed with corruption, quite literally cease to exist. How about that – Augustinian Moral Philosophy in a couple geeky movies!

Obviously, a great deal of Augustine's arguments are entirely predicated on a very specific understanding of the Christian faith, one's relation to and within it, and as such, are potentially not a universally applicable as the Platonic thought from which they draw their inspiration. Nonetheless, Augustine stands as an ideal exemplar of the thought process that we see toward the end of the Classical and the beginning of the Medieval Eras, in which the philosophical project is largely dedicated to integrating the thought of the Greeks with the developing doctrines of the Christian Church. Whether or not we accept Augustine's philosophical package in its entirety is going to be largely based on where we're coming from in our own faith background (or lack thereof), but at the end of the day, Augustine's unique perspectives certainly give us some interesting things to consider, and if nothing else, it makes for a unique counterpoint to the arguments put forth in works like Euthyphro, as well as a great many that will come in later centuries and the philosophical project continues…

Chapter 9: Thomas Aquinas

First, some perspective; in going from Augustine of Hippo to Thomas Aquinas, we're quietly skipping about eight centuries, which, to put it in context, is roughly the same amount of time that separated Augustine from Plato, and separates us from Aquinas. This means that Aquinas is separated by sixteen centuries from Aristotle, on whom he models his approach to Ethics; this would be like us taking up where Augustine left off, with little or no interlocutor. I point this out mainly to show that while the thought is still there and identifiable as Aristotelian, it's fairly impressive that it was able to remain so, given so much time passing in between them, not the least difficult part of that being the dark ages. What made the dark ages "dark?" It wasn't a sudden profusion of solar eclipses, or a paucity of candles available in medieval Europe, but the lasting effects of the Fall of Rome, coupled with a few other factors. In other words, another brief history lesson is probably in order...

We need to go back first and foremost to Constantine (again), as he is the Roman emperor responsible for splitting the empire and establishing and eastern capitol, modestly named Constantinople, what today is Istanbul in Turkey – when that was established, among his "housewarming" gifts were copies of all that wonderful Greek Philosophy, Mathematics, Logic, Tragedy, etc. When Western Rome fell and the Visigoths streamed in, folks necessarily streamed out, which led to a more or less semi-nomadic existence in continental Europe, certainly among the various barbarian tribes. One can imagine that it's fairly difficult to find time to pause for philosophical reflection on the moral happenings of the day when one is simply trying to stay alive and avoid conflict, hence, it was "dark," at least intellectually and philosophically, for quite some time following the Fall. Meanwhile, things are going on apace in Constantinople, which would stand until Ottoman Turks topple it (finally) in 1453 – nearly a full thousand years after their Western counterpart fell.

About two hundred years after the death of St. Augustine, a Saudi Arabian man named Muhammad would have revealed to him a message he would then record as the *Qur'an*. The religion and military religious state that arose from this man and his book would come to take over most of what had been that Eastern Roman Empire, within which they found they had ready access to all that Greek knowledge. Thankfully, they recognized its value, and began to "comment" on it, annotating it, translating it into Arabic, adapting the polytheistic notions for a belief in one God, and so on. So, while Europe was experiencing its dark ages, the Islamic world was experiencing a fantastic boom in scholarship. Gradually, the Muslim world would expand across the northern coast of Africa, across the Strait of Gibraltar, and into the Iberian Peninsula, modern day Portugal and Spain, and they would bring this adapted, modified, and commented-on Greek knowledge with them. Meanwhile, in a rather abortive[76] attempt to reclaim the "Holy Land," the Roman Catholic Church would launch a series of "Crusades" – at least four officially, possibly as many as seven or eight if you count

---

[76] Why abortive? Because they never managed to actually hold onto Jerusalem and the surrounding territory for very long, and because in the process of trying to get there, they actually ended up killing as many if not more Jews and Eastern Orthodox Christians than they did Muslims; they also sacked Constantinople and stole many of the Church's treasures, taking them back to Western Europe. Way to go, guys!

the lesser efforts, which would likewise bring back to Europe this Greek-come-Muslim body of information and texts. At this point there's a veritable flood of Greek (and Roman) knowledge into Western Europe, already conveniently adapted for a belief in one God (it's a pretty easy leap from Allah to Christ), and into the proverbial floodwaters wades Thomas Aquinas.

Aquinas was born to a noble family, received the best possible education, with the greatest teachers and at the greatest universities of his day, and wrote voluminously on topics philosophical, theological, and legal. He was in the best possible place at exactly the right time to "inherit" and employ the legal legacy of Cicero, Justinian (really Tribonian), and the developing Church canon law, but also the work of Aristotle, then so long lost as to have been nearly forgotten. When we read Aristotle, we typically read a translation straight from the Greek; when Aquinas read Aristotle, it was doubtless from the Greek to the Arabic to the Latin, which probably added a few subtleties at the expense of a few others. Needless to say though, the meaning came through, and we see a new lease on life for Aristotle in the thought and writings of Aquinas.

Scholasticism, the movement within Philosophy with which Aquinas is most closely associated and certainly emblematic of, held as its goal the rationalization of the teachings of the Catholic Church. While this is certainly not universally accepted as having been successful,[77] the profound influence it had on Western Christianity, especially Roman Catholicism and its protestant derivatives, is undeniable. The Thomistic (from *Thomas Aquinas*) project's intent is to combine the thought of Aristotle with the theology and tradition of the Roman Catholic Church, and on that count, he certainly succeeds. His writings would come to form the philosophical basis for much of subsequent Roman Catholic theology; a healthy portion of today's Catechism of the Catholic Church is practically verbatim Aquinas, much of the remainder is directly traceable to his thought and work. It is fair to say then, that without Aristotle, much of what today is recognizable as the Roman Catholic faith would be markedly different.

The End, the Good, and the Law

As an Aristotelian, Aquinas is predictably teleological in his approach to Ethics, and an emphasis is placed on the end of our actions, though in an updated and somewhat modified fashion. He continues the notion begun by Aristotle, whom Aquinas respectfully refers to as "the Philosopher," in identifying humanity as the rational animals, but uses the term "intelligent agents" to express this same thought. The rest of animate nature, my golden retriever included, falls under the other heading, that of "natural agents." All agents, whether intelligent or natural, are capable of action, and every action of every agent are directed at some specific end (aim, goal, design, plan, *telos*). Natural agents, because they are without reason, are directed at their natural ends, to which their instincts lead them; intelligent (rational) agents act for the sake of ends they intend. So we have a system in which all living beings are able to act instinctually, which is to say reactively, but where

---

[77] Eastern (Orthodox) Christendom has been, for the most part, content to ascribe to mysticism what Western (Roman) Christendom felt compelled to approach legalistically.

intelligent agents have the additional benefit (or burden) of acting intentionally, proactively.

That which is good is still defined as that which is desirable for its own sake, and we still pursue ends that we identify as such, but approach changes somewhat based on what is introduced at this point. Because ends are connected to that which is good, or that which they view as good as the object of their actions, Aquinas holds that every agent, again whether natural or intelligent, acts for the sake of some good that their action makes accessible to them. As intelligent agents, we are able to determine our ends based on what we desire, and pursue them because we see something good in them and about them. Because God is viewed by Aquinas as Himself being both the highest good and the source for all lesser goods, all things are ultimately directed at God as their final end. How do, or rather, how can we know what God expects of us, and which ends are acceptable for us to pursue? For that, we have the law(s).

There are two levels as it were, of the law, on Aquinas' account, the eternal and the natural. The eternal law presented a body of fixed laws, especially moral, but also physical, which direct agents, natural and intelligent, to their natural ends. This alone though, is insufficient, as the means by which we connect to and internalize these eternal laws isn't immediately apparent. Somehow, we have an intuitive sense or understanding of the eternal law, such that its precepts seem to us to be self-evident and are then reflected in the laws we create and live by. Essentially, the natural law is our participation in the eternal law – the way we, as rational creatures can use our reason (our *natural* reason) to discern between good and evil.

Summa Contra Gentiles

Despite the somewhat intimidating-sounding title, the best translation into English is probably something like (The) Truth of the Catholic Faith, and the book divided into those things accessible to our intellect, i.e., which can be reasoned through, and those things for which our intellect is insufficient, and we must accept on faith if at all. Thankfully for us, Aquinas considers morals, which he covers in his third book of this work, as among those things we can reason our way through and benefit from without recourse to leaps of faith. In the foreword to Book III, Aquinas tells us first that as God is perfect in being and causing, so He is perfect in ruling, in other words, God made the game, God gets the make the rules as well, and we, as the playing pieces, have only to follow them. Because the good and the end are (or ought to be) the proper object of our wills, whatever proceeds from a will must be directed to an end, attained by the action of the agent, but ultimately directed by God, who endowed us with the principles that allow us to act in the first place.

Having a will of our own, and with that will ostensibly being free, how do we know that this is an accurate account of how we come to act and what we intend by our actions? We know that by our action we intend some end – our efforts of any sort tend toward something determinate, sometimes the action itself, sometimes something beyond the act; this should sound familiar, because it's exactly what Aristotle told us (in the sex for recreation vs. for procreation example I gave earlier). We know already that every agent, natural or intelligent, acts either by nature or by intelligence, but our contemplative actions, they are always themselves an end. We read in Chapter III that every agent acts for a good which is the object of every appetite, and all action and movement must be for a good. Jumping to Chapter XVII, He informs us that all things are directed to one end, which is God, but the way he does so is characteristically Aristotelian, referring to that which is supreme in any genus being the cause for all things in that genus, terms "the Philosopher" himself not only would have approved of, but you'll recall, used. Right after this, we get another bit of Aristotle when we're told that the good of one nation is more godlike than the good of one man – something we saw before styled (in the *Nichomachean Ethics*) as "nobler and more divine."

The rest of this particular *Summa*, similarly numbered, wraps up and makes Aquinas' point very nicely, especially since Aquinas, ever the legal eagle, more or less summarizes his entire paragraph in his introductory statement for each, a method we'll understand more fully next, when we discuss his other *Summa*.[78] In XXX we're told that our happiness does *not* consist in wealth; XXXI – *not* in worldly power; XXXII – *not* in goods of the body; XXXIII – *not* in the senses; notice a pattern emerging at this point? In XXXVII, we're told that instead, our ultimate happiness is in contemplating God, and his word choice here is both important and characteristically Aristotelian with its emphasis on contemplation as our highest sort of activity. In XLVIII,[79] we make the final transition to the Christian approach to Ethics from that of the classical Greeks when we're told that our ultimate happiness won't even be found substantively in this life, but in heaven, and that the happy person, rather than adapting to fit the situation, must, as Aristotle had told us, spring from a "firm and unchangeable character," which Aquinas more imaginatively describes as *not* being a "kind of chameleon."

Summa Theologica

In writing the Summa (and this is the one generally considered by scholars to be, and referred to as *the* Summa), Aquinas intends to summarize the history of the universe, as well as to provide an outline for the meaning of life itself – you know, no big deal – sure we can do all that in one book. The order established is cyclical, beginning and ending with God, as one might reasonably assume and expect, given the author. The Summa is broken into three parts, the second part of which is itself broken into two parts. The first part is entirely focused on God and Creation, the highest point of which is humanity. The second part addresses the meaning of life for humanity, which is happiness; the Ethics here are unabashedly Aristotelian, which stands to reason. But because we can't live the ideal ethical life on our own, and in so doing reach God, we need a perfect man to bridge the gap between us and God, so God became man, and the third part discusses the life of Christ, as well as the sacraments, which Aquinas identifies as the means by which we learn from

---

[78] Together they're "*summa* kind of wonderful." See what I did there? ☺

[79] Here's a quick refresher on Roman numerals; when the bigger number is on the left, you add whatever's to the right, e.g., XI = 11; when there's a smaller number to the left, you subtract that, and *then* add whatever's on the right, so XLVIII is L = 50, minus 10, plus 8, so 48. There – now you'll always know which Superbowl it is.

Christ to approach God. As we are interested presently only in Aquinas' Ethics, we'll be looking exclusively at the second part of the Summa, which overall includes general moral principles, but specifically we're concerned with his approach to morality in particular.

The format of the Summa is nearly ideal in terms of presentation and format for debate – remember, it's written with a legalistic approach in mind to begin with, so precision and clarity are of paramount importance. Each part of the Summa is made up of a group of questions, and as you progress through them, each gets more specific, covering some subtopic of the question(s) before, so the overall effect is cumulative information of a very precise nature with regard to an overarching idea. Within each question a standard format is followed, which is as follows: First, a series of objections to the conclusion that will eventually be presented are given; this might seem counter-intuitive, but it's a great approach – especially for taking the wind out of the sails of whomever you're arguing with. Next a short counter-statement is given, invariably beginning with *sed contra*, "but instead…," which is then supported with a textual reference – usually the Bible, St. Augustine, or Aristotle. Only then does Aquinas make his actual argument, which at this point is generally just a clarification of the issue, based on what has already been presented. Finally, he replies to each of the objections that were already given, sometimes rather tersely, other times with some elucidation provided, further references, etc. The method is derived somewhat from the Socratic Method, perhaps a little bit from Peter Abelard's *Sic et Non* format, but most directly from the Muslim commentator Averroes, whom Aquinas refers to as "the Commentator," in much the same way he refers to Aristotle as "the Philosopher," titles of great respect.

Law

Aquinas gives perhaps the best definition of "law" that Ethics has ever seen or is likely to ever see, if for no other reason than that it is simple, direct, cogent, and entirely without ambiguity as to both what it means and what is implied by it. In Question 90, Article 4 of the second part of the Summa, law is defined as "an ordinance of reason for the common good, made by him who has care of the community, and promulgated." Pretty simple, pretty direct, but also amazingly well articulated because it is at once accessible and eminently scalable. What do we mean by scalable? Well, not that it's able to be scaled in the sense of climbed (though that would make sense also), but rather, that it's easily adapted to a wide range of subjects – from God, all the way down to any of us, without fundamentally altering the definition in any way. Let's start with the God, whom we'll argue has all of Creation[80] as his "community to care for" as per the definition; His laws are promulgated (that is, put into use) by his people. If we take the exact same definition, but scale down our understanding of whoever it is who's said to have "care of the community," it still works perfectly – for a nation, it's the president (or king, or what-have-you); for a state, it's the governor; for a city, it's the mayor; for a household, it's the head of the household, and so on. Nothing about the definition of law has to be adjusted, it stays constant and applicable, and we understand that it's an ordinance of reason, both the reason of whomever is generating the law, as well

---

[80] Everybody, now: "He's got the *whole* world, in His hands…"

as the reason of those within whom the law is intended to resonate and be internalized, without any loss of meaning or veracity. That's just pretty impressive.

All law (on a Thomistic account) comes from the eternal law of God's Divine Reason that governs the universe, which is understood by us and participated in by us, because we are rational beings, fit for the rule of law, as the natural law, which, when codified (that is, formatted in legal codes) and promulgated, is the human law. In addition to the human law as a product of our reason, we also have access to the Divine (eternal) law, which has been revealed to us that we may perform our actions in the proper way, in view of our final end, which is God. Human law is fallible in that it can't direct our conscience, can't prohibit our vices, and can't force us to act according to the letter of the law rather than simply the spirit. Furthermore, it's entirely possible that even the laws we arrive at through our reason can themselves be without any basis in the eternal law, in which case Aquinas tells us we're under no compulsion to follow them, unless they demonstrably aid the common good. Law is perhaps Aquinas' greatest direct contribution to Ethics, and even outside of and apart from a religious context, it's easy to see how and why Thomistic thought has been so influential in Western civilization – it's got a lot going for it, regardless of where one falls in the spectrum of religious belief.

Aquinas is perhaps a little more palatable to a broader range of readers than St. Augustine, simply because he makes relatively little recourse to matters of faith in defining his Ethics. That is, just about every Thomistic concept can be read atheistically as easily as theistically, with little of the impact and applicability lost – we still respond to an intuitive sense of right and wrong by means of our reason, and the definition of law, because it's so easily adapted, remains a reliable one. The warning is typically issued to students of Aquinas that he should not be read merely as a Roman Catholic gloss on Aristotle, and generally that's true, but with respect to his Ethics I think it's safe to say that there is here a lot of Aristotle shining through, and, with the exception of a few unique approaches, specifically as regards the law, there's not a lot of original material or information to be gained from looking at Aquinas exclusively. But we now have a sense of what was happening in Ethics during the high middle ages in terms of carrying forward theories of remote antiquity, and we ought to be satisfactorily prepared to proceed into the early modern era and see what changes await our moral thinking...

Chapter 10: The (Early) Modern Era

When most of us think of something as "modern," we probably think of that thing as existing or taking place "now," so it's a bit of a struggle for us to learn that historically and philosophically speaking, the modern era has been over for quite some time now. This is made somewhat more daunting to us when we come to learn that although it's definitely over and done with, there's really no agreed-upon start of end dates, either. For our purposes, I'm going to define the modern era as from 1500 (again, rounding up from Columbus' voyages) to 1900 (rounding down from the First World War), but these are dynamic, especially the end date, and will satisfy our purposes, especially since our final "modern" ethicist dies (conveniently) in 1900. Beyond the rough connection to historical events, especially in the case of the start date, the modern age marks a conspicuous departure from the classical and medieval era, if for no other reason than the confluence of environmental factors, religious, political, scientific, etc. that came to shape morality and moral reasoning in a way that was unprecedented, and quite simply unavailable to even the most advanced medievalist. Each of the events in the modern era conspired or at the very least contributed to the development of a time in Europe that was unlike any the world had ever seen, and the ethical theories that would be developed during this period are likewise unique and lasting in the impressions they have left us with.

Religion and Reformation(s)

We're all familiar with the protestant reformation of the 16th century – it's part of our Western Civilization 101 class, we know generally that they were protesting (hence the name) the Roman Catholic Church, in an attempt to reform it (hence the rest of the name), we probably even have a few vague notions about Luther and his having nailed something to a door somewhere, maybe a cute mnemonic about the fates of the wives of Henry VIII,[81] but unless you've made a study of it, that's probably about it. The fact that it's almost always referred to in the singular is a disservice both to the reality of what happened, as well as leaving us more or less in the dark about what the reaction to it was, as well as (in our case, at least) what any of this has to do with Ethics. It's better if we describe them as the protestant reformations – emphasis on the plural, as they are really best thought of as mutually exclusive, though chronologically simultaneous efforts on the part of a few main figures, to leave the Roman Catholic Church behind – one on the continent (of Europe), and the other on the island (of England). The former was primarily a theological dispute – Luther, Calvin, Zwingli, and others had problems with a few of the more questionably entrepreneurial practices of the papacy, disagreed with the notion that the Bible should not be made readily available in vernacular languages, and various other issues regarding the sacraments, source(s) of authority, and so on. The latter was very much a political dispute, with the church of England remaining very Catholic in appearance, with more protestant (and puritan) ideas evolving after the official break with Rome.

---

[81] For the curious, it's "divorced, beheaded, died, divorced, beheaded, survived."

In answer to this, there was the Roman Catholic Church's efforts at staging a counter-reformation, which was only marginally successful, but which did result, at least in part, in the formation of groups like the Jesuits, who would carry the philosophical program forward significantly in the decades and centuries to come. The significance of these events to Ethics has little or nothing to do with the nature of the disputes themselves, nor even of their outcomes; we're primarily interested in what results from the challenging of the most powerful, most wealthy, most ubiquitous institution of medieval society, the Roman Catholic Church, and what that would do for the furtherance of an academic agenda outside the scope of the Church's influence. The growing religious pluralism would make apparent the need for a new basis for morality that was not tied to a particular line of religious thinking or source of religious authority. It would also give rise to the now very popular notion that individuals can and do think for themselves without having to defer to established authorities, if only they're allowed to. This second point would extend not only to religion, but also to politics and the sciences.

Science and Politics

Regarding those sciences, it's worthwhile for us to note that the scientific and medical communities of the sixteenth and seventeenth centuries were also departing significantly from their medieval forebears. Despite the witch crazes and trials that would seem to give evidence to the contrary, the science of the modern era was much less dependent on the natural magic of the middle ages and early renaissance, and was beginning to explain symptoms of the body and events in the natural world in ways that would be more familiar to us – empirically and analytically. Politically, the paradigm is shifting as well. As we head into this era, we're firmly in the now deteriorating feudal system, so power is highly centralized in what amounts to absolute monarchies maintaining the divine right of kings. Now, we'll start to see all that power limited in the person of the monarch, or transferred, either in whole or in part to a parliament, congress, or other such national assembly. This wasn't typically a nice and neat transition, but more commonly occurred as the end or part of a protracted political struggle in which radical upheavals were fomented, revolutions were staged, civil wars were fought, and traditional power structures were ousted in favor of more "modern" arrangements.

The Effects on Ethics

So far, despite a few variations in definitions and understandings of the terms, all of our ethicists have had a more or less similar, or maybe even interchangeable definition for the good, a roughly equivalent understanding of virtue and the various virtues themselves, and all of this has been seen as something the individual must undertake for their own moral betterment. Well, all of that's about to get thrown out the window and replaced. We'll still encounter definitions of the good, but the new iterations would confuse or horrify most of our classical and medieval thinkers as fundamentally lacking somehow, insufficiently individuated, and fundamentally ill-equipped to address ethical issues in their respective worlds. In short, it's the perfect time to see where all the cultural changes we've just discussed will allow us to take our Ethics. The most notable emerging ideas are the idea of a natural law, and the notion of duty or obligation. We say an inkling of natural law theory in Aquinas, where it was presented to us as our rational participation in the eternal law, but now we're going to mean so much more than this rather passive approach. As for the ideas of duty and obligation, they, more than any other single factor, will come to shape and characterize modern Ethics through their various modes, targets, and understandings.

Duty (and Obligation)

There is an idea developing that more than anything else, morality imposes demands on us, and requires us sometimes to limit or forego our pursuit of our own good for the sake of others, of simply for those things which we feel compelled to do. This was a sort of thinking that was simply unavailable to the guys in the classical and medieval worlds, for the simple reason that whatever right conduct demands of us and our considerations of our individual good could not be thought of as mutually exclusive prior to this point in the history of Ethics. Now though, the authority or rather the influence of our principles that guide our right conduct are independent of our private good considered on an individual basis. Importantly, the focus of our modern ethicists won't be what our duties are in and of themselves, but rather, what they're based in and on, and how they can bind and limit our behavior. Because of this, most of the philosophers we encounter in this section won't be disagreeing about the content of morality as such, but about the grounding of our moral obligations, which in turn are going to be dependent on their understanding firstly of the nature of human nature, and secondly, on the influence and participation of our rationality in our Ethics.

With all the changes taking place in the Western world, religious, scientific, political, and social, it's important that our Ethics adjust similarly to reflect the changing world. We can't, after all, very well expect a world that no longer reflects the classical worldview, to limit itself to a classical ethical approach; ditto that for the medieval world applying seamlessly when the rest of conscious thought was no longer medieval in its mindset or approach. The philosophers and theories we're going to spend the next several chapters considering are thought to have had an ongoing impact on our moral thought – most of the professional philosophers working today are either proponents or critics of these theories, which goes quite a long way toward telling us that these are the theories of the greatest constant import to ethical thought. Indeed, even our contemporary moral thinkers, whom we'll end up with toward the end of the text, find their inspiration or starting point in the work of those whom we're about to consider and discuss. In other words, there's a very good reason that this is the only period of moral history that we'll be covering more or less exhaustively – it's had the most profound and lasting impact over history.

The Modern Philosophers

We'll be discussing each of these guys in greater detail as we go on, but let's briefly introduce each of them to get an idea of who we'll encounter and how they're doing something fundamentally new and different from their classical and medieval counterparts. Hobbes, with whom we'll begin, grounds morality on our rational self-interest. Hume will find morality to be a natural phenomenon, innate in all of us and grounded emotionally in our capacity to feel sympathetic. Kant will very importantly introduce another feature characteristic of the modern era, wherein we find (with a few exceptions) each of our philosophers responding to (and often rejecting) the philosopher who came immediately before him. Kant does not agree that human nature contains moral principles naturally, and argues for a rational basis expressed through the categorical imperative. Next up, those crazy, but frighteningly influential Utilitarians, Bentham and Mill, declare that actions are right when they carry favorable consequences that promote happiness. Kierkegaard, our first existentialist, finds the ethical life as merely a stage along the way to the religious life. Marx, as you might expect, approaches Ethics by way of an economic critique of capitalism, arguing for social change. Finally, Nietzsche, who will see us right to the dawn of the twentieth century, attempts to identify the origins of our moral terms, and determines that we're largely misguided at present. Needless to say, this is going to be a fascinating time in the development of Ethics, which is why we'll pay the bulk of our attention to these men and their ideas.

Chapter 11: Hobbes

It's unlikely that Thomas Hobbes would have answered to "ethicist," he seems to have considered himself, and is certainly considered by us, to have been primarily a political philosopher. The social contract theory[82] counts him as one of its major figures, and he approaches his position on the idea of obligation and the ideal basis of political authority by examining his particular take on the "state of nature" (more on this shortly). His approach is undeniably egotistical, but that's not necessarily a bad approach as we might interpret it – if anything, it's an honest and unvarnished approach, that, like many of our modern philosophers, we may not *want* to hear, but we probably *need* to hear. Hobbes is dark certainly, but with good reason; he was writing in the context of the English Puritan Revolution. Time for another history lesson:

Recall for a moment that in King Henry VIII's split with the Roman Catholic Church, he declared himself not only the political ruler of England, but also the head of the English (Anglican) Church.[83] When Henry died, he left only one male heir (from his third wife), who didn't live all that long; Lady Jane Grey then served for all of nine days; next up was his daughter, Mary – we know her as "Bloody Mary" for all the protestants she had killed in her attempt to bring England back to the Rome. She slunk into madness and died as well, leaving Henry's daughter by his second wife Elizabeth as the heir apparent. Queen Elizabeth brought England to its highest point since the Norman Conquest, culturally, intellectually, economically, and in just about every other sense – the Elizabethan Era was truly the "Golden Age" of England, and it was into this age, albeit toward the end of it, that Hobbes was born. As the "Virgin Queen," Elizabeth didn't leave and heir, so the crown then went to James of Scotland (the Bible guy), and then to Charles I, with whom our story takes up again. Charles' belief in the divine right of kings, as well as his preference for "popish" aspects of Anglicanism didn't win him many friends, and the country was thrust into a civil war – one he lost. He was handed over to the English Parliament, convicted of treason, and beheaded, at which point Oliver Cromwell becomes the "Lord Protector" of the nation until the Royalists returned to power following his death, and Charles II was restored to the throne.

Charles II's onetime tutor, Hobbes, witnessed the whole thing, and the colored his approach to Ethics in a way that can scarcely be underestimated. He writes Leviathan not only as a case supportive of an absolute monarchy, but as an indictment of war and the disastrous affect it has on society. In this sense, it's essentially a cautionary tale. Remember those "scared straight" videos from back in the day, where they sent middle school miscreants to prisons, and the enormous, tattooed felons would tell them to "hold their pocket in the

---

[82] This is exactly what it sounds like. You and I form a contract of sorts – I won't kill you if you won't kill me; then we'll meet some other folks, and we'll agree not to kill them if they won't kill us, and we go on like this, establishing rules contractually.

[83] Here in the United States, the Episcopal Church, and, to a somewhat lesser extent, the so-called "Continuing" Anglican Churches.

yard," and "put the Kool-Aid on their lips." Well, it's sort of like that; Hobbes wants the prospect of war, and certainly the costs of war, to scare us so badly that we never go to war ever again, as it would be tantamount to voluntarily entering a "state of nature."

The State of Nature

Contrary to what some have thought, the state of nature does not refer to an actual point in history; rather, it's something of a thought experiment in which we are asked to imagine what life would be like without any political or legal structures in place, a state of anarchy. This was a popular topic in Hobbes' day and beyond, and the various states of nature proposed were as varied as their authors; some, like Jean-Jacques Rousseau's, are idyllic, giving rise to the notion of the "noble savage," as yet uncorrupted by civilization. Needless to say, Hobbes' vision is a bit bleaker than that – closer to the post-apocalyptic visions of the Mad Max movies or the Walking Dead series of graphic novels and television series. In this version of the state of nature, just about everyone you meet wants to kill you, rob you, and rape you – and not necessarily in that order. Because of this, there's a level of mutual distrust that makes any cooperative social effort next to impossible, so anything requiring more than a single person, acting on their own, simply won't get done. It's a level of perpetual insecurity the likes of which we can only imagine, as there are no laws by which to govern our actions, and even if there were, there are no authorities to enforce them. Hobbes tells us that we run the risk of falling into a state of nature if we allow our existing social and political structures to collapse; to prevent this, out of the chaos, we establish and follow an absolute monarch – a sovereign to which we agree to be subject, since it's got to be better than the state of nature itself.

Leviathan

A leviathan itself refers to an Old Testament sea monster or creature – it shows up in Job, in the Psalms, and in Isaiah, as well as making an appearance long after Hobbes, in Melville's Moby Dick, which is closest to its modern definition, which is simply, "whale." On the frontispiece of the first edition of *Leviathan*, there's a fantastic illustration of a stylized Stuart Dynasty king (either of the Charles' would fit the bill), rising up out of the water off the English coast. Above the king is a quote from the Old Testament book of Job (41:24): "There is no power on earth to be compared to him."[84] He is depicted wearing a crown, brandishing a sword in his right hand, and with a crozier in his left. The king's body is shown as being made up of several hundred people – symbolic of the commonwealth (more on that momentarily). The meaning of the sword is fairly obvious – the king is the ultimate civil authority; the crozier, more often called the bishop's staff or simply the shepherd's crook, emphasizes that following Henry VIII, English monarchs were likewise the heads of the Church of England. The smaller illustrations on either side of the title and subtitle emphasize this – the king's castle is shown opposite the bishop's cathedral; the crown and the mitre; the canon and the wrath of God or excommunication (ironically depicted in

---

[84] It appears in the Latin of the Vulgate: "Non est potestas Super Terram quae Comparetur ei." The modern verse is actually found at 41:33 or 41:25, depending on translation and version, just FYI, in case you go searching and can't find it.

somewhat pagan terms as lightning); the piled weapons of the king's army, and the "weapons" of logic; the pitch of battle, and the ecclesiastical court.

The subtitle goes a long way toward enforcing this paired symbolism: "The matter, form, and power of a common wealth ecclesiastical and civil." In other words, the substance, organization, and impact of all our powers held in common (literally a commonwealth) with (authority over both) the church and the state. The other subtitle of the text (it wasn't uncommon to have several) is "Of the interior beginnings of voluntary motions commonly called the passions and the speeches by which they are expressed." So basically, the text is concerned with the passions by which we are moved, which begin from within us, and according to which we *choose* to be moved, and the words we use to talk about them. Hobbes goes to great lengths to explain the words he uses and why he uses them as he does, and this is helpful, as a great many of the words have either passed out of common use, or have radically changed meaning since the Elizabethan era.

Motions

Hobbes tells us early on that in animate nature (that is, us and other, lesser animals) there are two sorts of motions that only we engage in, one of which is vital, and the other, voluntary. The vital motions are fairly straightforward – they start at (or even before) our birth, and continue until we die – or rather, we die when they cease; these are things like our pulse and breathing, nutrition and excretion, and so on – none of which require any help from our imaginations, i.e., we don't have to think to keep them going. Voluntary motions are exactly what you'd expect – they begin in our minds, and are only then carried out by our bodies, when we speak, when we move, etc. Our imaginations, then must be the beginning of all our voluntary motions, and every endeavor we make. When they're toward something, we're said to desire or have an appetite for that thing – something we love; when it's away from something, we're said to have an aversion to that thing, and want it away from us, which develops into a hate for the thing when it's in our presence.

Whatever we neither desire nor hate we are said to contemn, which Hobbes calls an immobility, but which we might more accurately call a neutrality. Now it gets a bit more complex, not least because our bodies are constantly changing, our tastes and desires are constantly evolving, and so on. Because of this, Hobbes says it's impossible that the same things should always cause in us the same appetites and aversions. As an example of this, think of some of the foods you maybe hated as a kid, but might really enjoy now as an adult – for me, it's bleu cheese and mushrooms. Or, think of the opposite – I tried some of my son's candy the other day and was amazed that I had ever liked it. Now, think of this on a grand scale; how could we possibly get everyone to agree that the same thing or things is or are "good," and how would our understanding of the good need to adjust to make it so?

The Good

The definition of the good we find in Hobbes is a notable departure from those given in the classical and medieval era; no longer are we particularly interested in "that which is desirable for its own sake." For Hobbes, the good is whatever a person happens to desire, and what is deemed "good" is always from the viewpoint of the person making the statement, and so will be relative to them, and will obviously vary greatly from person to person. Because of this, there is no "greatest good" to be found, as he says, "as spoken of by the old moral philosophers," ironic, because to us, Hobbes *is* himself an old moral philosopher, but he's referring here to Socrates through Aquinas.

Human Worth and Commonwealth

Our power is our present means, our current ability, to obtain some future apparent good, and our power is either original or instrumental; original powers are the sort we're born with – our natural abilities, instrumental powers are those we acquire either through those natural powers or by good luck. The greatest of our powers says Hobbes, is that which is compounded of the powers of most men, united by consent, in one person, natural or civil, that has the use of all their powers depending on his will. This is the idea of the commonwealth, where quite literally, all our wealth – physical, intellectual, and so on, is held together in common, to be used at the whim of the monarch we establish. Why do we establish them? Because we view our worth in a certain light, and respect the sovereign as having the greatest power among us.

Our worth, or our value, is, as Hobbes notes, as with all other things, our price – what or how much would be given for the use of our power. He gives two very good examples – a general in wartime, and a judge in peacetime. As Bing Crosby pointed out so well in *White Christmas*,[85] "what can you do with a general, when he stops being a general," the answer, as you might expect, is "not much." In other words, during a war, we need generals to guide troop movements, make crucial decisions, and so on; if peacetimes, we have relatively little use for their particular set of unique skills. Likewise with the judges – provided there's peace, their decisions will be listened to carefully and carried out with earnest; very few are likely to find the time to do that in the middle of a war. We are, at the end of the day, worth whatever someone is willing to give for us, and for the use of our skills. Just like all those Franklin Mint commemorative plates your aunt collected, that the operator assured her would appreciate in value – they're really only worth what someone would pay her for them, which, when it comes time for the estate sale, is probably not a whole heck of a lot.

We rate ourselves at the highest value we possibly can – we want everyone to think we're as great as we think we are, but our true value is no more than it is esteemed by others. Because of this, as well as the limitations of our nature, Hobbes tells us that if there is any one general inclination that will be shared and participated in by all mankind, it is our "perpetual and restless desire of power after power, that ceases only in death." We want more and more power, and we don't stop wanting power until those vital motions we discussed earlier decide to stop. The monarchs among us, the sovereigns, whose power is greatest, turn their endeavors, that is, their motions, toward assuring it at home by laws, or abroad by wars. The monarch you'll recall, has the use of all our powers considered together, but for the most part, the difference between us, at an individual level isn't so considerable – we all have more or less equal abilities. We're with ourselves all the time, so

---

[85] If you haven't seen Irving Berlin's classic holiday musical, you're remiss – see it!

even though we might acknowledge that others are better in certain areas, we nonetheless still can't imagine anyone quite as good as ourselves, or better prepared for the myriad situations that face us daily. For my own part, Oscar Wilde was wittier than I am, Matthew Arnold was more eloquent, and J.R.R. Tolkien was more learned, yet I can hardly be brought to believe that any of them were as wise as I am, because I see my own wit at hand, but theirs at a distance. Can this be reconciled, and if so, then how?

War

Hobbes tells us that the most reliable sign that our abilities are equally distributed is that, with a few notable exceptions, we are all mostly contented with what we have. Somewhat contrary to what we might ordinarily extrapolate from this, this is precisely where he finds the origins of our conflicts – from our equality of ability comes our equality of hope that each of us will attain our desired end(s). Therefore, if any of us desire the same thing, which nevertheless we can't both enjoy, we become enemies. Hobbes' take on this might surprise you, because he's not inclined to stop there and argue for no war – he seems to want to draw things out to their logical conclusion and demonstrate for us exactly *why* he wants no more wars. As a consequence of our overlapping desires, roughly equivalent talents, and the necessity of augmenting our dominion over one another, Hobbes tells us that in a state of nature, we ought to be allowed that sort of a survival of the fittest approach – a Darwinian political perspective two full centuries before Darwin. We fight if for no other reason than because we can, and because we want others to value us as we value ourselves.

Remember that great scene in that not-so-great movie, where the Mongolian general asks a rather hirsute Arnold Schwarzenegger, "Conan, what is best in life?" and gets the reply, "to crush your enemies, see them driven before you, and hear the lamentations of their women!" Hobbes tells us that we find three main causes for all our quarrels, invasions, wars, in short, conflicts at every level: competition, defense, and glory. In competition, we seek to gain through violent efforts, to make ourselves masters of other people, their children, their positions, and so on; if defense, we seek to defend the same things from violent attacks. When we fight for glory, we're fighting for reputation, for trifles – sometimes even a word, a smile, a different opinion, or any other sign that our undervalue by others will be reversed and they will value us as we value ourselves. Keep in mind, Hobbes wrote about this nearly four centuries ago, and unless I'm very much mistaken, these are *still* the reasons we fight and go to war – that's a fairly far-reaching statement about the reality of human life and sources of motivation, if we haven't managed to change matters in that amount of time.

To make his point abundantly clear, Hobbes gives a nice list of those things which are simply unavailable to us in times of war, many of which are, as before, still quite applicable. Because his list is just about perfect and certainly still timely, I'll give it here as he does, with his statements in *italics*, and mine in normal type. In times of war... *There is no place for industry, because the fruit thereof is uncertain*; don't bother producing that product, as there might not be anyone to buy it from you, or they would simply take it if they were able to. *No culture of the earth*; there's very little point in planting fields if your crop is going to be trampled in battle. *No navigation, nor use of commodities that may be imported by sea*; this would have been a crushing blow to Hobbes' readers – the average Elizabethan gentleman was already becoming accustomed to the sorts of goods that only a proto-globalized economy can provide. *No commodious building*; the English, like most of us, simply loved to build palaces and parks, cathedrals and civic centers – it expressed their humanity, and Hobbes uses this to show how war would express their lack thereof. *No instruments of moving, and removing, such things as require much force*; remember, you're absolutely on your own in a state of nature – if you need help to complete a task, that task is quite simply not getting done. *No knowledge of the face of the earth*; this would have really struck the Englishmen's' pride, as they considered themselves the emerging mercantile economy, and were beginning to establish the British Empire that the sun would famously "never set upon." *No account of time*; because you're probably not going to worry too much about what day or time it is when you're in the middle of a battle. *No arts, no letters, and no society*; Hobbes' final statement would have been absolutely devastating to anyone who remembered the Golden Age of Elizabethan England – the age of Shakespeare, Marlowe, Donne, Milton, Bacon – men who produced some of the finest literature anywhere, ever.

Worst of all he tells us, continual fear and the danger of a violent death renders life solitary, poor, nasty, brutish, and short. Solitary, because we can't trust anyone; poor, because we're without quite a bit; nasty, because you don't have any of the things that make life comfortable and pleasant; brutish, because people are trying to kill you; and short, because one of them is eventually going to succeed. So what passions incline us to peace? Fairly straightforward ones – fear of (violent) death, desire of the things that make like pleasant, and the hope that the proper sorts of action can obtain those desired things. We're seeing the first inklings here of something that will come to its fullest fruition when we get to David Hume, next – the notion that what really drives us isn't our rationality as such, but those things to which we are passionately devoted, the preservation of our own life topping out the list by a fairly wide margin!

Law and Contracts

You will (hopefully) recall that Aquinas had defined the natural law simply as the rational agent's participation in the eternal law; Hobbes will depart from that significantly here, when he defines the natural law as the liberty each of us has, through the use of our own powers and abilities, as we decide ourselves, to preserve our own lives. He also refers to this as our "right of nature," which is our freedom to preserve and protect not only our lives, but our interests as well. The law of nature now becomes a general rule that our reason leads us to naturally, where we realize that we ought not to do anything that could interfere with our long-term self-preservation or risk our interests; in this sense, the ordinary moral rules we establish, both for ourselves and our societies are veritable "laws of nature." That is to say, we don't kill because we don't want to be killed ourselves, and so on. While we may be inclined to think of liberty as synonymous with freedom, to Hobbes, it is the absence of external impediments – nothing in our way to prevent our acting as we choose. Rights then consist in the liberty to do or not to do any given action; the function of law is quite different for him, as it determines and binds us (sometimes quite against our will) to one or the other – some things we *must* do by way of law, e.g., pay taxes, and some things we may not do according to the law, e.g., taking the life of an innocent other. And so law and right differ in this sense as much as obligation and liberty, which, when applied to the same instance, are obviously inconsistent.

If law is so limiting to our liberty, why then do we impose them on ourselves and each other so freely and so frequently? The Hobbesian[86] answer seems to be, out of a reasonable fear of falling into the state of nature, wherein everyone has a right to everything – even to one another's bodies. As long as the natural right of everyone to everything endures, there can be no security for any of us. The ideal rule as given by Hobbes is the "golden" rule – the Law of the Gospel – actually the law of just about every religion ever, as well as being a part of good old common sense; whatsoever you require that others should do to you, that do you to them.[87] We can certainly choose to lay down our rights to anything also, the term he uses here is a particularly apt one – to "divest" ourselves – literally, to take off (as in an article of clothing) of that right. What we are specifically giving up, on Hobbes' account, is our particular liberty (remember – our freedom from obstacles) of hindering someone else of the benefit of their own right to the same. Right is laid aside in this way (divestiture) by either simply renouncing it (stating that we voluntarily give it up on our behalf), or by transferring it to another (an example of which might be power of attorney).

The motive and goal for renouncing or transferring a right is to attain some measure of security for ourselves, our life, our means of preserving our life, etc. When there is a mutual transferring of right(s) between two or more parties, we call that a contract; if one part of the contract will be performed at a later time, we call that a pact or a covenant. We typically only encounter this latter term in religious terms, but the concept is one we see on a regular basis, e.g., "If you'll work for me this weekend, I'll work for you at date to be specified later." Hobbes tells us that whatever can't hinder us from promising the latter part of the covenant, ought not to hinder us from performing the latter part when the time comes. The notion of obligation enters here, especially in a civil estate, where there's a power of some sort set up to constrain those people who would otherwise violate the covenant, but the fear that this could happen is still reasonable, and it's addressed by stating that whomever is to perform their part of the covenant first, they are *obliged* to do so.

Justice

If we don't perform our assigned actions in the covenants we make, the foundation of all agreements would be baseless and the words would be empty, and it is here that Hobbes finds his rather unique approach to justice – by coming at it by way of its inverse. He defines injustice as the not performance of a covenant – not doing what you said you would do, reasoning from this that whatsoever is not unjust is, by default, just. Justice then is defined on Hobbesian terms as the constant will of giving to everyone their own – almost a

---

[86] Reflecting the thought of Thomas Hobbes, just as "Thomistic" reflects Aquinas.

[87] As with most everything, it sounds much cooler in the original Latin in which he presents it: *Quod tibi fieri non vis, alteri ne feceris.*

karmic[88] understanding of the term, somewhat far removed from Plato's definition (but not too different from Cephalus', where what is just is to pay what one owes), where it is just when we get what we have coming to us, presumably both good *and* bad. Therefore, where there is no sense of one's own, that is, no propriety, there is no injustice; and where there is no coercive power in place (which would trump our liberty), that is, where there is no commonwealth, there is no propriety, and all people have a right to all things. Therefore, on Hobbes' account, where there is no commonwealth (i.e., in a state of nature), nothing is unjust; we've heard this exact idea, presented in somewhat different terms – "all's fair in love and war," and it seems to be correct.

In a condition of war (or a state of nature) where everyone to everyone, for lack of a common power to keep us all in check and behaving, is an enemy, there none of us can hope to survive for long – someone will always be stronger, smarter, or simply sneakier, and will eventually overcome us, so it becomes necessary to form basic social contracts, if for no other reason than to prevent our own destruction. If we live in a society, it's because it can be reasonably expected of us that we'll behave in certain ways, keep to certain normative standards, and so on, and despite Hobbes' understandable trust issues, we see here a glimmer of hope that we can rationally expect those around us not to endanger our preservation, but it really depends on what evidence we have to go on…

The laws of nature present themselves to us in a frustratingly non-empirical manner – that is, we can't witness the thinking of someone and determine with any certitude what their behavior might be, whether or not we're at risk with them, if they're the sort who might violate a covenant with us, etc. This is simply because the laws of nature take place first and foremost in our internal forum – in our thoughts and considerations of the costs and benefits attached to a given course of speculative action. When those actions finally do take place, in an external forum, in which they're observable by others, this is when we can see them, and judge and act accordingly. Our danger then comes when we observe people who, feeling themselves to be sufficiently safe from reproach or revenge, while others observe the laws toward them, they don't observe them themselves. In other words, if we don't follow the laws ourselves, we ought firstly not to give them to others, and secondly, can't reasonably expect to be protected under them; as Hobbes says, they seek not peace, but war.

Peace

Hobbes rounds out the ethical discussion in Leviathan by telling us that the laws of nature are immutable and eternal, and that Moral Philosophy is nothing else but the science of what is good and evil, good and evil being the names that signify our appetites and aversions, respectively.[89] The same person, in diverse times, differs from themselves; from these fluctuations in our appetites and aversions come our disputes, our controversies, and at last, our wars. All that we seem to be able to agree on, in fact, is that peace is good, or at

---

[88] *Karma* – the Eastern idea of what goes around, comes around, or, more vulgarly, life's not a bitch until you're a bitch first. Not to be confused with *karma chameleon*.

[89] Next-up, Hume will disagree with the first part of this, but base much of his own theory off the latter part.

any rate, preferable. Therefore the ways that bring about peace, or the means by which we achieve peace, justice, gratitude, modesty, equity, mercy, and the vest of the laws of nature which we call moral virtues, are good; and their contrary vices are evil. In this, Hobbes is both echoing Aristotle and presaging Hume; we are reaching the point where it's not so much the virtues themselves that we're interested in per se, but rather what they enable, engender, or outright provide, which is a direct and appreciable good, but at the end of the day, they're just terms or assignations we make for convenience rather than set-in-stone dictates of our moral character.

The true doctrine of the laws of nature, says Hobbes, is the true moral philosophy, which we're used to calling law, but he says we do so improperly when we do. All they really are, he tells us, are the conclusions or theorems that concern what conduces to the conservation and defense of ourselves. Law, on quite the other hand, is properly the "word of him that by right has command over others." Note here the similarity but impactful adjustment of Aquinas' definition of law, who defined it as "an ordinance of reason for the common good, made by him who has care of the community, and promulgated." Now no mention of reason or goodwill is being made, there's no sense of community, and command takes precedence to promoting the common good. Furthermore, that which is commanded is not necessarily subject to promulgation, which implies at least a bit of voluntary action on the part of those who are ruled – that's absent here. For Hobbes though, this doesn't appear to detract at all from his understanding of what is owed by those subjected to the laws – he likens them in fact to the word of God, who by right as command over all things, and, in lock-step with the divine right of kings thinking of his time, has placed over the rest of us a sovereign monarch to rule and decree as he sees fit. This will be more or less that last such notion that we'll encounter, as we're about to enter the age of revolution, in which these divine rights are questioned, monarchs are toppled (or at least limited), and all the "old" wisdom with regard to Ethics is at once brought low and rejuvenated, to bring us thoroughly into the modern age, which we are undoubtedly the children of.

Chapter 12: Hume

Hume is far and away our best, "Dorothy, we're not in Kansas anymore" modern era ethicist – he's the guy who tells us how we *really* think about matters ethical, and it certainly bears little resemblance to what we've seen so far, from Socrates through to Hobbes. Is that a good thing? Undoubtedly, for it's in Hume that we discover the first glimmers of our human psychology, and how it uniquely approaches the moral problems presented to us, which, as it turns out, don't involve our reason nearly as much as most if not all of the earlier ethicists assured us it did. Does that mean that for Hume reason has no purpose in our ethical thinking? Not remotely – it merely means that reason will be taking a fundamentally different and certainly secondary role to those troublesome passions and emotions that Plato advised us to overcome through the practiced use of our rational power. As Hume will tell us, "Reason is, and ought only to be a *slave* of the passions."

The *Treatise on Human Nature* is at once impressive and troublesome – it's one of, if not the single-most important philosophical writings ever composed in the English language, but it's also dreadfully dull stuff to slog your way through at times, especially as Hume has a tendency to repeat himself frequently so we *really* get the point he's trying to make. It's important that we do get his point, though, since it's so unlike what we've seen so far; Hume has a skeptical[90] position with regard to both our scientific and moral claims, and he denies that either have a legitimately rational basis. We can extract two things from this: firstly, that means that everything we've accepted as valid up to this point, if it's been based in reason, is potentially false and must be reworked to establish what actually is and isn't the case; and secondly, if Hume is going to suggest an alternative, he's going to have to work doubly hard to convince us he's correct. Hume will find the origins of both our claims to general knowledge, and especially our claims to moral knowledge, rooted in what we today identify as psychology. When the *Treatise* was first published, it fell flat (surprise, surprise) – even Hume reported that it "fell dead-born from the press." I'm willing to give him a bit of leeway, considering he was only twenty-six when he wrote it, and I'm midway through my thirties now. He revised it a few times, and it still wasn't particularly well received. Be that as it may, there are several points that we can certainly benefit from them to inform our Ethics – let's take a look...

Ideas and Impressions

Remembering that Hume is an empiricist,[91] he first divides all our sense perceptions into ideas and impressions. He explains that simple impressions cause simple ideas, and form simple ideas we form complex ideas, all of which takes place most of the time

---

[90] Remember, in Philosophy, **skepticism** = "radical doubt," i.e., no knowledge is possible, and if it were to be possible, it would remain improbable.

[91] Remember, in Philosophy, **empiricism** = "sense-based," i.e., all we can know is that which we directly experience in a sensate manner, seen, heard, touched, etc.

subconsciously, without our really even being aware that such connections are being made. Sometimes, these are restricted to the same sort of the corresponding complex impressions – those events that have impacted our lives substantially, e.g., births, deaths, accidents, etc., are likely to have made very strong impressions on us in the form of memories. Other times, we rearrange the things we've seen or otherwise experienced in new combinations, which we call imagination; we've seen or experienced things with a single eye, with a single horn, that fly, that occasionally attack and eat people, and from all this, we can imagine the "one eyed, one horned, flying, purple people eater" you might have heard a song about.[92] Descartes, writing about a century before Hume had made the claim that the only reason we have an idea of God is that God himself must be the inspiration for it. Hume explains that God is a complex idea formed form simple ideas that themselves come from simple impressions, and the idea of God then neither requires God nor proves His existence, as we have ideas about a great many things that may not necessarily exist. This is probably a good time to mention what you may have already figured out – while he never explicitly claimed to be, it's generally agreed that Hume was an atheistic, and, while he's certainly not as snide about it as some of his modern counterparts, it certainly does seem to inform and influence his approach to Ethics.

Hume likewise rejected another of Descartes' more infamous theories, that of innate ideas, arguing instead that we come into this world without any knowledge, and we then have knowledge only of those things which we directly experience. Before you get your mind working toward torpedoing the theory, probably from the perspective of history, let's take a look at an historical occurrence that while I did not directly, i.e., personally experience, I nonetheless have direct experience of. Confused? Not to worry – while I was not on any of Columbus' ships, I still have knowledge of them based on experiences, in my case, of having read, been taught, seen movies, and so on, all about them. So he's not quite so slavish to the empirical model as it might sound, but it nevertheless informs and directs his Ethics in important ways. Specifically, all the perceptions that our senses present to us can be divided into two distinct groups; they're all either robust, lively impressions that have formed from direct sensory input, or they're fainter, hazier ideas, which have been copied from our impressions. For instance, if you put down the book momentarily, you'll have a fairly strong impression of what color the shirt you're wearing is; but, think for a moment (without googling it) which color is on top in a traffic light.[93] We've all seen traffic lights, but since our attention has probably rarely been drawn to which color surmounts it, we have a fainter idea rather than a stronger impression.

Sentiments

Hume was one of a whole group of British sentimentalists, a group which included other greats like Shaftesbury, Hutcheson, and a handful of others, all of which were more or less approaching the problem of conduct in the same way, but Hume is undoubtedly the most influential of them. Now, "sentimental" doesn't mean Hume watched a lot of Lifetime made for television movies, or read a lot of Hallmark cards; it does, however, mean that all our

---

[92] See what I did there? ☺

[93] No – I'm not going to tell you; either go for a drive or look it up – sorry.

ethical thinking is directed not by some dusty collection of abstract moral principles, but rather by our feelings. Here's what he means by this – think for a moment of everything you've had to learn and keep in mind up to this point – very specific definitions and understandings of the good, of virtue, or justice, and so on. These are all abstract notions in the sense that they're very general, and while they can be applied to a great many things with a good amount of variety, they start to get a bit hazy when we try to apply them to specific instances while maintaining the same level of accuracy and aptitude as they can lay claim to in general. Plus, they're just an awful lot to remember and sort through, as to which definition was held by which philosopher, how differences in definitions affect the Ethics that result, and so on, a good example of which is Plato's versus Aristotle's notion of virtue, and Aristotle's versus Augustine's notion of the highest good. Contrasted with this convoluted collection of confusion in the making, think for a moment about your feelings. No one had to teach you how to feel, how to interpret your feelings, or what feelings are appropriate in a given situation. Hume and the other sentimentalists reason from this that this must be a more natural, and by extension, a more sensible (pun intended) approach to Ethics.

Sympathy

Unlike everything we've heard from every ethicist up to this point, Hume tells us that reason has absolutely no power to motivate us to act; we can still be rational animals, and our rationality can still inform our decisions secondarily, but it can't make us do anything at all, as it has no motivating power whatsoever. Moral judgments, on quite the other hand, motivate us (or rather, *move* us) on regular basis. When we're watching or reading the news, hearing an event related to us, and so on, we react viscerally to it – we have (as the term implies) a "gut" reaction first and foremost – sometimes we quite literally feel sick to our stomachs if the story is sufficiently disturbing to us. According to Hume, this is because our moral judgments are based not on reason, but on our desires, those things which we relate to passionately, and on our feelings, those things which affect us emotionally. The feeling at issue here is one of sympathy. Because this is a confusing term sometimes, let's take a momentary aside, this time not into history, but into the English language itself...

Remember the old, "ethos, pathos, logos" bit from the Literature class you probably slept through more often than not? Well, we're interested again in the second term there, "pathos," which we typically translate as "feeling," but really means something closer to a sense of "yearning" or "striving;" the "sym" part just implies that we're striving, yearning, feeling etc. along "with" someone. Now, a few things to note: one, don't mistake this with "empathy" (more on this momentarily), and don't fall into the temptation to think of this only in negative terms. How does sympathy differ from empathy? When we're sympathetic, we're acknowledging what another is going through because we can imagine what it would be like to experience that ourselves; when we're empathetic, we understand what they're going through because we've been there ourselves. So I can be sympathetic to my wife's labor pains, but no stretch of physiological wonder no imagination would ever allow me (thankfully) to be empathetic to them in the same way. As for the second temptation, we typically today think of sympathy only in its negative sense – someone passes away, and we send their surviving relatives a sympathy card. It can certainly be this, but as Hume sees it, it can be in positive terms as well – when our friend gets that job they've been hoping for or the promotion they've been counting on, we can sympathize with them in positive terms also. So where I might feel pride in having accomplished something,[94] the operation of sympathy allows you to feel esteem on my behalf.

Social Needs

With apologies for all the references to other disciplines in this chapter, think for a moment about your Psychology class,[95] specifically about that Maslow chap and his famous "hierarchy of needs." At the bottom there's the basics (duh) – survival-type needs like finding food and water, shelter, and clothing, etc. Next, we have safety needs – making it through the day in relative safety, and so on. Then there are social needs, and this is where Hume places what we call Ethics, but more on that momentarily. Fourth we have esteem needs, wherein we develop the desire for those whom we're socially connected with to like us, and maybe even love us. Finally, there's the level of self-actualization, where we start thinking about the meaning of life, whether or not there's a God, and so on – all the stuff we normally consider a part of Philosophy in general, though what Hume will call the "speculative" branch thereof – more on that a bit later.

How does this relate to Ethics? First, forget everything we've been told by our ethicists from Socrates through Hobbes, especially all those specific definitions of the good, virtues and vices, even what makes a given action right or wrong, ethical or unethical, good or bad, etc. For the Humean,[96] all these notions of what's right and wrong, what's virtuous and vicious, are just the predispositions that lead certain actions and certain character traits to arouse our sentiments of approval or disapproval – that's it, and that's all. In other words, these terms are not fixed entities, but merely tendencies associated with actions and personalities that evoke an emotional response from us. But wait – some people seem to be naturally more sympathetic than others, how can Hume account for *that*? – BANG – owned! Not quite – our feelings of sympathy do indeed vary from person to person, but the judgments we make, e.g., calling an action good or bad, doesn't necessarily vary all that much from person to person in a given society. Let's say that I decide to invite all of you reading this over to my house for dinner, where I'll be serving dog as the main entrée. Or if I were to show up to my lecture seminar in my underwear and a pair of flip-flops.[97] I'm certainly capable of doing either or both of these things, and there are parts of the world where either or both might even be considered perfectly socially acceptable, but generally speaking we frown on these types of behaviors here, and unless I'm very much mistaken, share the judgment that they're unacceptable. Why? Because we have a social need for shared judgments about things we label as good or bad and virtuous or vicious – it's one of the primary things, along with food and language, that helps us to identify as part of a group of people.

---

[94] Finishing this book would certainly be nice…

[95] See – that liberal arts education your engineering major buddy said was a waste is suddenly becoming useful! (Especially if he's having to read this book for his job.)

[96] Same idea as the Aristotelian, Hobbesian, etc. – you're getting it!

[97] Brain bleach available upon request – please write the publisher for details.

The Judicious Spectator

Here Hume introduces the concept of the judicious spectator; as the name implies, they're watching, and they're sensible to our actions, which either merit their esteem or don't. In other words, what would someone observing our behavior objectively (so far as it's ever possible, it seems to be so here) and impartially (with nothing to gain or lose) say about a given course of action or character trait being exhibited? Hume says this is the basis from which we make our moral judgments, and we make them based on the feelings that are stirred in us, of either approval or disapproval, when we reflect from a common point of view. How, then, do we become ethical individuals? We don't become habituated to acting ethically as Aristotle had said, but instead, we become accustomed to acting in certain ways that are ethically approved, our Ethics having been directed by custom, rather than by habit. Without direct impressions of a metaphysical self of the sort Aristotle seems to have required, Hume tells us we have no actual conception of the self; what we call the self ifs really just a bundle of sensations that we associate with our notion of "self." This involves a little bit of Locke (whom we haven't studied here, and only need to borrow a single concept from), where the mind is perhaps best thought of as a linear record of what we've done, and what's been done to us. This in turn borrows heavily from Plato's definition of existence, where something is said to exist if it's capable of acting, or being acted upon; we are capable of acting, and we, as well as objects, are capable of being acted upon. It's really not a bad way of looking at this – we approach ethical situations within the context of our specific experiences, background, knowledge, upbringing, personal politics, religious beliefs, etc. Even when we invoke the judicious spectator, all of that is present at some level.

Starting with Reason

Up to this point, it would be fair to say that a person could be considered virtuous, provided they conformed to a particular understanding of both virtue and virtuous conduct, regulated by reason as a necessary effect, the cause for which was and is existence as a rational animal and agent. In other words, you're born, welcome to the species, please accept this lovely gift of rationality, and act accordingly. Hume doesn't want to accept this simply and leave things there, and makes a good point in reminding us that all these abstract definitions and even the demonstrative reasoning that frequently accompanies them never really influences our actions – all it can really do, in fact, is perhaps direct our judgment about causes and effects we witness and connect, but even then, it does so only secondarily, following our feelings of approval or disapproval. It works for or less as follows:

Carrying forward an idea we saw first in Plato, echoed again in Aristotle, Augustine, and Hobbes, and will see in its fullest expression a few chapters from now when we discuss the Utilitarians, Hume sees a definite impact of pain and pleasure on our Ethics. I, like most of us, learned a very young age, not to touch the hot stove – Hume would say it left with me with a very strong sensory impression to back up Mom's warning on the matter. Now, whenever I have a prospect (or a good likelihood) of experiencing pain from any object or situation, I feel a consequent emotion of aversion, and I'm moved to avoid whatever it is that will give me that pain, as it creates in me a feeling of uneasiness. Likewise, I know that I really enjoy ice cream, and so when I have the prospect of feeling pleasure, I feel a consequent emotion of propensity that carries me to embrace the source of what will be my satisfaction. Now, the distractions of hot stoves and yummy ice cream aside, it's fairly obvious even the most staunch rationalist that these impulses we feel don't arise out of reason, but at best, are only directed by it. It's from the prospect of pain or pleasure that we feel aversion or propensity toward any object – at this point, we simply aren't interested in ascertaining causes and effects, and for Hume, that's the only function of reason – it's nothing more than the discovery of facts.

Reason, on Hume's account, can never by itself produce any action or give rise to a choice on our part; at the same time, it's also incapable of preventing us from doing either of these things, or of disputing our preference with regard to passions, emotions, or even options in the case of choice. Nothing, in fact, can oppose a passion, but a contrary passion. Think of it like we did Aristotle's notion of virtue – we find it at the balance point between vices of excess and deficiency; in this case, we find reason informing, but not giving rise to, contrasting passions of, for example, love and hate. If the contrary passion came from reason, then it would have to have an original influence on the will, and would be able to cause or stop any act of choice on our part, but it doesn't actually work that way, so the principle that opposes passion can't be the same as reason. This is precisely why Hume tells us that reason is, and ought only to be, a slave of the passions – all it can do is serve and obey them.

Passion… and Reason

A passion is an original existence – they arise in us spontaneously, as a gut reaction, without having to stop and think about them. Accordingly, it's impossible for any passion that we might feel – any passion whatsoever, can be opposed by or contradictory to reason. The only time, Hume says, that a passion can be contrary to reason, is when the passion is accompanied by some judgment or opinion. He even allows that sometimes passions themselves are unreasonable; let's take a quick look at the examples he gives, exactly as he gives them, and how they can be understood in modern English. Passions, such as hope or fear, grief or joy, despair or security, are unreasonable, Hume says, in one instance, if they're founded on the supposition of the existence of objects which really do not exist. For example, let's say your significant other has been staying "at work" late into the evening, is slipping into the next room to take phone calls from "no one," and racking up some strange charges on the credit card statement, all of which would lead you to understandably suspect they're being unfaithful. But what if they're staying out late planning a romantic getaway for the two of you, taking calls from their travel agent, and booking the bed and breakfast on your Visa – then your passions have been founded on the suspicion of something that didn't exist, and are, on Hume's account, unreasonable.[98]

---

[98] Seriously – you really ought to see it. While you're at it, watch *Idiocracy* too.

The second example of an unreasonable passion given by Hume has to do with the means by which we seek our ends (plans, goals, desires, aims, etc.). He says when we exert any passion in action, but we have chosen means insufficient to attain our designed end, and deceive ourselves in our understanding of causes and effects, then our passion is unreasonable. Back to my admitted fondness for ice cream – let's say I really want an ice cream sundae right now (incidentally, I do!), and instead of hopping in my car, driving to the shop and buying myself one, I decide to stay here and meditate it to me – if I just concentrate hard enough, I can *will* that the ice cream come to me, instead of my having to go to it. Obviously, that would be unreasonable – but wow, it would be super cool if it worked that way! So where does this leave us? Hume reasons, correctly, that when a passion isn't founded on false supposition(s), and it hasn't chosen means insufficient to achieve its end, that our understanding, i.e., our reasoning can neither justify nor condemn it.

To illustrate this, Hume gives 3 further examples of things, that, while we would ordinarily be tempted to rationally label as "unreasonable" are nonetheless, according to his understanding, are *not* contrary to reason at all. It's not contrary to reason (read: unreasonable) according to Hume, to do any or all of the following: "to prefer the destruction of the whole world to the scratching of my finger, for me to choose my total ruin, to prevent the least uneasiness of an Indian or person wholly unknown to me, [or] to prefer even my own acknowledged lesser good to my greater, and have a more ardent affection for the former than the latter." Now, those are certainly very extreme examples, but I prefer the one found in the 1993 film, *Demolition Man*; wait – stay with me here. There's actually a lot of really good Philosophy found here, not what you'd expect in a Stallone/Snipes star vehicle, but nevertheless. At a great point in the movie, Dennis Leary's character, Edgar Friendly, goes off on a bit of a rant and rattles out a whole litany of the exact sorts of things that Hume has just said are not contrary to reason. And what's the reason he gives? "Because I suddenly might feel the need to, okay, pal?!" and this is a perfectly acceptable explanation from Hume's perspective, and one that, gosh – seems to make a lot of sense, when it comes right down to it. In fact, what he describes as "trivial" goods can, depending on the person and their circumstances, give rise to the greatest and most valuable enjoyment. Think of your guilty pleasures; mine, if you haven't already deduced this, are stupid movies – the cheesier, the better.[99] Granted, they're not going to be winning any Palm d'Or awards at Cannes, but I enjoy them, and for me, that's enough. Remember, since a passion can never be rightly called unreasonable unless it's founded on a false supposition or chooses insufficient means to reach its desired end, then it's impossible for reason and passion to oppose one another.

Further proof of this can be demonstrated through the application of reason itself, or through a few further examples of our reason in action. It's a fair place to note, perhaps, that for a guy who claims to have little use for reason, Hume sure seems to be employing an awful lot of it to prove his point, but I digress. Consider some of the activities we engage in that require the use of our reason, such as a multi-step mathematics problem or breaking

---

[99] This is why I have to read relatively profound books – to maintain balance in the cosmos; if I didn't finish reading the *Treatise*, then immediately watch *Police Academy* or *Roadhouse*, who knows what might happen!

down, even diagramming a sentence (and here we pause for a shudder at the memory of doing either or both). When engaged in either of these activities, your frustration (in which you're not alone), or your enjoyment (geek) isn't derived from the reason being put to use, but from your aversion to or desire for the activity itself. To add to the difficulty here, while we're ultimately interested in pleasure and pain, and in what we consider to be good in a given situation, we can, and we very often do, act against our interests – engaging in activities that we know are bad for us, and where our thoughts on the greatest possible good don't really influence us. This is where Hume is significantly different from Bentham and Mill, our two Utilitarians who will use his work as a starting point, but will view the greatest good as quite a bit more important and influential.

Practical Philosophy

Hume says all Philosophy can be divided into two main categories, speculative, and practical. The speculative side is exactly what you would expect – that's where we question the meaning of life,[100] ultimate truth, and all the sorts of things that really never have application outside of the lecture hall, but that which rely almost exclusively on our rational powers; thankfully, he includes Ethics in the practical side – the area where something can actually be done with the Philosophy we engage in – it can't be practically applied in real life. Morality is supposed to influence both our passions and our actions, and to go beyond the judgments of our reason; morals have an influence on our actions and affections, but can't be derived from reason. Morals excite passions and produce or prevent actions – reason can inform this process but can't do either of these things. The rules of morality therefore are not conclusions of our reason, and as long as we realize that reason has no influence on our passions and actions, we shouldn't pretend that morality can be deduced through the use of our reason.

Reason, for Hume, is nothing more than the discovery of truth and falsehood about the world, and because of this it can't tell us to do anything, except in relation to some desire. Truth or falsehood consists of an agreement or disagreement either to the real relation of ideas or the real existence of matter of facts about the world. What this means is that whatever is *not* susceptible to agreement or disagree or is incapable of being true or false, can never be an object of our reason. Now, consider any passion or emotion you've ever experienced, and the only one who could speak authoritatively on whether or not you actually felt it is you. Why? Because our passions, choices, and actions aren't susceptible to being agreed with; they can be acknowledged as having taken place, but that's about it – each is complete in and of itself, and implies no reference or requirement to other passions, choices, or actions. It's impossible then, Hume argues, for them to be labeled true or false, and are neither contrary to nor conformable to reason, which he holds to directly prove that actions aren't given merit for conforming to reason any more than they're blamed for being contrary to it.

Furthermore, reason can't prevent or produce actions by contradicting or approving of them, so reason can't be the source of moral good and evil, because our morals can and *do*

---

[100] Didn't we already cover this? It's 42.

produce or prevent actions. Actions can be deserving of our praise or blame, but Hume maintains they can't themselves be reasonable or unreasonable, for the simple reason that moral distinctions don't come from reason. Reason is entirely inactive when it comes to our moral thinking, and could never, according to Hume, be source of such an active principle as the conscience or a sense of morals. About the furthest Hume is willing to go is to say that our reason and judgment can be the mediate cause of an action, but only by prompting or directing some passion of ours.

Our Unreasonable Morality

At this point we might very well be wondering exactly what Hume has left us where we might be able to discover the origins of morality. If we trace his reasoning through, we find him reminding us that if our thought and understanding were by themselves incapable of establishing boundaries of right and wrong for us, then the basis of virtue and vice can be reduced to two possibilities.[101] Either virtue and vice consist in some relation of the object toward which they're directed, or they are simply matters of fact, the latter of which ought to be discoverable through the use of our reason. At this point, he's more or less destroyed any hope we might have had for making a case for reason, so he reasons (the irony is terrific) that virtue and vice must consist in some relations. If the relations are susceptible to certainty and demonstration, we have to limit ourselves to the following instances where relationships apply within our reasoning: resemblance between them, contrasts in their degree and quality, and proportions in their quantity and number; but since morality doesn't consider *any* of these relations in making moral claims, and is also not discovered through considering them, he quickly eliminates this possibility too. Remember that for Hume, all reason or science is simply the comparing of ideas, and the means by which we discover their relation(s) to one another – the same relations may have different causes, but the relations themselves are of the same sorts, and as discovering them isn't usually accompanied by a moral judgment one way or other, notions of right and wrong don't arise from nor are they connected to, their discovery.

Recall for a moment Aristotle's understanding of humanity as the rational (and social, and political) animals, separating us from the rest of animate nature because we're able to reason in a certain way that renders us fit for the rule of law, and Hume doesn't seem to quite agree with that. Think of an action that would criminal, or at the very least, morally blameworthy, if perpetrated by a human; now imagine an animal doing that same thing. The animal, lacking the rational factor that would allow it to identify the action as something that ought not to be done, can proceed unencumbered by its conscience, especially since, on Aristotle's account, it doesn't have one to begin with. Man, on the other hand, being endowed with the faculty that ought to restrain us to doing our duty morally and otherwise, should know better and avoid that action, based entirely on our having reason. Hume very rightly points out that this is a circular argument – if our reason were sufficient to prevent us from committing immoral acts, then we wouldn't be having this discussion. Every animal that has sense, and appetite, and will is susceptible to all of the same virtues and vices; case in point, I have a dog that seems "guilty" whenever something

---

[101] Note the similarity in his method here to St. Augustine's approach.

blows into the yard that she thinks shouldn't be there, and I have a cat who for all intents and purposes is greedy – he eats all the food he can before the other cats can make their way to the bowl, and even if he then throws it up elsewhere, he still got to it first! I'll admit to anthropomorphizing[102] my pets a bit here, but the point stands, relatively without question, just as Hume makes it.

If we can't rely on reason, then how are we supposed to be able to think about things that we normally include under the headings "moral" or "ethical?" Hume presents a process for thinking about actions that we might otherwise be inclined to call "vicious" for instance, and proceeds to show that the actions themselves are really morally inert, but the actors committing with them are what we really take issue with. These shouldn't properly be thought of each as steps necessarily, but as premises followed by the conclusion (there's that ironic use of reason again). The breakout is as follows: 1) take any actions considered to be "vicious" by most people; 2) examine it in all lights; 3) in whichever way you take it, you find only certain passions, motives, volitions, and thoughts on the part of the actor; 4) there is no other "matter of fact" in the case, and 5) the vice supposedly present entirely escapes you, as long as you consider the object. So for the sake of example, let's take a look at an act that while not necessarily illegal, is seen by many if not by most to be immoral – adultery. Sure, we could certainly consider murder or lying or whatever, but we run the risk of spiraling way out of control with all the situational vagaries, so this is just easier in the long run – trust me. So anyway, we've got a situation of adultery taking place, we'll assume for our case that it's one-sided, perpetrated against an unknowing spouse, with the conscious participation of a knowing partner. Hume's point is that no matter how we look at this act, we can talk about the passions involved – love, lust, etc., what their motives might be – a dead-end marriage, some sort of physical issue, etc., their volition – the choice they made to engage in this sort of behavior, the thoughts they must be having, and so on, but that's it. The vice that this would seem to embody on Aristotle's account doesn't enter into the equation with regard to the act itself – just the actor. So for Hume, while the adulterer may themselves be vicious, the act(s) they engage in are morally neutral, inert, etc.

The position Hume seems to be advocating here, although he doesn't label it as such, as one of amoralism – the position occupied by an amoralist,[103] in which, as the "a" implies (as in asexual, atheistic, apolitical, and so on) means without morals. Now, we have to be careful here – this doesn't mean the person holding this position is themselves without morals, but rather, they hold the position that actions have no moral status attached to them – only the actors who carry out the actions. For example, murder is neither praiseworthy nor blamable, but specific murderers, Ted Bundy for instance, certain are to blame. This same notion extends to words as well, specifically that there are no "bad" words; there are bad intentions, bad feelings, and so, but the words we use to describe them are simply collections of vowels and consonants that have no independent moral standing.[104] A good

---

[102] The tendency we so often have to give non-human things human characteristics.

[103] When we get to Nietzsche, a few chapters from now, he'll claim this for himself.

[104] The late, great George Carlin espoused a similar notion, and no doubt would have been thrilled that Hume suggested something similar.

example of this would be racial epithets as used by the comedian as a member of the race in question as compared to a bigot using the same word in a derogatory manner. This may not seem immediately apparent given the wide range of actions and words that we frequently and confidently label as vicious or otherwise morally deplorable, but it's a sound theory when one takes the time to think it through.

Virtue and Vice

Carrying forward themes we first saw in Aristotle, Hume turns his attention to virtue and vice and tells us that the distinction between them, like morality in general, is not founded on the relations of objects, and (predictably) isn't perceived by our reason. Here's where we're at so far: since virtue and vice aren't discoverable by reason, and our decisions concerning moral rightness and wrongness,[105] and all our perceptions are either strong impressions or faint(er) ideas,[106] we can conclude from all this that morality is more properly felt by us than arrived at through the use of our reason in judgment. Really this comes down to, and I can't help but squint slightly, and say this in my best "Dirty Harry" impression, "Do you feel virtuous? Well, do you, punk?!" To have a sense of virtue, on Hume's account, is nothing more than the feeling of a certain kind of satisfaction when we contemplate the character of the actor carrying out the action – that's it, and that's all. The feeling itself constitutes our praise or admiration, but we don't infer someone's character to be virtuous simply because it pleases us; but in feeling after a particular manner, we in effect feel that it is virtuous. He's echoing Aristotle here, remember – an action isn't virtuous simply because it's performed; it has to be performed in the way a virtuous person does. It's no less confusing getting this from Hume than it was from Aristotle, but it's about to make at least a little more sense to us than Aristotle managed...

According to Hume, all virtue is the power of producing love or pride; when we do something we feel is virtuous, we're proud of having done that, when we observe others doing it, we love that they're acting that way. Vice works similarly, but produces humility or hatred; we're humiliated by our vicious behavior, and hate others'. In every case, he tells us, we judge one by the other, in the same way as something being an impression precludes it from being an idea. Here's where he (again) differs from (or improves upon) Aristotle; remember, Aristotle, while thinking of the virtues as the mean, and the vices as extremes to either side, still thought of them as a fixed idea, what Hume calls a constant principle. Actions themselves, Hume tells us, not proceeding from any constant principle, have no influence on love, hate, pride, or humility, and are themselves never considered in morality – there's that amoralist position again. He tells us, quite correctly, that when we're looking into the origin of morals,[107] we don't consider actions, only the quality of character of the actor who performs the action. Actions are better indicators of our character than our words, wishes, or sentiments – as we say now, "actions speak louder than words," and indeed they do, as Hume proves.

---

[105] Hume uses the terms "rectitude" and "depravity" respectively, which are arguable cooler, but now somewhat obscure.

[106] According to Hume, if it's not one, then it *must* be the other.

[107] This will be the case when Nietzsche looks into the origin of our moral terms too.

Sympathy Revisited, and Artificial Virtues

You could tell he was leading up to this; Hume tells us next that the *true* origin of morals lies in the nature and force of sympathy, and he makes a pretty good case for the psychology of our morality, about three centuries before we even had a classification for things like that – not bad. The operation of sympathy turns out to be a causal (not casual) relationship – nothing more than simple causes and effects operating within our minds, and it works like this: When we see the *effects* of passion in the voice and gesture of another person, our minds immediately pass from the effects to the causes of them. This, in turn, forms in our minds such a lively idea of the passion that it's presently converted into the passion itself. In other words, we see how they're feeling, get an idea of why they're feeling that way, and we experience the same feeling through our sympathy, simply because our minds move almost immediately from the cause of any emotion to conveying the same emotion in ourselves. This still doesn't require our reason – we are only sensible (remember – Hume is an empiricist) of the causes or effects, and from these we infer the passion, and consequently these give rise to our sympathy – it really is as simple, and direct, as that.

Sympathy can, in fact, do quite a bit more than we might initially be inclined to give it credit for, or for having an influence on. It's from sympathy that we get the esteem that Hume says we pay to all the artificial virtues, a statement that probably calls for a brief aside of its own. The virtues, and by extension, the vices, are artificial because we made them up – they're not fixed terms, but merely convenient labels that we've come up with in order to be able to speak about these concepts. Back to sympathy, it's fairly obvious what a powerful principle this is in human nature – it even has an influence over our aesthetic senses, as we're more likely to watch, listen to, or eat things we might not ordinarily care for, depending on who's with us when or influencing us to do so. Ultimately, it is sympathy that produces our sentiment of morals with regard to all of what Hume persists in calling artificial virtues (though it does sort of rub off on you after a while – he's got a point). It's safe to assume, then, that sympathy also gives rise to many of the other virtues, and that certain qualities of character get our approval because they tend toward the good of mankind. Hume even tells us that where the quality we approve of really *is* beneficial to society, a *true philosopher* will never require any other principle to account for the strongest approval and esteem on our part; and we'll pardon his not-so-subtle dig on anyone and everyone who doesn't explicitly agree with him.

We have some fairly good evidence that the virtues, while real, are nonetheless artificial; why then, do we react the way we do to them? If we didn't have natural sentiments of approval and blame when we consider certain actions and characters, then they could never be taken advantage of people intent on keeping us at odds with one another. The adjectives we use like laudable, praiseworthy, odious, and so on, would be unintelligible to us if we lacked this natural capacity. "Real life" examples of this present themselves on a daily basis – especially in politics and otherwise political issues. Think for a moment of a few of the more divisive ones that receive a lot of our attention – abortion, stem-cell research, immigration issues, music piracy, etc. If our Ethics were tied to our reason alone, then provided we were all provided with equal access to the same set of data then we would all arrive at the same conclusions with regard to the moral issues in question. The fact that we arrive at vastly different conclusions gives pretty good evidence in support of our emotions and these natural sentiments having quite a bit more to do with them. We are, first and foremost, emotionally inclined to one side or other on these divisive issues; we may reason and judge later, but first, we emote.

The good, or that which results from every virtue, arises from every single act we engage in, and is the object of some natural passion we feel. For example, a single act of a specific virtue, justice for instance, considered in itself, may often be contrary to the public good, but hardly anyone would deny that law and justice, both as concepts and forces, are advantageous to society. If you're inclined to disagree, go back and reread the chapter on Hobbes' state of nature, and with a view to this advantage of having them that we have established them by our voluntary conventions, i.e., we made them up because they beat the alternative(s).

Sympathy versus Esteem

For obvious reasons, we sympathize more with people nearest us, and less so with people remote from us – I'm more concerned with (or at least more directly affected by) what's happening in my neighborhood than I am with events transpiring half the world away from me. Sympathy varies without any variation in our esteem though, and so Hume reasons (again – correctly) that our esteem can't come from sympathy. Our approval of certain moral qualities comes from a moral taste, and from certain sentiments of pleasure and disgust which arise within us when we contemplate or see particular qualities or characters. Sort of piggybacking on Hobbes' point that we're all so different that we can't possibly agree on a highest good, Hume notes that each of us occupies a peculiar (unique, in this instance) position with regard to everyone else. In order to prevent continual contradictions, and arrive at a more stable judgment of things, we fix on some steady and general points of view, and place ourselves in them, whatever our present situation may be. Something similar can be found in Aristotle, where he cautions us to seek precision only so far as the subject at hand makes it possible, i.e., find an ethical position that will be correct more often than not, nine times out of ten, etc.[108]

In general, all our sentiments of praise and blame are variable; from the influence of characters and qualities of those whom we encounter, we base our praise or blame of them. We are able, and very often called, to overlook our own interest, and by reflecting on this, we correct the sentiments of blame that are inclined to rise up in us when we meet opposition. We find many contradictions to our sentiments in society, and in conversation; the phenomenon of Facebook comes quickly to mind in evidence of this. Hume tells us we blame equally a bad action which we read of in history with one performed in our neighborhood the other day, which seems to lend some support to the notion that it is our emotional response, rather than our rational reflection, which really influences our

---

[108] Of course, Aristotle uses the infinitely cooler Greek phrase, *hos epi to polu* – "for the most-part," or "sorta-kinda-maybe."

sentiments with regard to any given action or character. What does seem to influence us directly and reliably, and Hume is unknowingly presaging the Utilitarians we'll discuss two chapters from now, are pleasure and pain. We experience pleasure from the view of the character of others, or ourselves, and in those things which are simply agreeable to others, and to ourselves. Though the pleasures of other people influence us more faintly than our own, they are more constant and universal, provide a counterbalance to our understanding of our own, and are alone what Hume will admit to and identify as the standard of virtue and morality, but we'll encounter that soon enough…

Chapter 13: Kant

If you found Hume entirely too emotional for your taste, don't like the idea of there being exceptions to every rule, and tend to be a black and white thinker with regard to your Ethics, where reason triumphs and trumps all contenders, no matter how compelling, then Kant is your guy. He wrote extensively on Moral Philosophy, but the piece that most interests us is one of his shorter works – more of a longish essay than a book, really, but nonetheless, an extremely influential one, the *Groundwork*[109] *of the Metaphysics of Morals*. If Hume's *Treatise* is one of the most influential works in the English language, then it's fair to say that Kant's *Groundwork* is one of the most influential works in *any* language. That's not to say that it's the end-all, be-all of Ethics – far from it; as we'll see, it's got some rather glaring problems with it, but this is where we see a fundamentally new approach to Ethics appearing on the scene for more or less the first time ever, and that approach is a deontological one. From the Greek word *deon*, meaning duty or obligation, this approach has us ultimately ignoring both our inclinations and guesstimated consequences and doing what we do not necessarily because we want to, but because we must. Kant wanted to find a (or rather, *the*) "supreme principle of morality" – that which would remain if we were to jettison all the minutiae we've accumulated so far in our study of Ethics – all the religious aspects, politics, personal emotional psychology, etc. In other words, what is the single element that we could maintain and still be said to be ethical?

For Kant, whatever moral duties we are subject to must apply both necessarily and universally to be considered valid, and to have any claim at all on commanding our allegiance to them. We'll look at each of these on their own momentarily, but for now, we should understand that duties present requirements (also referred to as practical laws) for us because they hold for the will of every rational being. He's carrying forward a bit of Aristotle here – you're born, congratulations – welcome to the species; because you're a rational sort of animal, it's Kant's contention that his Ethics automatically apply to you. Now, whether or not you choose to accept that premise is entirely up to you, but that's where he's coming from, and he's quite serious about it. The notion of necessity implies that our duties, whatever they may be, will always override the other reasons that compete for our attention and allegiance. In this sense, it really doesn't matter what we want out of a given situation, or whether our interests and ends are being served – all that matters is whether or not we're doing our duty. Duties also apply to us "universally" simply because we're rational agents and our actions ought to be those which conform to universally valid principles. Because of this combination of necessity and universality, Kant will claim that moral requirements can't be based in features of our human nature,[110] specifically in our

---

[109] Variously translated as the *Foundation* also, but really – to-MAY-to, to-MAH-to.

[110] Which may seem a bit odd, considering he's also arguing that our rationality is a special feature of our human nature too, the accusation he levels at psychology.

human psychology (as Hume had claimed). Instead, our morals must, to Kant, have an *a priori*[111] basis in rationality.

The Good Will

Kant begins in a way that perhaps we would assume he would, given his nearly obsessive focus on our rationality; he begins with the concept of our good will, and defines it as our disposition to act on our judgment of what is the morally correct course of action, simply because it's the right thing to do. Now, this is an odd way to phrase it, especially as we often think of our disposition as having more to do with our state of emotional health than with our rationality, so it may be a bit of a stretch, but this is his starting point, so it's worth our while to spend a few moments examining it. Kant tells us that nothing in the world – indeed, nothing even *beyond* the world – can possibly be thought of as good which could be called "good" without qualification, except a good *will*. His inclusion of "beyond the world" has been examined a few different ways, and whether he's implying God, alien life, or something altogether different, he seems to be saying that it holds true that this is the proper (read: rational) whatever might be presently outside our understanding, i.e., if we discover some new species, provided they're rational, they'll reason as we do. If the good will can be called "good" without qualification, that is to say without evidence or support, firstly it's one of those things which we can know *a priori*, and secondly, it will be for Kant the indispensable condition even of worthiness to be happy in the first place.

So if we have any hope of reading Aristotle's vaunted *eudaimoniac* state, Kant tells us we must first be in possession of a good will. Some qualities – what we have to this point referred to as the virtues – seem to be conducive to this good will and can facilitate its action, but in spite of that they themselves have no intrinsic, unconditional worth. So what he's saying here is that all the virtue terms we like to bandy about – justice, temperance, fortitude, courage, generosity, and the like, while they may help us outwardly manifest and express our good will, are not themselves good independent of our putting them into use. This is a far cry from Plato's association of justice as being in the highest category of good things, wherein they're desired for their own sake and not for any consequences arising from them. Be that as it may, all these virtues seem at the very least to presuppose a good will, i.e., they're not likely to be present in or employed by someone whose will is not good. But, because we don't value them on their own, what Kant refers to as limits on their esteem, they can't be held to be absolutely good in the same sense as the good will can be and is.

The question should arise right about now, "What makes the good will *good*?" Kant tells us the good will is not good because of what it makes possible or accomplishes, and not because of its being able to achieve some particular end that we might propose. The good will is good only because of its willing, that is, on the Kantian[112] account, the good will is good simply because it is good in and of itself, which matches up with our classical

---

[111] "Prior to (experience);" things that are true by definition, e.g., "all bachelors are unmarried men." This is as opposed to *a posteriori*, "after (experience);" things which can only be known given a certain level of personal experience with them, e.g., "some bachelors are very happy."

[112] Just like Humean, Hobbesian, etc. – you get the idea (or you ought to, by now).

definition of the good where it is defined as that which is desirable for its own sake. Because of this, the good will can't be made any better, no matter how useful it is for us, and it won't be in any way diminished if it proves, in isolated instances, to not be particularly useful to us. In this way it remains constant, and so does its intrinsic worth, regardless of the circumstances in which we're call on to employ it.

Reason, Duty, and Happiness

Elsewhere, Kant had credited Hume for having awoken him from his "dogmatic slumbers," and we can see a lot of the Scot's influence in the Prussian's work – look for it in his approach to reason, our desires, and so on, and it's readily apparent. There is, finally, a great deal of Hume in Kant, but not a lot of Kant in Hume, something that may lend itself handily to anyone trying to ascertain which of them has been ultimately more influential and useful to us, but I (yet again) digress. We see a bit of this in Kant's understanding of the limitations and role of reason – he believes it isn't competent to guide our will safely with regard to its (the will's) objects and the satisfaction of all our needs, simply because it is a practical faculty only. Reason has been given to us to employ practically (as opposed to speculatively) in order to get such things as we need to make it from day to day, and its influence on our Ethics is reflective of this role and limitation. Reason's proper function on Kant's account is to produce a will that is good in itself – since reason is absolutely essential for this production, and reason will not produce one that is good only as a means. The good will then isn't the only good or the complete good, but is the highest good, and the necessary condition he places on all other goods, even of our desire for happiness.

Happiness, by now, should be a familiar theme running through Ethics, keeping a nice pace alongside the good, the virtues, justice, and the like. Kant approaches happiness a bit differently than we've seen so far, by telling us that we have a duty to preserve our lives, and all of us, with a few rather noteworthy exceptions, seem to have a direct inclination to do so – you might say we're moderately hooked on this whole living thing. Since we're living anyway, we might as well enjoy ourselves, and so to secure our own happiness is at least indirectly a duty also. Even if we momentarily don't consider duty (Kant will surely forgive us), all of us seem to have the strongest and deepest inclinations to happiness, because, as Aristotle rightly surmised, in the concept of happiness, all of our other, dare I say lesser, inclinations are summed up and expressed, or at least made possible. But let us say, even if for only a moment, that if the universal inclination to happiness that Kant is suggesting were not allowed to determine our wills, and if our continued lives and health were not at least a necessary factor in calculating this sort of thing, there would, he argues, as in all other cases, a law (of sorts) that we ought to promote our happiness, not from an inclination, but from duty. Presuming this to be the case, only from that law[113] would our conduct have true moral worth – more on this concept shortly.

---

[113] Kant doesn't seem to mean either a juridical nor a physical law, but the sort that inheres in the Greek word *nomos* – closer to what we might think of as a natural law, in the same sense as Aquinas or Hobbes thought of it, or as best expressed in Sophocles' play *Antigone*, wherein our allegiance to the law trumps even patriotism.

Moral Worth and the Will

Moral worth, for Kant, is an attribute an action acquires when it is done from duty, a direct result from the actor having been moved by their recognition that the action is inherently right and ought to be done. It's a special characteristic that the action takes on, and it elicits our esteem, sort of like Hume's judicious spectator, because we realize that's it's been done right and for the right reasons. To that end, Kant makes two important propositions that lead along the way to identifying his supreme principle of morality; the first of which is, to have moral worth, an action must be done from duty or obligation. This stands to reason, based on what we know about his thinking so far – actions don't acquire their moral worth simply because they're done, but because their done out of a sense of obligation on the part of the actor. The second proposition follows from the first; an action done from duty doesn't have its moral worth in the purpose to be achieved through it, but in the maxim by which it is determined – more on maxims momentarily. So the moral value of anything done by anyone doesn't depend on the object acted upon itself, but on the principle that guided our volition, without any consideration of the objects that might otherwise direct our desires. So basically, it doesn't really matter what we're trying to obtain or achieve, but it is of the utmost importance that our principle(s) guiding us are of the right sort.

To illustrate this, Kant imagines the will as standing at a crossroads, faced with a decision as to how we ought to act, with our principles on the one hand, and the incentives that might otherwise guide us on the other. The principle is *a priori* and formal, that is, it exists for us only as an idea; the incentive is *a posteriori* and material, that is, it is something actual that we can focus on and desire. So on the one hand we have what we've told ourselves we would do in a given situation, e.g., "no matter what, I'll never steal;" on the other hand, we have the reality of our situation, e.g., "my family is starving, and I have no means by which to provide them with sustenance other than stealing." So we're stuck between what we established for ourselves as a principle before it was tested, and the present reality of it being tested, and into this already difficult mix, walks Kant. He tells us her that since our action must be determined by something, if it is done from duty, it must be determined by the formal principle of our volition, as we should view every material principle, our incentives, as having been withdrawn from it – we are not to allow them to influence our decision one way or another, but must instead stick to our proverbial guns.

The third principle Kant presents as a consequence of these first two, and this that duty is the necessity of an action done from respect for the law, as the law itself is the proper object of our respect and therefore presents a command we must obey (if we want to maintain our status as rational agents, that is). According to Kant, an act from duty excludes, or rather, ignores, the influence of our inclinations and the objects that our will might otherwise be inclined to desire, and so nothing remains which can determine the will objectively except the law and subjectively except pure respect (expressed as duty) for this practical law. By objective, we're referring to something that will affect everyone without preference for an individual, just as a thermometer is an objective tool for measuring temperature; by subjective, we're speaking of those things that impact us directly, on an individual level. The subjective element in this particular instance is the maxim that we should follow such a law, even if it goes against all our inclinations. The conclusion Kant reaches here is that the moral worth of an action is not in any way influenced by the effect that is expected from it, nor is it influenced by any principle of action that has to borrow its motive from that expected effect.

Maxims, Respect, and the Law

Now is probably as good a time as any to discuss exactly what Kant is talking about when he refers to a "maxim," and no – it's not a men's magazine. A maxim, in Kantian deontological terms, is a principle or rule that we establish for ourselves, and which directs all our actions. Our typical instinct, this being Ethics, is to proceed under the assumption that all our maxims must necessarily be of the utmost magnitude and carry with them profound ethical gravity that will extend to every situation we encounter, but this simply isn't the case. Kant's maxims, in a nutshell, could be summarized roughly as being those actions which would remain ethical when done by anyone, at any time, in any place, under the same or similar circumstances, without any loss of rightness. And they don't necessarily have to be earth-shattering sorts of things with any philosophical profundity attached to them – they could be simple things that would make the world a better place without any substantive cost, such as smiling, saying "please" and "thank you," and, perhaps most importantly, using your @#$% turn signal! In short, these are principles that we've established for ourselves to live according to, that by definition and extension we think everyone else ought to be following as well.

The greatest good, on Kant's account, can only be the idea of and participation in the law itself, and this can only be present in us as rational agents, so far as our wills are determined by and grounded in the law and not the effects we hope for in our day-to-day lives. That same greatest good, which he calls moral, is already present in the person who acts according to the idea of the law, so it doesn't have to be expected first in the result. In other words, unlike Aristotle's insistence that we don't become virtuous until we exercise a virtue, e.g., we're not generous until we do something that requires generosity on our part, Kant is saying that we have this as a special feature of our rationality right out of the gate. Incidentally, Aristotle had to take an extra step to reach this point, by positing our *epistemonikon* – the special feature of our rationality that makes us fit for the rule of law in the first place, and only then can we proceed to be virtuous, etc. Accordingly, Kant tells us that it's under this condition alone that our will can be called absolutely good without qualification, and this must admit of no exceptions. In this sense, Kant could well be thought of as the anti-Sir Mixalot, i.e., no but(t)s! If we're inclined by our good will, which itself is directed by our rationality, to always act in a certain way, then we can admit of no exceptions or special, extenuating circumstances whatsoever; Aristotle referred to this same basic notion as our action proceeding from a firm and unchangeable character, the notable difference being that here we don't have to habituate ourselves to acting this way, we simply follow our maxims from the outset.

Respect is, for Kant, a feeling, but lest we worry that he may be slipping into Hume's empiricism, he assures us that it is not received through any outer influence, which is to say, not felt in the empirical sense of the word, but rather, brought about independently by a rational concept. Aretha Franklin's notions on the concept notwithstanding, respect for

Kant is what we witness in the direct determination of the will by the law, and the resulting consciousness of that determination. In plain English, respect is best thought of as the effect of the law on us as rational subjects, and not as the cause(s) of the law itself. Because of this, all respect for a person, either ourselves or someone else, is really only respect for the law, of which the person provides an example. Take just a moment and realize what he's saying here – essentially, all our so-called moral interest is really just respect for the law, a position so legalistic and directly impersonal in and of itself even Aquinas probably would have cringed!

The Categorical Imperative

At long last we're presented with Kant's (in)famous categorical imperative, but before we get too excited, this is just the first iteration he presents, and not one he seems particularly happy with, so we'll be coming back to this a little while later. Nonetheless, he gives us the first version as, "I should never act in such a way that I could not will that my maxim should be a universal law." Okay, no problem – sounds good, even, so what exactly does he take issue with? He tells us immediately following this that it's soon clear to him that such a maxim is (as yet) based only on an apprehensive concern with (potential) consequences. So it's back to the drawing board for now, and his approach to the temptation we face when presented with an opportunity to lie will help him "think out loud" and dial in his definition a little better as we go on. In other words, prepare yourselves for encountering this same notion, only a little tighter, a few more times until he's satisfied that we're not going to be distracted by the possible outcomes and potentially influenced to act in a way that would not truly reflect a respect for the law.

If you've never in your life told a lie, please lay the book down momentarily and raise your hand so you can be counted. If you did so, congratulations – you've just lied – welcome to the club, we're growing all the time. We all lie, almost without exception, but the question we need to address before we can dive back into Kant's arguments is *why* do we tell lies? Usually, or rather hopefully, it's generally to spare someone's feelings, avoid a socially awkward situation, or preserve a level of peace that to us (at least at the time) probably is in closer accord with our respect for the law than the lie itself would risk and engender. Despite this, and again, almost without exception, our lies are nearly always found out and we're faced with the uncomfortable proposition of explaining ourselves to one or more people to whom we've now lied. Kant doesn't quite get to this level of psychological consideration, and limits himself instead to considering our reasons for being truthful. He says we're either truthful from duty, or we're truthful because we have a fear of disadvantageous consequences, and he appears to be correct in this assessment.

Back to why we lie, or rather *when* we lie, and especially if it's a whopper, our next step, after having told the lie, is inevitably our attempt(s) to justify our actions, usually to ourselves, sometimes to our co-conspirators if they were in on the lie as well. We say the usual sorts of things like, "I had to," and "anyone in my same situation would have lied," or "it's better this way," possibly even, "they'll never find out, so it's okay." Kant would most likely remind us that our urge to justify our actions is as good as an admission on our part that we've done something we know full well is wrong, and we're trying to soothe our

92

aching conscience rather than restore order to the cosmos, and he'd be right. To be truthful from duty, on Kant's account, is an entirely different thing from being truthful out of a fear of disadvantageous consequences, because when we're truthful from duty we have in mind the law, the concept of which contains an explicit law for us to follow. When we're truthful only out of our fear of the potentially negative consequences, we've got to look around first to see what results might be connected with it when we're ultimately found out. We see immediately that while we can justify our actions and make claims like those above – we had to, anyone would have, etc., we can very easily will the lie itself, but we can't will a universal law that anyone may lie whenever it benefits them, even though we've just done exactly that. In other words, and specifically Kantian words, our maxim would necessarily destroy itself as soon as it was made a universal law.

Kant tells us that he is "inexperienced in the course of the world," and "incapable of being prepared for all its contingencies," and this is quite true, but bears a bit of explanation. Suffice to say, Kant didn't "get out" a whole lot – he was born, grew up, was educated, employed, retired, and died, all in Konigsberg, Prussia,[114] and doesn't appear to have had much of a social or family life outside his work life, so he means his caveat to be taken quite literally. All he can do is ask whether or not he can will that his maxim become a universal law, and if not, it must be rejected, not because of any personal disadvantage, but because it could not be entered into universal legislation. To duty all our other motives must give place because duty is the condition of having a will good in and of itself, a worth that transcends everything for Kant. Wisdom – the *sophia* part of *philosophia*, a sort of which we're engaged in here – consists more in acting than in knowing, something very similar to what we heard from both Hobbes and Hume with regard to our actions speaking louder than our words.

The Role of Reason

On Kant's account, reason functions very much as it does in Aristotle, issuing inexorable commands without promising anything to the inclinations; his choice of words here is important – if we break "inexorable" down, it implies something that we can't (in) talk ourselves (orable) out of (ex). So despite our tendency to justify things to ourselves (as in when we lie), when our reason directs our actions according to duty, we are unable to do otherwise – according to Kant. Reason disregards, and holds in contempt (something else we saw in Hobbes) those claims that are so impetuous and yet some plausible, that can't be abolished by any command. In other words, those thoughts we're inclined to have along the lines of, "I could get away with it," "no one would ever find out," etc., have to be put aside, as they're not in accord with the sort of universality Kant requires our decisions to be based on.

It's observed by Kant, again quite rightly, that everything in nature works according to laws – physical laws, natural laws, and so on – only we, as rational beings, have the capacity to act according to the conception of laws, i.e., according to our principles. We don't have to be in the middle of viciously murdering an innocent other, only have someone else come along

---

[114] Which is today Kalinigrad, Russia, as it's been since 1946.

and tell us that murdering is wrong, and we ought not to do it, then stop and learn the law – we are able instead to be told that murder is wrong and that we ought not to do it, and go from there, based entirely on our understanding and conception of the law implied. The capacity that allows us to do this is, again, Aristotelian; Aristotle had referred to *epistemonikon*, a special feature of our rationality that makes us fit for the rule of law; for Kant, this exact same capacity is our will. Our will is what allows us to choose only that which reason, independently of our inclination, is recognized as practically necessary, i.e., as good, right, moral, and so on.

But if our reason doesn't determine the will, and if the will is subjected to our subjective conditions that don't always agree with objective conditions, then the actions we recognize as objectively necessary will always be subjectively contingent. Yes – that was English just now. Here's what he means: There are things that are necessary for the rest of the world, i.e., that benefit humanity on the whole, and these are the objectively necessary things. When we use "objective" in this context, we're referring to those things which are not subject to our personal interests, in the same was as a scale is an objective measure of weight; no matter how much I want it to read as my slim(mer), trim(mer) college weight, it now (cruelly) registers my weight as a college professor instead of as a student. Back to Kant, we can reasonably assume that because the objective aspects of life are not going to change, and in fact, are *unable* to change, that it is our subjective desires that must instead bend to fit the objective reality of our situation. In saying that those things which are objectively necessary are subjectively contingent, Kant is reminding us that that which is good for the world is very definitely dependent on our willful participation in it. This idea of an objective principle acts to constrain our will – it places limits on the options we have with regard to our actions – there are some alternatives theoretically available to us that we simply can't take in actuality because our principles won't allow us to.

Imperatives Revisited

The conception of this objective principle, so far as we allow it to constrain our will, is a command of reason, and the formula that the command is expressed by is called an imperative. Kant tells us imperatives are easy to spot – they'll always include an "ought;" functioning a lot like should, no longer merely a suggestion, but now a command, order, directive, etc. The practical good is what does, or at least what ought to, determine our will. And so a perfectly good will, if there could be such a thing, would be equally subject to objective laws, but would have, as part of its objective constitution, a natural inclination to do the right thing. In other words, if Kant's Ethics are correct, then they're not needed – if we always acted in the way he seems to be describing, we wouldn't need to have this discussion. But for now, we'll hold off judgment and see if he can rescue his theory. If the imperatives are only formulas expressing a relation (a theme we've seen since Plato) of objective laws of our volition in general to the subjective imperfections of our wills (our tendencies to *not* always act in the best possible way), then all imperatives must issue their command either hypothetically or categorically.

Now remember, Kant sees actions in quite the opposite from the way Hume sees them – actions, independent of actors, are themselves either good or bad, right or wrong, and have moral worth on their own merits, or don't. Anyway, back to the actions, if the action in question is good only as a means to something else, the imperative is hypothetical; but if it's thought of as good in itself or desirable for its own sake (remember the Classical definition for/understanding of "the good"), then the imperative which commands it is categorical. All the hypothetical imperative says, therefore, is that the action is good to some purpose, possible or actual. So what's the problem with that? Don't we choose actions like that all the time? Nothing is necessarily problematic about it, and yes – we do choose actions like this all the time. Think for a moment about your going to the dentist (stick with me here) – all that time spent reclined in the chair, getting scraped and drilled on, maybe even flossing like you're supposed to (I never remember). Let's say you've done all this, and some afternoon you're on public transportation – a nice bus with the metal bar on the back of the seat in front of ours, and suddenly the bus comes to a stop, but, due to inertia, you don't. You don't, that is, until your very well-cared-for teeth contact that metal bar and cease to be quite so nice as you'd like for them to be. All those hours spent reclined in the chair, brushing, flossing, and the like, were just wasted; you were acting according to an end that wasn't going to be realized, and now never will be, despite your best efforts.

The correct course of action, then, must be the one we arrive at by way of the categorical imperative, which declares actions to be themselves objectively necessary, without making any references to be a purpose to be achieved beyond the action itself. Because this imperative directly commands us, without making its condition some purpose to be reached by it, this is what Kant identifies as the supreme principle of morality, and this is what the *Groundwork* set out to find to begin with. Law alone implies the concept of an unconditional and objective and hence, universally valid necessity, and the commands that result are laws which must be obeyed by us – even against our inclinations, simply because the categorical imperative is restricted by no condition. There are other types of imperatives, certainly – technical, and pragmatic, as well as moral. Technical imperatives are the sort that guide architects and electronic engineers in knowing where to place load-bearing walls or in which direction to orient transistors in a printed circuit board. Pragmatic imperatives related to our general welfare – these are the imperatives that remind us, "if it ain't broke, don't fix it." Moral imperatives, the categorical included, belong to our free conduct – those actions we perform or forbear from performing, guided to their proper ends by our will.

Why can't the moral imperative be hypothetical and be just as moral as the categorical variety? Just what would be wrong with basing our actions, moral and otherwise on the achievement of goals? Kant tells us that no matter how self-aware and attuned to our goals we might be, it is impossible for us to form a definite concept of that which we *really* will. In short, we're not capable, on the basis of any principle, and with complete certainty, or ascertaining what would make us truly happy – omniscience would be needed for that. This is very similar to something we encountered in Hobbes, who reminded us that very often we want different things at different stages of our lives, so it's impossible that we could all want the same thing. In Kant's take on this, our lack of clearly-defined and precise goals makes truly hypothetical imperatives almost mindless on our part.

So we have arrived at the point where the categorical imperative is identified as the only thing that can be thought of as a practical law; other things (such as the virtues) can be called principles of the will, but are not themselves laws. We get a clarity from the categorical imperative that other types of moral principles seem to be lacking – when we think of a categorical imperative in the positive, e.g., "I ought always to tell the truth," or in the negative, e.g., "I ought never to lie," we know immediately what it contains, and by extension, what it excludes. At long last, Kant arrives at what we call the first iteration (restatement) of the categorical imperative, and it's this: "Act only according to that maxim by which you can at the same time will that it should become a universal law." There will be a second iteration shortly, but it shouldn't be thought of as replacing this one, but rather, as supplementing it. This one refers to how we determine which actions are moral and ought to be performed; the next will have to do with our interactions with other people.

Duty

In every decision we make, whether we're conscious of it or not, we are carrying out our decision(s) with some respect to duty – either following it, or ignoring it. Kant breaks our decisions with respect to duty down into four distinct categories, each of which involves a dutiful action, but which focuses in a slightly different way with regard to how this sense of duty impacts our decision to act in the way(s) we do. The first instance involves actions that are themselves contrary to duty, such as stealing.[115] The second example involves actions that are dutiful, but done only out of fear of the penalty or sanction(s) that await us upon their discovery, such as paying taxes – I don't like sending in my tax return, but I don't want to be Wesley Snipes' cellmate, so I dutifully mail them out each spring. The third option involves those actions that are in accord with our duty, but which we're already inclined toward because we find them pleasurable in some way, such as a labor of love. The final possibility involves actions that are in accord with duty but are contrary to our inclinations, and this is where, in its more extreme examples, most people tend to part company with Kant, as we'll see shortly. Kant maintains that *all* duties, so far as the kind of obligation (not the object of their action) is concerned, have been completely exhibited in these instances by their dependence on the one principle. And, while we have that tendency to attempt to justify our actions, to ourselves if no one else, when we observe ourselves in any transgression of a duty, we find that we don't actually will that the maxim we were following in that instance be made a universal law.

The question then becomes a very practical one for us to consider – is it a necessary law for all rational beings, that is, us, that we should always judge our actions by such maxims that we could ourselves will to serve as universal laws? In other words, would it be practical and practicable to go around constantly testing all our active endeavors against this criterion, or would that hopelessly delay getting anything done, as we'd be in a nearly continuous state of testing and deliberation? Kant doesn't seem to think so, and compared to Bentham, who we'll encounter in the next chapter, it may even seem quite reasonable to ask this of ourselves and each other. The reason, for Kant, that this is so imperative upon us[116] is that we, i.e., human beings, are the only ones who have the faculty of reason for use

---

[115] Regardless of circumstances – remember, on Kant's account, if an action's wrong, then it's *always* wrong.

[116] See what I did there (again)?

in determining our conduct, carrying forward Aristotle's notion of humanity as the rational animals. As such, we are the best equipped, or at least significantly more-so than my golden retriever, to ignore, or at least not focus solely on our subjective ends, which rest on incentives, in order to focus on and follow our objective ends, which depend on motives valid not only for ourselves, but for every rational being. At least that's how Kant hopes it will work out; being somewhat more cynical we can agree with him to some extent, while realizing also that it very often doesn't – we are entirely too caught up in our subjective ends – those things that are relative to us, which we're reminded (often too late) are grounds for hypothetical imperatives only.

Treating Others as Ends

In general, humanity, being comprised of rational beings, recognizes that each of us exists as an end in ourselves, and not merely as a means to be used by another's will for another's own purpose, and this recognition carries with it a certain weight that Kant argues ought to be respected by us. Humanity (momentarily) aside, the worth of any object to be obtained by our actions is at all times conditional, so if there is going to be a supreme practical principle and categorical imperative for our human will, it must be one that leads to our forming objective principles of the will from the conception of that which is necessarily an end for everyone, simply because it is an end in itself. From this, Kant develops his second iteration of the categorical imperative – act so that you treat all humanity, whether in your own person or in that of any other, always as an end and never as a means only. In other words, don't use others as a means to achieve ends you desire for yourself if doing so would not respect them as ends in themselves. But wait – there's more – Kant extends the same requirement to how we treat ourselves, saying we may not use ourselves as means to an end either! Now, whether this was always thought of as implied though not expressed, or if it simply didn't occur to earlier moral philosophers is unclear, but it doesn't seem to have been treated or discussed up to this point, so Kant's contribution is both unique and thought-provoking.

To illustrate his point, Kant provides us with some examples of what he considers to be immoral behavior either toward another or toward oneself, with regard to treating all rational beings as ends and never as means. The first, and arguably the most contentious, involves one who is sick of life and contemplating suicide – we'll come back to this one and give it its own treatment shortly. The next example, and one that's fairly obvious, is borrowing money that you have no intention of ever repaying – the same would go for that buddy who always seems to "borrow" tools, books, games, etc. that never make their way back home. The third example, while not nearly as contentious as the suicide example, nonetheless upsets people, and it involves not pursuing a special talent that has the potential to benefit society. Say for instance that you have "gifted hands," and, while you could be a great neurosurgeon or something on that order, you opt instead to become an abstract sculptor in a rural artists' colony – Kant would contend that you're wasting talents that could otherwise be put to use to benefit all of us, and this objection of his may or may not be trumped by his own notions of autonomy – more on that shortly. Finally, Kant calls out those who are financially secure by who don't donate to charity; ostensibly this would extend to the other virtues as well, e.g., those who are courageous but engage in pacifistic activities, or who are prudent, but work in Vegas – whatever. Each of these, on Kant's account is an instance of using others or ourselves as means to an end rather than an end in and of ourselves, which he considers to be wrong, but which we probably consider to be simply the way things sometimes turn out.

Alright, back to the suicide example; Kant maintains that one who is sick of life may not commit suicide on those grounds alone, and we may agree with him there, but he also extends this prohibition to those who are suffering unbearable pain and seek death as a means of escape from their torment – which is where most people part company with Kant. Before we judge for sure, let's try to understand just where he's coming from on this. Here's what I take to be Kant's contention: let us say, for the sake of argument, that you have one of the more slow and painful terminal diseases – you're going to die, probably pretty awfully, and all you're really looking for is to end your suffering sooner rather than later. Kant says you may not do so; why? Because it would be tantamount to using yourself as a means to an end instead of respecting your own rational humanity for its own merits. It's not a particularly compelling argument, but he may have a point. Let's say we were to make it a maxim that if you're in unbearable pain, you may end your life – no questions asked. Let us further say that you've lead a particularly sheltered life, and one day, breaking the trend of your relatively pain-free existence, you stub your toe on the coffee table or step on a Lego for the first time, get your first hangnail, or what have you – you're in unbearable pain, and you just want to end it all, rather than endure it. Now, please understand, this is not at all meant to make light of those suffering from otherwise horrific and/or terminal diseases, but the question is still begged – who's to say what qualifies as "unbearable" to the extent that life can be ended? If you can't say that a certain group can do it, then on Kant's account, no one may do it. This is the same logic behind extreme gun restrictions; if guns can be used to shoot innocent others, let's take them all away, thus preventing anyone from being shot. It's not popular in that instance either, but it's not a whole lot different from the logic behind the suicide issue, and again – this is where many readers decide that Kant has missed the mark.

Autonomy and the Kingdom of Ends

For Kant, the principle of every human will as a will giving universal laws in all its maxims is very well adapted to being a categorical imperative, provided it's otherwise correct and functioning normally. The will is able to issue these imperatives because of its autonomy; taken from two Greek words, *auto*, meaning self, as in automobiles, which are mobile all by themselves, and *nomos*, law, we get the notion that the autonomous individual is one who is quite literally self-lawed, self-ruled, self-guided, or self-governed. This is as opposed to the effect of heteronomy, which, exactly like you might think, is the state of being ruled or directed by others. It's specifically our autonomy, and that of others, that is being respected when we act so as to treat all people as ends in and of themselves, and never as means to an end. We have autonomy as a feature of our rationality – just as Aristotle defined that *epistemonikon* as what makes us fit for the rule of law, our autonomy, on a Kantian account, serves the same function – we are able to obey and create laws for ourselves and others.

When we create these laws, either for ourselves or for others, by positing a maxim that could be willed as a universal law, we do so within the context of what Kant refers to as a "kingdom of ends," which is interchangeably referred to sometimes as a "realm of ends" – same difference. We belong to the kingdom of ends as members when we give universal laws that we ourselves are subject to. In other words, the old axiom of parenting, "do as I say, not as I do," simply has no place in Kant's Ethics. Rational beings must always regard themselves as legislative in the kingdom of ends, because through all their actions they are declaring universal laws, wrought through their freedom of their wills, but they belong to it simultaneously as members subject to the laws, and as sovereigns giving the laws.

Dignity, and Autonomy Revisited

Morality, on Kant's account consists in the relation of every action to the legislation through which alone a kingdom of ends is possible, or more plainly, morality has to do with what we do and why we do it, with the categorical imperative as the final word on whether or not our actions are moral. To this end, everything in the kingdom of ends is considered by Kant to have either a price or a dignity; the absence of one is a compelling case for it being the other. Whatever has a price can be replaced by something else as its equivalent; if I back out of my driveway and over your toddler's tricycle, I can give you a new tricycle to present them with, give you the cash value, etc., and we're square. Whatever is above all price, and therefore admits of no equivalent, has a dignity; if I back out of my driveway and over your toddler, I can't simply give you another toddler in their place, nor can I (probably) compensate you monetarily for their loss. For Kant, this indicates that only morality and humanity (so far as humanity is *capable* of morality) have dignity. The legislation which determines all moral worth, i.e., the categorical imperative, must have a dignity too, which is to say it has unconditional and incomparable worth, and the basis of the dignity of both human nature and every rational nature is autonomy.

Interlude: From Deontological to Utilitarian

It's pretty obvious that Kant's ethical thought has some serious problems when it comes to practical application. Kant is the quintessential "in a perfect world" philosopher, and I attribute a lot of that to his not having gotten out a whole lot – he very definitely suffers from the ivory tower syndrome that so afflicts some academics, in that his moral theory would be practically ideal if only people actually thought like he suggests we ought to. It's not to say that it never crosses our minds that our actions ought to be able to be equally extended to all others in order to count as moral, but it won't be until John Rawls (our final ethicist) that this basic notion will be described as "justice as fairness," and even then, it will take a somewhat convoluted thought experiment to make it (sort of) work. At the end of the day, we live in a world that sometimes admits of special conditions, extenuating circumstances, the making of exceptions for what might otherwise be unethical behavior, and one in which we frequently use one another as means, not out of rancor, but out of purely pragmatic thinking. Kant is not without his uses, certainly, and his was the dominant philosophical approach in the German-speaking world for over a century (at least until Nietzsche); his thought strikes us as perhaps more ideal than real, but it is the hope for an ideal and ethical world that keeps us coming back to his work, as well as it not hurting a bit for us to stop every once and a while and question whether what we're doing can really be considered ethical on his account.

As I mentioned before, one of the defining features of the modern era is that each of the philosophers will, to a lesser or greater extent, be responding to the one immediately before him, and the leap from Kantian to Consequentialist thinking is no exception to this pattern. Our two Utilitarians, Jeremy Bentham and John Stuart Mill are in effect, responding solely to Kant in their rejection of a deontological approach to Ethics, and their arguments, perhaps not surprisingly, have been incredibly influential in the English speaking world. From the 1860s to the 1970s (again – until John Rawls), the dominant mode of thinking in the United States, England, and Her colonies/countries was Utilitarian in nature.

Now, let me be perfectly honest and come completely clean with you – I consider Utilitarianism to be a fallacious theory, an excuse to marginalize the minority on weak philosophical grounds, and a general waste of time. So why am I going to be discussing two philosophers of this ilk? Certainly not because I want to, but rather, to show what the response to Kant's moral thought was, and also, to provide a nice segue from deontological thinking to existentialist philosophy. To that end, I'm going to move *extremely* quickly through Bentham, and moderately quickly through Mill. You may find as we go along that some of their ideas make a lot of sense, and may even reflect your thinking – there's certainly nothing wrong with that, and you're not a defective or anything, but there are some very real problems with this line of thinking that should give just about anyone with a conscience a great deal of pause when considering applying this to any issue of great import, whether in a personal, political, national, or really any other capacity. That admission, admonition, and caveat aside, let's get starting with these guys...

Chapter 14: Bentham

We have to accept right from the start that Jeremy Bentham was probably quite insane. Well, perhaps that's not entirely fair, but he wasn't "quite all there;" there was a pyschobiographical study several years ago[117] that arrived at the conclusion that Bentham was probably an undiagnosed sufferer of Asperger's syndrome, and he may well have been, but that was certainly the least of his problems. His is a particularly peculiar approach to Ethics, an undeniably quantitative approach, and I suspect what led the researchers to their conclusion is that he seems completely devoid of either emotion or common sense in his application of his own ethics. He is admittedly a psychological and ethical hedonist, and there's several compelling reasons to believe he was more than a little bit of a megalomaniac. As a social reformer, he actually did some good, having been influential in the direction of the Reform Bill of 1832, which transferred some political power away from the landed aristocracy in Britain, perhaps presaging Marx's efforts a bit.

All that aside, what he is probably best known for today can be found through a simple google image search. Go ahead – put the book down momentarily and do a search for "Jeremy Bentham Auto Icon." Yeah – I know – it's pretty grisly. Far from being the only thing that inclines me to call him insane, the fact that Bentham had himself publicly dissected as part of an anatomy lecture, his skeleton stuffed-out with straw, dressed in his clothes, accompanied by his walking stick, and topped with his own poorly-preserved head, makes him more than a bit "off" when compared to even our most eccentric other thinkers. Bentham's idea seems to have been that this would be remarkably popular, and we would have whole museums of these auto icons (from the Greek for "self," and "image") to walk amongst and draw inspiration. The fact that his head is perhaps the worst example of taxidermy the world has ever seen didn't help the popularity of this plan. Incidentally, it was stolen several times by students at University College London, where it's on display – yes, even today – it's in the south cloisters there, now with a wax head instead. On the centennial and sesquicentennial of the College, it was wheeled into the board room and listed as "present, but not voting." Bentham himself suggested in his will, where his instructions were given to preserve him thusly, that should his friends desire to gather to commemorate the founder of his theory, he could be conveniently brought in to them for reverencing as well, which would have been entirely possible, since it was kept in the home of one of his "disciples" for nearly twenty years following his death, prior to be donated to the College, and that's just creepy. Anyway, on to his Ethics...

---

[117] I'm afraid the exact citation of the source eludes me at present ☹

Hedonism - Quantified

Because Bentham is a hedonist, he holds that all human action (and he means "all" quite literally here) is motivated by the desire for pleasure – either directly, as in, action = pleasure, or indirectly, as in action is the initial step of many that will ultimately lead to pleasure(s). Because of this, pleasure is thought of by him as the sole good, and anything else that we might call or consider to be good, is only labeled or thought of as such because it can be a means to our pleasure. So obviously, right away, any idea we might have associated with Aristotle, Augustine, Aquinas, even Hobbes goes right out the window. I suppose one could consider Bentham to be sort of in the tradition of both Aristotle *and* Hobbes, as the highest good is a sort of happiness (or *eudaimonia*), and would necessarily differ (at least in its object) between individuals, but none the less, it's a very concrete notion of what qualifies something as good, and, while it might be (sadly) realistic, it seems to lack the idealism of classical Philosophy, but that's just my personal bias creeping in.

For Bentham, all pleasures are qualitatively on par and are of equal value, i.e., one pleasure is just as good as *any* other, and the only real difference between *any* two pleasures is the quantity. Think about that for a moment – now the Mona Lisa and the dogs playing poker are on par with one another, and so are Mozart and Nascar, *Madame Bovary* and Snooki's autobiography. If that last example doesn't make you cringe and shed a tear for literature, then you may have no soul. Anyway, the point he's trying to make is that if we consider any two experiences that contain equal amounts of pleasure, no matter what other differences there may be between them, neither experience is in and of itself better or worse than the other one in terms of quality. That is to say if we had several dogs playing poker (and I believe Coolidge[118] painted a series of three of them), and only one Mona Lisa, then the puppies playing stud[119] are going to win every time a Benthamite[120] is calculating the pleasure to be gained in the viewing of either or both.

Utility

As a working definition that will extend into Mill's take on Utilitarianism also, albeit with a few slight (and somewhat redeeming) alterations, utility is, for Bentham, the tendency an action has to increase the happiness of the individual(s) performing the action or affected by it, "utility" being just another word for "usefulness" or "happiness," in this case. By extension, "general utility" is the tendency of that same action to promote the happiness of all individuals affected by it, and this is the concept that will see some improvements made by Mill, up next. With these working definitions in mind, Bentham formulated what he liked to call his "greatest happiness principle," but which today is more commonly known simply as the "principle of utility." It states that an action is right to whatever extent it promotes the happiness of all individuals affected, and obviously, this could be likewise applied to a

---

[118] No, not the president, but a different Coolidge, arguably with more of a sense of humor.

[119] Pun intended.

[120] Same as a Humean, Kantian, etc., but come on – it even *sounds* creepier.

particular governmental policy, social norm, or what have you, just as easily. Rephrased, the "fundamental axiom"[121] that Bentham is searching for here comes out something like this: "the greatest happiness of the greatest number is the measurement of right and wrong." There are some obvious problems with this, but we'll address those a bit later.

Why is Bentham doing all of this, and what does he hope to achieve? He was trying to create what he referred to as a pannomion (from the Greek words *pan* – "all" and *nomos*, which we've seen before – "law"), i.e., a complete restatement of all laws, everywhere, which would be reoriented with the greatest happiness principle as the determiner of its ethical efficacy. It's certainly a noble ambition, and not even a particularly bad plan, except for the glaring problems with the principle itself, which again, we'll get to here in just a bit. His foundational notion for all his is undeniably Humean, but taken further than Hume seems to have been willing to, and it ties ultimately to pleasure and pain, which Bentham identifies as the "two sovereign masters nature has placed mankind under the governance of." As he sees it, they establish the standards for all we do, all we say, all we think, and so on, and are the foundation not only for our moral standards, but for causation itself, as he understands it (in a sort of warped Humean way).

Principles of Legislation

The book in which Bentham promotes most of these notions is entitled *Principles of Legislation*, which should give us a fair amount of insight into his intentions for his theory's application – he really wants this to be the basis upon which all laws are codified, promulgated, and upheld. Remember, his principle of utility considers as "good" whatever produces the maximum amount of pleasure and the minimum amount of pain; and "evil" (we've apparently skipped "bad" entirely[122]) as whatever produces the most pain without compensating adequately with some sort of accompanying, balancing pleasure. In other words, we can tolerate evil, provided we have some amount of compensatory good associated with it. When Bentham is referring to pleasure and pain here, he means physical sorts that probably come foremost to mind for most of us, but also the intellectual or "spiritual" pleasures that are to be had from certain activities, and included among them are the moral pleasures. All of this is, on Bentham's account, limited to "civilized" societies, which brings up another criticism of Bentham; despite being a liberal and progressive thinker with regard to the average Englishman of the day, he and his friend, James Mill (John Stuart's father) were notoriously Anglo-centric, perhaps even egregiously so, which is quite an accomplishment (and not in a good way), seeing as they were smack in the middle of a British Empire obsessed with the "white man's burden," absolutely flush with rather infamous colonial practices and abuses.

The Hedonic Calculus

The question tends to arise that if pleasures are the sorts of things that are qualitatively identical and must be quantified in order to be accurately assessed, how exactly does one

---

[121] Notice the similarity to Kant's "groundwork" or "foundation" for morals.

[122] See Nietzsche, a few chapters ahead, for why this might have been...

go about quantifying pleasures? Bentham's answer is the provision of a set of criteria for measuring (objectively, on his account) the amount or extent of pleasure and/or pain that a certain decision, action, or policy will give rise to, allowing one to act accordingly. He calls his method the hedonic calculus, but it's also known as the utility calculus, the felicific calculus, and the hedonistic calculus, and, as the name implies, it's an algorithm for determining the amount of measurable pleasure and pain a specific occurrence is likely to cause. Remember, as an ethical hedonist, Bentham believed that the moral rightness or wrongness of actions is directly tied to the amount of pleasure produced by them, and so this calculus could, theoretically at least, determine the ethical status of *any* act we might care to consider and apply it to.

When I teach this in lecture, I refer to this as "calculating pleasure with Uncle Jeremy," and I can't help but think of Herbert, the neighbor on Family Guy, when I go through this, so there you go – continue reading, trying *not* to picture *that*. Bentham divides his calculus into seven different variables (sometimes referred to as "vectors" by scholars, and as "dimensions" or "elements" by Bentham himself), directing us that for each we should assign a value (I always picture a 1 to 10 scale, but however you like is just fine for our purposes). The solemn seven are as follows: **Intensity**, or the strength of the pleasure – is it quite literally orgasmic, or just a passing "oh, that's nice." **Duration**, as you might expect is how long it will last – a few seconds, a few hours, in perpetuity, etc. **Certainty** is where we run into problems like Kant associated with hypothetical imperatives – how likely (or unlikely) is it that the pleasure in question will actually occur. **Propinquity** (by far the most fun to say aloud – try it) is more often rendered as "remoteness" today – how soon the pleasure will occur, i.e., how soon it can be expected – a few seconds, a few years, etc. **Fecundity**, a term borrowed from the biological sciences, in which it refers to sexual reproduction, Bentham applies this term to quantify the probability that sensations of the same kind will follow the initial pleasure. **Purity** is the likelihood that the pleasure will not be followed with pain.[123] And finally, **extent** is the measure of how many people will be affected by this particular pleasure.

Great, so we've got all our vectors, all with numbers having been neatly assigned to them; what do we do now? Bentham tells us we're to take an account of the value of each distinguishable pleasure which appears to be produced in the first instance, do the same for the pains, and then repeat the process for every pleasure that appears thereafter, the pain, and so on – to establish the fecundity and purity. Then, he wants us to sum up all the values of both the pleasures and pains (picture a "T" chart) and see which side has the higher value once all the vectors have been calculated – it's as simple as that. If the balance is on the side of pleasure, then the act is good with respect to the interests of the individual affected; if on the side of pain, the act is bad. He's serious, folks. Then, repeat this entire process with anyone else involved or affected by the action in question; if there are several, I guess you'd have to average them out somehow. Did I mention he's serious? So basically, Bentham wants you to walk around all the time with a Big Chief tablet and a #2 pencil, quite literally calculating the expected pleasure and pain of all your actions to determine whether or not you should go through with them – seriously. Suddenly, Kant having asked

_____

123 You know – unless you're into that.

us to always ask ourselves whether our maxim could be willed as a universal law seems remarkably mild by comparison.

But wait – there's more. Bentham, I suppose realizing that some might be a bit taken aback by a moral and social life quite as math-heavy as he was willing for his to be, devised a cute little poem to help us remember the process. You can't make this stuff up. He called it the "mnemonic doggerel," or "memoriter verses," and it goes like this:

> *Intense, long, certain, speedy, fruitful, pure-*
> *Such marks in pleasures and pains endure.*
> *Such pleasures seek if private be thy end:*
> *If it be public, wide let them extend.*
> *Such pains avoid, whichever be thy view:*
> *If pains must come, let them extend to few.*

That's right – not only does he want you walking around doing math to decide if you're acting morally or not, but he wants you to be simultaneously reciting his little poem to help you remember how to go about this whole business. According to Bentham, these verses "synthesized the whole fabric of morals and legislation;" according to most, though, this just (further) marks him as a kook.

Applications and Criticisms

So what's been done with Bentham's Philosophy? Surely everyone realized what a nutter he was and quickly jettisoned as many of his contributions as were encountered before they could be put to widespread use, right? Well, yes and no, and while I'm somewhat loathe to admit it, some of Bentham's thought has actually had a few positive impacts – in his own time, as well as into ours. Bentham has been somewhat influential with regard to our criminal justice system, specifically, how we view punishment – whether it will create more pleasure or more pain for the society in which it's enacted. Very rarely do people come out of the prison system genuinely reformed, and the hot check writer that gets tossed into general population at county is probably going to come out somewhat worse for having been there. Bentham suggests that instead of suppressing acts considered evil by society, we ought to turn our focus to laws that may in fact be unnecessary, the punishments for which might ultimately lead to new and more dangerous vices than those being punished, and he's got a point here. Bentham's criticisms of extant legal codes were more fitting in the England of his time than ours, and apply only in a limited fashion to the United States' laws, but they're still worth mentioning. He notes that laws based in antiquity, religion, metaphor, fiction, fancy, antipathy or sympathy (with apologies to Hume) should not be the pattern upon which we base our legislation. Instead, he argues that when enacting legislation for a society we ought to be concerned first and foremost with maximizing pleasure and minimizing pain for the greatest number of people.

That last point, "for the greatest number of people" brings me to what is probably the most persistent and problematic criticism of Utilitarianism in general, but of Bentham's version of it especially – it willfully allows for the minority in any given situation to be marginalized, provided the greatest good has been achieved for the greatest number. To illustrate this, look at it in reverse: the best (or most moral) outcome is the one in which we allow the fewest number of people to be completely screwed over. Phrased that way, it's unlikely to win many adherents, but that's essentially what he's saying. We don't take issue with killing 1 to save 99, but how far are we willing to take it – could we kill 30 to save 70? What about killing 49 to save 51? The problem with Bentham generally is that in an extreme example, provided the majority is placated, anything that results could be labeled as moral. Want further evidence of Bentham's impact and influence in the modern English-speaking world? You need only look at most governmental and corporate policies – provided the majority is taken care of, the minority may be sacrificed, and that's just the way it is. So there you have it. And I readily admit that I have a nearly psychotic hatred for Jeremy Bentham's ethical "Philosophy" of a level that most well-adjusted adults reserve exclusively for the Internal Revenue Service and the French, but I'm strangely comfortable with it. Now, let's move on, and see if Mill can salvage anything remotely useful based on what Bentham's left him with...

Chapter 15: Mill

A bit of background on John Stuart Mill is probably in order. Firstly, it's important to get an idea where he's coming from in terms of his specific approach to moral philosophy, and Utilitarianism. He had been homeschooled by his father, James Mill, an Anglo-centric imperialist author and economist, and by Jeremy Bentham, whom we've just discussed, and whose influence on Mill is readily apparent. Mill will at once draw inspiration from Bentham's philosophy, finding a theoretical justification for his political views (considered somewhat radically liberal at the time), but also a need to redeem Utilitarianism – from the depth of craziness Bentham had taken it to, in order to see if we can somehow profit from its ideas and put them into practical application. While Mill isn't nearly as "out there" as Bentham had been, he's still facing something of an uphill battle in terms of convincing his reading audience that his is a practicable approach.

Even our old friend and recurrent theme of justice gets a new and very different treatment from Mill. He has an essentially Hobbesian understanding of justice, in that they're based in our interests, but rather than predicating them as being based on an avoidance of the state of nature (as Hobbes had), they're (for Mill) a set of rules that protect our essential (self)interests, and whose enforcement as a result, has a very high utility for us. Justice is no longer a concept that stands apart from us as an abstract concept desirable for its own sake, but is now more or less a list of the things we can reasonably expect, and even demand that society protect on our behalf, but will also include those things which can be expected of us. So for Mill, seeking the greatest good for the greatest number will, as a side effect, and by extension, produce a just situation and society. This may prove to be a tough sell, however, because we still have that glaring problem of the minority that Mill never quite satisfactorily addresses.

The Principle of Utility – Version 2.0

Mill picks up more or less where Bentham left off with the principle of utility, but alters it subtlety to effect a significant change in meaning and application; he tells us now that actions are right *in proportion* as they tend to promote happiness, wrong as they tend to promote the reverse of happiness. What exactly do those two little words do to what is otherwise unchanged from Bentham's presentation? Now the principle implies that the morally right action is the one that does the most to promote the happiness of *all* human beings – not simply the majority, full stop. By extension, his definition of the good is updated to "pleasure," and, in a very Epicurean way of approaching things, "freedom from pain," which, taken together, he refers to as a "theory of life." But now our interest gets piqued, as Mill departs significantly from Bentham in telling us that we must look not just at the quantity of pleasure, but also at the overall quality of pleasure, with priority given to those pleasures which are of a "higher" quality, and thus (ought to be) more desirable – more on this shortly...

It's important to note that Mill really wasn't known in his own time for his Utilitarian Ethics, at least not primarily; he was a notable philosophical liberal, and continues to provide a theoretical basis for liberal philosophy, but his book *Utilitarianism* contains his only major discussion of this ethical theory. It appeared first in serial form, and was later collected and reprinted as a single volume, eventually going through four editions and revisions, but remains one of Mill's comparatively minor works, as compared to *On Liberty*, and his various proto-feminist works, which quite notably were co-written by his wife, to whom he gave a level of credit very uncharacteristic of the age. He begins in a straightforward way, wanting to define the term and make sure his readers understand precisely what Utilitarianism claims and how it judges actions. He's predominantly writing it as a critique and an apology,[124] responding mostly to deontological (read: Kantian) opponents. In the very first chapter he breaks all of Ethics into two broad categories, which we might think of as the mental and the physical; he places *both* Hume *and* Kant in the former, since they're based on intuition and reason, respectively, and places himself and Utilitarianism in the latter category because he claims it's based in experience, and is, at its base, an empirical mode of Ethics.

Higher versus Lower Pleasures

The notion of higher pleasures isn't entirely foreign to us, though, like a lot of other things, we probably have a tough time, when pressed, defining exactly what we mean by "higher." For Mill, the higher pleasures are available only to humans, carrying forward Aristotle's rational animals idea, because our distinctive human faculties – our intellect, imagination, moral sentiments and judgments, etc. – are ultimately what allow us to approach and appreciate them. In other words, my golden retriever is unlikely to appreciate Baudelaire at the say level I do, nor is he able to make an assessment of something as deserving of our moral approbation. The lower pleasures, as we might expect, are those available to all of animate nature, and they're based in our sensations; we find pleasure in good food, good sex, and so on, because our rationality isn't (necessarily) engaged in these activities.

Mill's famous quote about higher and lower pleasures goes like this: "Better to be a human being dissatisfied than a pig satisfied; better to be Socrates dissatisfied than a fool satisfied." In other words, our rational capacity, beyond differentiating us from the rest of animate nature, has something about it that is to be appreciated and promoted regardless of our emotional state. Echoing Plato's behavioristic approach, Mills says that it's for this reason that we have to be brought up and educated in a certain way, and be knowledgably curious about the world; in other words, to have an education more or less exactly like his, which wouldn't necessarily be a bad thing, minus the influence of Bentham. As long as we're on him, Bentham's (in)famous quote regarding his take on the same basic idea was "quantity of pleasure being equal, push-pin[125] is as good as poetry." So basically, if a child's activity like skateboarding brings more pleasure to people than a night at the theatre, it is imperative upon society to devote more resources to building skate parks than putting on

---

[124] See previous footnote clarification as to what we mean by this in Philosophy.

[125] Presumably a Georgian era (1714-1830) children's game, but, because I have no idea what it consisted in or how it was played, I always envision "whack-a-mole." ☺

productions of Shakespeare plays – Mill and I collectively shudder at the notion, I'm sure – perhaps our one moment of solidarity. So Mill is responding to, and dare I say, correcting this notion, from the perspective that those who appreciate the "simple," i.e., lower, pleasures more, do so only because they lack sufficient exposure to and education in appreciation of the higher pleasures, and therefore are not in a position to judge. My inner art and literature snob grins gleefully at this.

Qualitative Thinking

Because Mill's is a qualitative (as opposed to quantitative) account of happiness, utility is something that we can think of in relation to ourselves as progressive beings – we're in the process of becoming something better than we were. As part of this ongoing process, we're expected to develop and exercise our rational capacities as part of our striving for a higher plane of existence; interestingly, this somewhat presages our next thinker, Kierkegaard, as we view the ethical life as only an intermediary stage on the way to a higher existence, but more on that later. As part of our continuing education and betterment process, Mill calls for the rejection of censorship and paternalism – we ought not to be denied access to anything that might help develop us, nor ought we to be told what to do or not do, but instead allowed to find out for ourselves. Most of us can probably agree with both of these notions, but for Mill, their absence provides the prerequisite social conditions for achieving the sort of knowledge that will make us ethical, especially with respect to seeking and appreciating the higher pleasures, and will allow the greatest number to develop and exercise their full rational capacities, especially those that involve deliberation (as in between moral right and wrong) on our part.

Mill and Aristotle

As you probably picked up on before, I'm a big fan of Aristotle's from way back; this in turn makes me, albeit somewhat grudgingly, a bit of a fan of Mill's too – up to a point. I mentioned earlier that Mill had received a classical education, and his ability to read the Attic Greek no doubt gave him a leg up over others who would only have translations available to them. That's probably neither here nor there, and I mention it only in passing, but Mill's understanding of Aristotle is impressive, and I feel obligated to acknowledge it, whether I like Utilitarianism or not (and it should be obvious by now that I don't). Anyway, a handy way to clarify what Mill is getting at is made a little more accessible, and perhaps a bit more palatable, by comparing it alongside Aristotle's Virtue Ethics.

Both Mill and Aristotle (and Hume, and Kant, and really, most of the others too, but I digress – yet again) make a compelling argument that we naturally seek happiness as our objective in trying to attain the best possible life. To some extent then, Mill can claim that the principle of utility is proved through human nature itself; just as Hume had argued that we naturally feel before we're taught to judge, Mill shows that we're naturally inclined to seek the most good, in the form of utility. In a similar way, Aristotle had made the claim that virtue is a natural human function when it takes the form of *arête*, but for him, virtues are a means to securing the end of *eudaimonia*. Mill's criticism of this approach is grounded in the notion that this remains for Aristotle an abstract concept, hopelessly separated from the happiness it ultimately seeks, because means, by definition if not practice, are necessarily different from the ends they seek. Mill wants a more tangible happiness, so people can be happy and know it,[126] not so they can embrace an abstract principle and hope they've hit the mark through their virtues.

Remember that one reading of Aristotle's Nichomachean Ethics has us only being truly happy retrospectively – that is, after we die; Mill wants the living to be happy – here and now. According to Mill, and in my estimation, this is more than a little hubristic of him, the mistake that all the preceding moral philosophers, including Aristotle, had made, was that their systems of doing Ethics were really based in the principle of utility, but they were either unaware of this fact, or simply unable to understand that and make the connection. I guess you've got to, at the very least, give Mill credit for making this gutsy, though I would contend, fallacious, claim – talk about chutzpah! Mill claims that his principle of utility is the true principle of morality, and the defining mark of humanity that makes it possible for the greatest number to have the greatest happiness. Needless to say, Mill and I are going to have to agree to disagree on this one.

---

[126] It ought to be obvious to the casual observer – there'll be a noticeable increase in the number of people clapping their hands.

Interlude: Existentialism

Kierkegaard is the first of three existentialists we'll be taking a look at, but as something new in Moral Philosophy, it deserves a bit of quick explanation before we delve into the individual ethicists. There are certain features of existentialism that show up in Kierkegaard that will come to differentiate it from what we've seen so far – virtue theory, social contract theory, deontology, utilitarianism, and so – and indicate that something new and different is being done. So I'd like to take a brief aside and cover some common features that are seen among and between the three we'll be discussing, before we look at each of them in detail in the chapters to come.

Personal Responsibility

Existentialism, as the name would tend to imply, is fundamentally concerned with our existence – yeah – it's really that straightforward. It's sometimes called the philosophy of personal responsibility, or the philosophy of no excuses, and in Ethics, that has some rather important ramifications, especially when we seek to assign praise or blame, call an action or policy right or wrong, etc. To that end, each of us, on a completely individual level, is entirely responsible for our impact on and interaction with the world. We are responsible for what we do, who we are (or at least who we present ourselves as being), for the way we approach and deal with the world, and finally, for the way the world is. In other words, if you do something and it doesn't turn out as you'd planned, own it; if you're a jerk, it's because you've chosen to be one; if you're a pessimist, it's only because you've decided to be; and if you think the world is a hopelessly defective, generally crappy place, it's because you've either allowed it to become this way, or allow it to continue to be this way. Let's face it – life can be tough, circumstances can seem doubly so, obstacles in our path (many of which we place there ourselves) may seem insurmountable, but all of this aside, we are nonetheless entirely responsible!

But wait – can't we just shift the burden of all this responsibility onto God, on the myriad shortcomings of mother nature, or just ascribe it to "the way it is?" No – not in existentialism, at any rate. More on the religious stance of existentialism here shortly, but for now, suffice to say that if there is a God, we make the active choice to believe in Him, and are equally free not to. If nature made us a certain way with regard to our physical abilities (or lack thereof), then it's up to us to decide what we do with what nature has given us. I'm a diehard Game of Thrones[127] fan, and this is the perfect philosophy to sum up Tyrion Lannister;[128] he's an ugly little dwarf, more or less despised by his family and everyone he meets, but he absolutely revels in it, and has a great time of things because he

---

[127] If you haven't read these books, you are remiss. Get back on Amazon.com and place your order right now!

[128] Played by the awesome Peter Dinklage in the HBO television adaptation.

knows he's always the smartest person in the room – the perfect little existentialist.[129] Whether we go along or fight back, modify nature to suit ourselves or ultimately transcend it, is all entirely up to us.

The Individual

Kierkegaard is frequently quoted, primarily on mopey t-shirts and "emo" wall hangings, "Had I to carve my own epitaph, I would ask for none other than "The Individual,"" and that does a nice job of emphasizing what is perhaps the most marked feature of existentialism – a strong emphasis on the significance of the individual. Although this is variously defined and understood depending on which of our existentialists we're reading at the time, as a theme, it runs through them all, and they're certainly distinctive on an individual level, for their eccentricities perhaps as much as for their contributions to the philosophic project. Beyond their own personalities, these philosophers challenge and encourage us to discover who we really are, and then to *become* that person, a theme that will be especially strong when we get to Nietzsche, and which is hinted at in Kierkegaard's examination of what it means to become (note: not *be*) a Christian.

Passion

With the exception of David Hume, we've had it hammered into our heads thus far that the passions and emotions ought to be assiduously hunted down, and, if left with any role at all, it had better be one that can be exercised from the confines of the deepest, darkest dungeons of our minds rather than daring to assert itself. Well, existentialism turns that right around; that's not to say that it jettisons reason entirely, but instead that a significantly greater emphasis is placed on passion and living passionately. Specifically what is sought is a passionate commitment – to something, in some readings, to anything, provided you're passionate about whatever it is. Me? I'm a foodie, a fan of needlessly convoluted cocktails, a voracious reader, and a board game geek, none of which is admittedly all that earth-shatteringly exciting to most folks, but what matters is that I'm passionately devoted to all of them. For the existentialist, if you're going to live at all, you had better be living passionately!

Freedom

Kant, in his groundbreaking though blessedly short essay, *What is Enlightenment?*,[130] answered his own question with a single word – freedom, a theme that quickly became a bandwagon leapt upon by the likes of Fichte,[131] Goethe,[132] Schiller,[133] and many others,

---

[129] George R.R. Martin, if you're reading this, I would really appreciate those final two volumes of the series you've been promising us for years… Just saying.

[130] In the original German the title is rendered as, *Was Ist Aufklarung?* – say it loud and angry – it's better that way.

[131] Who tells us that we know we're truly free when we're first told that we may not do something, but up until that point, it's more or less anything goes. Party!

much to our benefit. There's a bit of background required for this, so permit me another brief historical digression, bearing in mind that most everything in the modern era of Ethics is addressing something that came before it, and either replacing it or rehashing it. Okay, so Kierkegaard, in addition to be our first existentialist (a title be didn't abrogate to himself, but which we apply retrospectively, especially once we get to Sartre), was part of what we call the Romantic movement, many participants of whom are also referred to as *Aesthetes*.[134] To couch this correctly, the Romantic rebellion is a rejection of and reaction to the Enlightenment, which itself was a rejection of and reaction to the Scholastic movement. Recall from our discussion of Aquinas that Scholasticism was the attempt to rationalize the teachings of the Roman Catholic Church, and if the findings didn't support the sought conclusion, then the experiment was altered rather than the belief attempting to be supported. Bacon, Descartes, and company came along and found that understandably frustrating, mostly because, while it had logical rigor to it, the scholastic approach neither encouraged nor allowed for much by way of the power of legitimately scientific discovery. Thus, the Enlightenment is born, setting itself up against the authority of received wisdom, the powers of rank, the unquestioning acceptance of tradition and antiquity, and we date it more or less from the birth of Descartes in 1596 to the death of Kant in 1804, and during which all the greats we associate with science would be working, among them Galileo, Newton, Locke, and so forth.

The Romantic criticism of the Enlightenment is that in the wake of Newtonian understandings of the world, everything has become entirely too mechanistic, and so, while we can explain the physical and astronomical processes at work when the sun rises, we are left unable to account for what it is about a sunrise that we consider beautiful. Because the sciences are based on our empirical observations, and because our observations can be mistaken, revealing only phenomenal and not noumenal reality,[135] science has built-in limitations. In place of the fabricated scientific answer, the romantic thinker wants to emphasize the creative power of genius as it reveals itself, along with the transcendent aspects of our sense of beauty and wonder. So anyway, back to the existentialists, they're concerned with our personal freedom – both on the level of free will (especially as regards our ethics), as well as our political freedom, and the relationship that obtains between our freedom and our reason is what is particularly at issue. Going back to a point I made earlier, traditionally, and up through Kant, being free is synonymous with acting rationally, and we act emotionally we're discounted as slaves to our passions; now that gets turned on its head, when the existentialists argue that we're most ourselves and live the best possible lives when we're *both* free *and* passionate.

---

[132] Particularly in *Faust*, where the eponymous character is so free he can give up his freedom to Mephistopheles in exchange for a completely novel experience.

[133] Who tells us that we are our truly authentic selves when we're just playing. ☺

[134] Remembering that in Philosophy, something aesthetical can appeal to *all* the senses, not only to vision and our thoughts on beauty as it's come to be used today.

[135] One of Kant's more troublesome propositions; the *phenomenal* reality is the experience the object creates in us as percipients, but the *noumenal* reality is the thing as it really is, hidden from our senses, but approachable by our reason.

Absurdity and Subjectivity

One of existentialism's more quirky emphases is on the irrational aspects of life – those features which simply don't add up rationally, but to which we're undeniably and inexplicably drawn, which Kierkegaard approaches in two ways. The first is his emphasis on subjectivity, having taken our subjective truth, that is, what we establish as true for ourselves, to be the central element to a meaningful and ethical life, because, simply put, we can produce only subjective answers to the question, "How should I live, and how ought I to conduct myself?" To be subjective is to look inward and to have passion – to take hold of our lives by choosing to commit ourselves passionately to something. The second approach, which builds on the first, is presented in our religious beliefs. Despite the bad rap it sometimes gets, existentialism is not an atheistic or anti-religious philosophy;[136] Kierkegaard was devoutly religious (though is his own unique way), and seems to have thought that faith itself, rather than which religion it was devoted to, was of paramount importance.

Faith, regardless of the religion toward and within which it's directed, is not rational – it's just not; if it were, it would be called reason, not faith, and any distinction between the two would be more or less empty, but a quick glance at the television news assures us it is not. Inherent to faith are the many paradoxes that almost without exception make up its body of beliefs and accepted teachings – thing that rationally cannot possibly have occurred in the manner in which they're recorded, but that are accepted regardless. You cannot, for instance, argue someone into a faith position using reason or logic – the scholastics tried and failed; rather, all that remains is for them to be gently coaxed toward an acceptance of the belief, and Kierkegaard seems to have realized and more or less mastered this – his readings aren't arguments as such, but elaborate seductions requiring a leap of faith on our part.

Existence

It being existentialism, it seems at least a modicum of attention probably ought to be paid to what it means to exist, and what is referred to by existence. As per the usual, and with all our other key terms, this is going to vary depending on which philosopher is being discussed, but since we're starting with Kierkegaard, it stands to reason that we begin with his definition first, and cover the others as we encounter them. Not surprisingly, he defines existence as a life that is passion-filled, self-understanding, and committed, which, in an odd work-around connects reasonably seamlessly with Nietzsche's definition of becoming who we really are. However life is lived, the existentialist approach urges us to live it to the fullest, though again – what that entails exactly will necessarily vary. In part due to this variance the issue of contingency arises; something is contingent if and when it is

---

[136] People usually get hung up on Nietzsche's having said "God is dead," but only because they don't then read what we wrote after that. No – I'm not going to tell you – go look it up for yourself, it's in his *Thus Spake Zarathustra*. Sartre will tell us that he's an atheist, but he's what I call a "reluctant atheist" – you'll see why when we get to him. Anyway, the point is that existentialism really leaves it up to the <u>individual</u>.

dependent upon something or someone else – okay, so what does that tell us? Let's find out...

We are firstly contingent in the sense that we might never have been born. This isn't just something to ponder after the crowds go home and you're still at the party, more or less deeply in your cups after a long evening of adult libations, but a very direct, real, and, especially for our purposes, good, question. Would someone else be "you" – wearing your clothing, doing your job, calling your mother, "mom," and so of? What if you were born on the steppes of Mongolia or the jungles of Uganda instead of whatever relatively urban or barely rural setting you're statistically likely to have hailed from, given that you're reading this?[137] How might life be different if you found yourself in the middle ages, particularly amid all their superstitions, or far into the future, into some vast dystopia even science fiction struggles to imagine?[138] If you're male, you're female, gay – straight, black – white, and so on, all the way up to the real clincher – what if, for instance, you were, either from birth or from mystery, no longer human at all, ala Gregor Samsa?[139] In other words, existentialism largely rejects the very Cartesian[140] notion that our existence is as tied up with thinking as the Enlightenment folks were so unwaveringly certain it was. Now, with existence and existentialism more or less understood by us, let's make our way to and through the thought of our first (of three) existentialists...

---

[137] With apologies to my inestimably cultivated Mongolian and Ugandan readers.

[138] And which, according to Hume, will be under no obligation to mimic the past...

[139] The protagonist of Kafka's *Metamorphosis*, who awakes one morning to discover he's been turned into a giant insect, and whose primary concern is getting to work.

[140] Referring to Descartes, just like Millian, Benthamite, Humean, etc.

Chapter 16: Kierkegaard

First things first, Kierkegaard stands out a bit in that he doesn't fit neatly into any of the categories of Ethics we've spent the bulk of our time together establishing and describing, so, while he's not himself a systematic philosopher, a system, or rather, a sensibility – a sort of responsiveness arises out of his work and comes to define this new and nifty thing we call existentialism. Like all of our modern era philosophers, he is responding to someone else's work, but in this case, it's not one that we've read too, since, well, Hegel is unimaginably dull for all but Hegel scholars, and really doesn't write a whole lot about Ethics, either, so we're safe there. Here's what we do need to know in order to couch this correctly – Hegel had asserted that the world, and the history with which it's recorded, are essentially logical, and therefore can be understood by our reason, especially when employed objectively. For Kierkegaard, this was quite obviously the reverse of what the facts of the matter were and are, and he argued that the world is fundamentally irrational, and if truth can be found, it won't be through the use of our objective reason, but rather, through our subjective and passionate personal commitments to ideas.

Kierkegaard, somewhat setting the tone for the rest of his existential friends in that they'll feel compelled to explain their own religious views, was a deeply religious thinker, but in his own distinctive way. All (or nearly all) of his philosophical writing can be seen as a treatment of what emerges as his central theme – "what does it mean to *become* a Christian?" But wait – why not "be" a Christian? He rejected the idea that simply being born into a Christian family was sufficient, noted that most Christians display no real passion for their religion at all, dismissed most of what we would identify as organized religion as being a sort of "herd phenomena," and said that the appropriate response to the paradoxes of Christianity isn't to try to rationally understand them, but rather, to base our passionate religious belief around them. Now, before you allow any of this to sour you on Kierkegaard, regardless of your religious position (or even your absence of one, suspense of judgment, etc.), you can apply this to just about any religion you like; you can even apply this to agnosticism or atheism if you're persistent. What is at the heart of the matter here is (again – and you're going to get sick of seeing this) passion. Even on a religious level, for Kierkegaard, passion is more important than praise.

Gilleleie

Gilleleje, with a "J" is the northernmost town on the same island on which is situated Denmark's capitol city, Copenhagen; *Gilleleie*, "with an "I" is a journal entry made by Kierkegaard in 1835, ostensibly while visiting said city. It's a relatively short entry, but by now a famous one, and he includes a few phrases that are really useful when we're attempting to understand his moral philosophy. The overall focus of the entry is the difference between something being "true" in the sense of objective knowledge, and something being "true" in the sense of an individual religious experience. Without quoting the lines to you (it's all I can do to encourage you to read the primary source texts yourselves), Kierkegaard first seems to tell us that there are so many things that we claim a willingness to die for; why aren't we *living* for those exact same things?! Certainly a good point when it comes to both our religion and our Ethics.

Kierkegaard cautions us on constructing worlds in which we don't really live, but only hold up to the view of others, in other words, we sometimes create facades with regard again to both our religious practices and our Ethics, and when we do so, both fail to have any deeper significance for our lives beyond this thinly-constructed veil. If we really want to make an impact, religiously and ethically, remembering always that for him, the ethical life is simply one stage along the way to the religious life, then we have to recognize an imperative (the first of several Kantian references we'll encounter in him) that the practice(s), of both religion and Ethics, must be taken up into our lives as the most important thing(s).

Either/Or

Here's a bit of a switch from what we're used to seeing- Kierkegaard isn't really going to give us a theory of Ethics; he's not going to tell us how we ought to be or become ethical, or really even mention Ethics directly in the sense that we've become used to seeing it. His is a radically different approach, and one that I have to admit, I'm partial to, if for no other reason than its simplicity and elegance – it truly is a gentle seduction as opposed to onslaught of rational argument. As regards the title, he tells us that there are very few instances where the either/or we're frequently inclined to apply are actually appropriate, and in many cases when and where we do apply them, they're actually ridiculous when put into perspective (not that that stops us). He points out to us that we listen(ed) with childish trust to the talk of our elders, and the instant of [ethical] choice was solemn and venerable, although in choosing, we were only following the instruction(s) of another person. This is a good point; when do our Ethics become truly ours, rather than just the regurgitated "truths" we know are expected from us from time to time? Kierkegaard doesn't provide an answer to this, but it's delightfully characteristic of his approach to point this out to us, and then give us a basis on which to ponder when our Ethics become our own.

For Kierkegaard, the only situation where an either/or has absolute significance to us is the one in which we have concrete examples of good and evil lined up on either side of us, or, as he so wonderfully puts it, truth, righteousness, and holiness" up against "lust, base propensities, and obscure passions," which, with a little imagination, paints quite the panorama of mental images. He then tells us that it's always important to choose rightly, even between those things which we might consider innocent choices, always acting as if at some point we might be brought back to that instant of choice and called to account for our decision somehow.

Now in case you think that it's ever going to be simply too late for you to choose, Kierkegaard assures us that it would be foolish for us to think this, if for no other reason than because when we choose, our personality make itself known to us and to the rest of the world. The problem is, the longer we put off the decision (*any* decision, for that matter), the easier it is for us to alter the character of what we're considering or be distracted by a whole series of "what if?" type questions. Kierkegaard tells us, quite rightly that we don't have time for thought experiments, e.g., imagining states of nature, creating maxims, and calculating pleasure, so we had better decide pretty quickly before the choice is made more difficult from the addition of too many superfluous complications and considerations. To illustrate this, he gives the example of a captain on his ship; there's a storm coming up, and he must either steer toward the shore, and risk getting dashed on the rocks, or toward the open water, and risk getting swept out to sea. Simple physics tells us that the boat's not going to stay stationary while he decides, and unless he decides quickly and acts accordingly, nature's going to decide for him and one or the other will happen, but beyond his control.

At that point, there's no longer a question of an either/or, not because the captain chose, but because he neglected to choose. Kierkegaard reminds us that this is equivalent to saying, because others (or in this case, another force) has chosen for him, that he has lost his *self*. No – this isn't just poor grammar on either of our parts, but an essentially Kantian way of looking at things – let's take a look. Recall for a moment the concept of autonomy from Kant – that idea that we're self-ruled; for Kant, that defines us as much as our rationality does for Aristotle – if we allow ourselves to be guided by others, i.e., heteronomy, we have lost ourselves essentially. The act of choosing is therefore the most stringent expression of the ethical, and the only absolute either/or is the choice between good and evil, which is likewise absolutely ethical.

The Aesthetical versus the Ethical

In (most of) the rest of Philosophy, something aesthetical refers most commonly to something being aesthetically pleasing with regard to our visual and other senses, and Kierkegaard could be understood to see it similarly, but it's got deeper ramifications. On the one hand, when he thinks of one living aesthetically, he's referring to our tendency to immerse ourselves in what is immediate, sensory, and momentary – our impulsive tendencies, for instance in the checkout line at the grocery store, where we've got everything on our list and we're ready to go – until we see that king size candy bar! There's nothing necessarily wrong with this, but the impulsivity involved keeps this from being an ethical choice. On quite the other hand, when we live ethically, we have committed ourselves to an ethical framework in which good and evil take on significance for us, as we establish guidelines for our own conduct, and imply what we can reasonably expect of one another.

When we make an aesthetic choice, it's either entirely immediate, or it begins to lose itself in the varied options that we present to ourselves; let's face it – if we're inclined to be impulsive, it's also easy to be distracted by options that present themselves – especially when it comes to the candy example. The ethical choice is therefore in a certain sense much easier, because it's a choice between only two options – good and evil, but in another sense infinitely harder, because the choice we make has further reaching implications for us. How's that? Well, when we make a decision for good, it's very telling with regard to our personality, and the same is true when we choose evil.[141] Kierkegaard describes this as being not so much a question of choosing the right, as it is the energy, the earnestness, and the pathos with which we choose – remember that from literature class? We strive or yearn in a certain way that isn't quite so easily changeable once we start down a particular path – the personality is consolidated as good or evil when our choice is made for one or the other. It's because of this that he tells us that even if we were to choose wrongly, we would almost immediately discover, because of the energy with which we chose, that we have chosen wrongly.

The Crossroads

Kierkegaard wants to be very clear that in distinguishing his either/or, he's not making the distinction between good and evil, but rather, bringing us up to the point where the choice between the evil and the good acquires significance to us, because everything hinges upon this. He tells us that as soon as we stand at the crossroads in such as a position that there is no recourse but to choose, we will choose the right. Now, a couple of things are going on here, and we should take a look at both to really understand what he's getting at. Firstly, he doesn't seem to mean that we never make the wrong choices, but rather, that we always choose what we consider to be the right course of action – we do what we think best in the situation, even if it later proves to have negative consequences. Secondly, you'll recall we've seen this before – again, in Kant, where he describes us as being at a crossroads between our *a priori* principle, e.g., "I'll never steal," and the *a posteriori* incentive, e.g., "my family is starving, and I must steal to feed them." Kierkegaard is here less strict than Kant, who told us we must slavishly stick to our maxim without a thought for consequences, implying instead that we ought to do the right thing, even if that means making an exception. So we have either to live aesthetically, in the moment, or we have to live ethically, which is to say universally.

Universality

Existentialism, as we've seen, places the greatest emphasis on the individual and our subjective decisions to act ethically; this poses a potential problem for us when we consider how we might have problems reconciling that to everyone else's subjective decisions. Kierkegaard accounts for this through his unique approach to the universal, which provides social norms for us, and according to which we gauge our character and behavior for acceptability within the context of our society. Ethics is universal in the sense that it consists of a set of rational rules that apply to all individuals within a given society. These in turn provide the final objective standard against which we measure our subjective choices determining how we interact with others. In this way, even if our subjective inclinations are to do something beyond the pale or unacceptable in our society, we are

---

[141] Kierkegaard refers to this as marking us with a *character indelebilis*, a term encountered in numismatics (coin collecting) and in Roman Catholic sacraments. When a coin is minted, the image can't (easily) be rubbed or washed away; likewise, when we're baptized, confirmed, or ordained, it can neither be undone nor redone. It's the same when we make a decision for good or evil – it marks us, indelibly.

able to temper them against the subjective measure of what is acceptable, allowed for, and by extension, ethical.

To Gain the Whole World...

We're reminded by Kierkegaard that we very often have no real conception of what the "self" is that we're potentially risking when we refuse to make a choice between good and evil, and it would be of very little use to any of us if we were to gain the whole world and lose ourselves in the process. Okay, time for a bit more popular culture – think of Brian DePalma's *Scarface*, starring Al Pacino as the eponymous antihero – it's a very existential film in this respect (*SPOILER ALERT*). It's the end of the film, and Tony Montana has everything he's ever wanted – the big house, the hot wife, all the power and money he could ever dream of, and none of it is worth anything anymore. His big house is being overrun by his enemies, who are about to kill him, his hot wife can't give him the child he so desperately wants because she's too strung-out on cocaine, he's just killed his best friend, and his sister hates him. So in a sense, he's gained the whole world, but lost himself in the process. As if to really hammer this point home for us, when he's fatally shot and falls over the balcony into a fountain, he lands next to a massive globe circled with the phrase, "the world is yours," perhaps the ultimate irony. Now go watch the movie again, and thank Kierkegaard right along with DePalma and Pacino!

Aesthetical Neutrality

Remember, the either/or doesn't in the first place denote the choice between good and evil; it denotes the choice whereby we choose good and evil, or *exclude* them, and it's this notion of exclusion that we need to look at now. The aesthetical is not the evil, but the neutrality – that should sound familiar, because we heard something similar from Hobbes, remember? "That which we neither love nor hate, we're said to contemn, contempt being nothing else but an immobility" (which is to say, a neutrality) – sounds more or less the same as what Kierkegaard is telling us here. In *Either/Or*, this is why it is the ethical that constitutes the choice. Here's what all this tells us, and it's best if we think of it as something of a flow chart, working from top to bottom, it works out as follows. The either/or takes us to the point where we either make a choice or exclude it, i.e., we refuse to choose. If we make a choice, that choice will be between good and evil, and this is the ethical; if we refuse to choose, that is, to maintain a neutrality, then this is the exclusion, and that is the aesthetical – the momentary or the impulsive, and not the ideal way to live.

Fear and Trembling

The question Kierkegaard wants us to address in *Fear and Trembling* is whether or not there can be a teleological suspension of the ethical, so let's take a minute and review what all that's involving and implying. The Greek word *telos*, you'll recall, implies a plan, goal, aim, design, or end. Specifically here he's applying the concept to the story of Abraham and Isaac, and asking whether the events described there represent a teleological suspension of the ethical, i.e., can we put our ethics on hold and do something immoral or evil, for the sake of a greater end being achieved, in this case, our obedience to God? If we can suspend our normative ethical or social values to achieve a higher aim, he tells us that would represent a higher expression of Ethics, but one that couldn't be comprehended rationally by us.

We need a bit of background to understand just what's going on here. Take a moment to look up and read *Genesis* 22:1-13. Okay, now he's a bit of background: Abraham is the Biblical patriarch who first established ethical monotheism as he leaves Ur for Canaan; he's quite old by the time of this story, had wanted a son for years, had more or less given up hope of ever having one with his wife, Sarah (he already had one by his wife's slave, Hagar). Finally, he gets his son, Isaac, and loves him more than anything in the world. So when God tells Abraham to sacrifice Isaac to Him as a burnt offering, it has to have come as quite a shock, but nonetheless, he prepares to go through with it, stopped at the last minute by the Angel of the Lord, sent by God, who realizes that Abraham's faith runs as deep as he had hoped it did. No mention is made, however, of the years of therapy Isaac would undergo if we were to update this pericope[142] to today.

Universal, Individual, and Paradoxical

Provided we accept that Ethics are or ought to be universal in the Kantian sense, we accept the notion that they are valid at every moment, and can't be conveniently set aside, regardless of what our aims or plans might otherwise dictate. As individual beings, immediate, physical, and spiritual, we have our *teloi*[143] in the universal, and our ethical task is to express ourselves continually in the universal – to strip ourselves of individuality in order to become universal – not with regard to our rights, but definitely regarding our ethics. Because of this, we can give up our rights in a few different ways – as Hobbes had described, where we voluntarily transfer or renounce our rights in accordance with our will; but also contrary to our will, such as if (or when) we're arrested and our rights are suspended – hopefully only temporarily. We can't likewise give up or be relieved of our ethical responsibilities, nor can they be taken from us in the same way – we're more or less stuck with them and subject to them all the time.

The paradox in question with the story Abraham and Isaac is that as an individual, Abraham somehow made himself superior to the universal – and we just can't wrap our minds around that. Abraham is thought of as the father of three of the world's great religions – Judaism, which traces directly to him as its founder, Christianity, as a branch or evolution of Judaism, and Islam, which claims descent from Abraham's firstborn son (with his wife's slave, Hagar), Ishmael. So Abraham represents, or is the embodiment of faith, and yet his life is the most paradoxical Kierkegaard can think of – so paradoxical that it can't be thought of at all. Abraham acted by virtue of the absurd, because it's absurd to think of the individual as superior to the universal.

---

[142] A particular reading from Scripture – usually one that contains a whole story, sometimes across several verses of a given chapter.
[143] The plural of *telos*.

121

The Tragic Hero(es)

Kierkegaard introduces the concept of the tragic hero as an understandable counterpoint to Abraham, who he says must be either a murderer (even if his attempt wasn't carried through to fulfillment) or he's the truest believer ever. He lacks the intermediary condition that saves the tragic hero, who can be understood by us fairly easily; we can't, however, understand Abraham, although, as Kierkegaard says, we can admire him more than any other man, if for no other reason than for the depth of his faith – not many of us would so quickly or willingly answer God's call in the way Abraham is depicted as having done. But how are we best to understand where he was coming from? In terms of Ethics, his relationship to Isaac can be expressed simply as the father ought to love his son more than himself. The task then is to see if a higher expression of Ethics can be found in the *Genesis* account that's capable of explaining his behavior ethically, and which would provide the justification for his having suspended his ethical duty toward his son, without going beyond the teleology of Ethics itself.

To help us put all this in context, Kierkegaard gives us the examples of three tragic heroes, whose behavior Abraham's can be compared to in order to identify the difference(s) and what keeps their actions within the realm of Ethics, but places his outside it; they are Agamemnon, Jephthah, and Brutus. Now, Kierkegaard is working under the assumption that we're all conversantly familiar with all these characters through literature, though that's rarely the case today. In order to better understand what he wants us to get from each of these guys, we'll take a look at them individually and in order, to examine their cases and see if we can identify just what it is that makes them tragic heroes operating ethically in comparison to Abraham.

Agamemnon, known to most of us as one of the antagonists of Achilles in Homer's Iliad, also features prominently in a Euripidean tragedy and in Racine's seventeenth century update of the story in his play *Iphigenia in Aulis*. This provides some of the backstory that didn't make it into the screenplay of *Troy*, starring Brad Pitt as Achilles and Bryan Cox as Agamemnon. Here's the set-up in a nutshell: Agamemnon, the king of the Greeks, has just told Achilles that his daughter, Iphigenia, won't be married to him as they had previously planned, but that instead she's going to scarified to appease the goddess Artemis,[144] who will then allow the Greek ships safe passage across the Aegean to Troy. So you know the middle part of the story already – they go, they fight, Agamemnon gets his victory, Achilles gets killed (darn that weak heel!), and they come back to Greece... where Agamemnon's wife, Clytemnestra is waiting for him, and kills him, because he had killed their daughter. In other words, classical Greek literature has everything you might expect and hope for in the most modern television soap opera, but more violent.

Jephthah and his daughter fall into the category of "weird stuff you probably had no idea is in the Bible," and he is the second of Kierkegaard's tragic heroes. Jephthah, a Gileadite

---

[144] Apollo's sister, and female counterpart.

judge of Israel in the Old Testament book of *Judges*[145] is fighting the Ammonites,[146] and having a rather tough go of things. To that end, he promises to the Lord that if He will give the Ammonites into his hands, upon returning home to Gilead,[147] he will sacrifice whatever comes out of his door to the Lord as a burnt offering. Ostensibly he was expecting to be greeted by the family pet, but was instead met by his daughter (you had to see that coming). So, true to his promise, Jephthah carries through with the sacrifice of his daughter – and she doesn't even get a name! Now, what makes this different from Abraham's case (because you know you're wondering) is that Jephthah undertook to do this entirely of his own accord – God never asked him to.

Brutus, probably the most familiar to us culturally of the three provided by Kierkegaard, is in a slightly different boat, as it's not his daughter whom he kills, but his father – sort of. Brutus, as most of us probably know from Shakespeare, along with Cassius and a handful of senatorial coconspirators, stabbed Julius Caesar; contemporary rumor and some modern scholarship contends that Caesar was actually Brutus' illegitimate father, which would make sense, given his romance with Brutus' mother, as well as the closeness of the bond obvious between them. So basically, Brutus killed his father – sacrificed him, really, to preserve the Roman Republic and prevent it falling into a despotism, which ultimately it did regardless, but anyway. As an interesting literary note, if we read Dante's Inferno, we find Brutus and Cassius, along with Judas Iscariot, being chewed in the three mouths of Satan, in the lowest pit of Hell, but that's another discussion...

As Kierkegaard tells us, at the decisive moment when Agamemnon, Jephthah, and Brutus "heroically overcame their suffering," when they had "heroically lost what was dear to them," and when they had then only to accomplish their exterior sacrifice, then "surely every noble soul will shed tears of compassion for their suffering and of admiration for their deed." Well, maybe not quite so easily as he envisions us doing, but I suppose we can at least see sort of where he's going with this – it was a selfless sacrifice on their part, even if a profoundly disturbed one. The point, as has already been pointed out, is that they acted of their own accord, and were decidedly not simply following a command God had issued to them.

Tragic Heroes versus Abraham

There is a striking difference between the tragic heroes (these three, and others) and Abraham; they remain within the realm of morality, where he does not. Abraham gave to an expression of Ethics a *telos* in an even higher expression of Ethics – one that transcends Ethics itself. There was no question in Abraham's case of appeasing the wrath of a goddess, saving a nation, or defending the idea of the Republic. Abraham's entire action stands in no relation to the universal and was a purely private undertaking – where the tragic heroes are great through their *moral* virtue, Abraham was great through his purely *personal* virtue.

---

[145] His story appears in *Judges* 11:29-40, in case you want to go read it for yourself.

[146] In modern day Jordan.

[147] Also, in modern day Jordan. Contention is nothing new to that part of the world.

Remember, in the life of Abraham, there is (or at least ought to be) no higher expression of Ethics than that the father should love his son more than himself; here there can be no question of Ethics in the sense of morality. The question ought to arise right about now… why did Abraham do this?! Kierkegaard tells us he did it for God's sake, but also, and identically, for his own sake; for God's sake because God had demanded proof of his faith, and for his own sake because he wanted to furnish the proof God had demanded. A temptation, on Kierkegaard's account, is something which tries to stop us from doing our duty, but in the case of Abraham, it is Ethics itself which tries to prevent him from doing his duty, which for him, is the expression of the will of God.

The tragic heroes never enter into a private relationship with divinity – to them, Ethics is divine, and so the paradox their behavior presents can be mediated in the universal. The tragic hero has no certainty that his actions will be effective, because he has been given neither directions nor guarantees by God or the gods that his actions will elicit their desired outcome. The tragic hero has need of our tears, and in fact, demands our tears; while we may have a tough time feeling too bad for Jephthah, and Brutus seems cold and distant from his task, Agamemnon, at least as Racine presents him, is an incredibly tragic figure that you almost can't help but weep with, if not for. The tragic hero acts in a specific time, but accomplishes something timeless – he makes us realize that our own troubles aren't nearly as bad as his, and reminds us that life could certainly be worse, no matter how bad we think we have it. But even as the tragic hero draws out our tears and emotions, Kierkegaard tells us that their heroism continues through to our actions, and they tell us not to cry for them, but for ourselves.

Where does all of this leave us? According to Kierkegaard, either Abraham was at every moment a murderer, or we stand in the presence of a paradox which has to be superior to all meditation, i.e., no matter how hard we concentrate on the facts of the matter, we'll never be able to fully and truly understand what's taken place here. The story of Abraham therefore involves a teleological suspension of the ethical – he has placed on hold that which he would ordinarily consider immoral for the sake of a higher goal – obeying the commands of God. Given existentialism's focus on the individual this is particularly problematic, because as an individual, he has become superior to the universal, and therein lies the paradox which can't be understood. But it doesn't end there – it is just as impossible for us to explain how he entered this state as it is to explain just how he remains there. If this is not the case, then Abraham is not a tragic hero, but a murderer.

Final Thoughts

I have a certain partiality for Kierkegaard – I'm intrigued by his thought, and especially by the way in which he provokes *my* thought. Remember – he isn't trying to argumentatively convince us of anything, but rather to gently coax us into a deeper understanding of why we might look at things in the unique but limited ways we currently do. To that end, his work is, to my way of thinking, the most literate and readable of all of the moral philosophers – it can be read as literature and enjoyed on that level, as well as on a philosophical one, in a way that thinkers like Kant simply can't be, or at the very least, often aren't. In the end, his Ethics are Kantian to a certain extent, but whereas Kant was our "in a perfect world" philosopher, Kierkegaard seems to have a bit more realistic application of this approach to Moral Philosophy, and because of that, he's perhaps a bit easier for us to digest, and we might be just a bit more inclined to approach things deontologically if we're able to do so from an existential perspective.

Chapter 17: Marx

Marx may seem, and certainly could be, an odd inclusion for an Ethics text, not least because he was not himself an ethicist, surely didn't self-identify as one, and would, in all likelihood, probably not appreciate our including him in and amongst a group of philosophers, as he doesn't seem to have thought of himself as one. He had studied Philosophy, and was unquestionably well-versed in it,[148] but was and is known more for his socio-political thought, revolutionary tendencies and writings, and is today of course, most closely associated with Marxism,[149] Socialism, and Communism. Now then, about those associations, it's important for us to realize and remember that it's not Marx that man that we tend to take issue with in the modern Western world, but what has been done with Marx's thought. That is to say that he, while perhaps not wholly innocent – after all, he must have had *some* notion of what would happen if someone read his work and took it seriously – is not nearly so much to blame as those who read his work as a handbook rather than as theory. Be that as it may, and it's an aside we will likely return to later, Marx should be read and benefitted from for what he presents to us directly, and not necessarily for what we associate him with retrospectively because of guys like Stalin and Mao.

So back to why we ought to include Marx in a discussion of Ethics, it's for two basic reasons, the first of which carries forward a theme, and the second of which makes him absolutely unique. The theme that is carried forward is one that we first saw in Plato, and that has come up with some regularity all the way through our discussion, and provides the point we'll end with – the theme is justice. Marx doesn't provide us with a theory or even a definition of justice, but what he does give us is a notion of what it ought to be, and how he says modern civilization actively prevents it from being, so we can approach our understanding more or less in the reverse, i.e., through his critique of how things are we get an idea of how he thinks they ought to be. Secondly, Marx has the unique, if infamous, distinction of being the only one of our ethicists whose theories has had enforced application over a significant period of time. No one (that I know of) has ever tried to run a society based almost exclusively on Kant or Hume for instance,[150] but we have nearly a century of data with billions of people, and a geographically significant portion of the world functioning as essentially a giant sociology lab, empirically testing the efficacy of Marx's theories. Generally speaking, they've been tried and found (severely) wanting, but the fact that we have the data at all is interesting and makes him undeniably unique.

Now, you might be surprised to learn that we're not (at least not here) particularly interested in his most (in)famous works, *The Communist Manifesto* and/or *Das Kapital*; I do

---

[148] His doctoral dissertation, from 1841, was written on the difference between the Democritean and Epicurean philosophy of nature, and yes - it's every bit as dry as you'd expect, aside from some interesting speculations on the notion of time.

[149] I've heard and read that Marx was once invited to address a group of Marxists, but declined, stating that he was not himself, a Marxist, and so could not.

[150] Geez – that would certainly be interesting!

encourage everyone to read at least the first of these, no – not so you'll become a little communist, but so you'll know what it is and isn't, placing you miles ahead of the ignorant masses who confuse it with fascism, think of it as necessarily synonymous with socialism, etc. Anyway, the writings we're interested in aren't even completed works, don't have titles, and are typically just referred to as the "Economic and Philosophic Manuscripts of 1844" or sometimes as "The Paris Manuscripts" – you can find them pretty easily online. They were never completed, are roughly edited if at all, and are more or less fragmentary, stopping sometimes in the middle of a thought, and characteristic of his early work. Most interestingly, while we can see where they're headed, they never specifically mention the "solution" Marx offers to the problems he identifies – the emergence of the ideal, classless society, following an upheaval or revolution of some sort.

Capitalism

Specifically, Marx seems to be replying to a particularly Smithian[151] scheme, in which workers have been alienated as a result of the social structure inevitably engendered, imposed, and sustained by bourgeois capitalism. So here a few clarifications are probably in order, not the least of which will have to include some vocabulary. Smith, in his *Wealth of Nations*, didn't *invent* capitalism, just as Darwin didn't *invent* natural selection – he merely described a process he observed as being already operant in the world. As for bourgeois (and please make sure you're never pronouncing this as "burg-ee-oys"), this is the adjectival form of *bourgeoisie*, a wonderful word we've borrowed over from French to describe the social class characterized by their ownership of capital and the means of generating more capital. If you recall your French Revolution history from high school,[152] this is the group referred to as the "third estate" (the previous two being the clergy and the aristocracy, respectively); for Marx, this gets updated to include all those folks who have exclusive control over the means of production. The proletariat, borrowing the Roman term that meant the same thing in their day, refers to the laboring class of wage earners who depend on the bourgeois for work.

Remedial Economics 101

Alright, time to revisit our high school Economics class – you know, supply and demand, and all that, to figure out exactly what Marx's problem with capitalism is, and how it came to be that way. Marx presents an economic scheme in which commodities and money are exchanged, and that remains the case all the way through our brief economic history, with only their roles and importance changing somewhat, with relation to our labor considered as we go on. In the simplest form of economy, barter, we exchange one commodity for another, e.g., "I'll trade you this fish I caught for that grain you harvested;" money later emerges as an intermediary in the same situation, e.g., "I'll sell you this fish and then use the proceeds to buy that grain." When intercontinental travel becomes the norm and the

---

[151] Referring to Adam Smith, specifically to his *Wealth of Nations*, yet another book to add to your bucket list, especially if you have any interest in economics or politics.

[152] And if you don't, I'd recommend reading Thomas Carlyle's masterful history of it, to get what you missed when you skimmed through *Tale of Two Cities* in high school.

world first experiences what will come to be call globalization, we enter the age of mercantilism, where money is an abstraction, replacing the concrete utility of the commodities themselves as the goal of economic exchange. Finally, capitalism as we now think of it emerges when labor itself comes to be treated as a commodity subject to sale, trade, manipulation, devaluation, and so on.

Invention and Alienation

How did all of this come about? The blame can be laid fairly solidly at the feet of those Industrial Revolution[153] inventor sorts, darn them! Now, I know eighth grade was a long time ago, but think back to that poster you probably made that you mom might still have up in the attic. If we consider guys like John Kay and Eli Whitney, the inventors the flying shuttle[154] and the cotton gin, respectively, we get a bit of an idea what Marx is upset with, especially considering he's writing at the end of their era. These inventions, and several others like them all resulted in an increase in efficiency, sometimes an exponential one, that enabled a single person to perform the work of sometimes dozens or even hundreds of people. Ordinarily, that strikes us as being a good thing – think of how much more we can get done – but to Marx, it has a very negative affect, especially with regard to our basic social organizations, and which ultimately resulted in a heightened alienation of workers and consumers.

Okay, but how did all of *that* come about then? The increase in efficiency comes at the cost of the artisanal approach, which today we probably associate with very exclusive items, but which were commonplace before these inventor sorts got involved. If your family produced a certain sort of cheese or boots, or sprockets, or what have you, then it was very likely that you too would produce that item when you came of age, and you were much more likely to have a certain pride of ownership (or at least craftsmanship) in producing said item. Fast-forward to capitalist forms of production, and workers no longer control the means of production, but are now free to sell their labor to whomever they can, the result being they're less closely tied to a level of expertise in their work or craft. Workers will also become alienated from the products they produce or service they provide because they're highly unlikely to feel any sort of close artisanal connection to them that they would have before, and throughout most of human history. In other words, that guy making your sandwich down at the shop no longer has any real reason to care whether or not it's the best he could possibly make, if for no other reason than to him it's just another place in what will likely be a long line of places that will purchase his labor until he moves on.

So inevitably, under capitalism, all workers become alienated, and in three main ways – from their products, from their activity, and from their humanity. We're alienated from the products of our labor because ultimately, they're not controlled by us but by capitalists, and as soon as we produce them, they take on a life of their own as commodities, that just like our labor can be bought and sold. We're alienated from our productive activity because it's not really satisfying to us, and instead is only a means for our physical subsistence – more

---

[153] Roughly 1760 to 1840, or thereabouts.

[154] No – not the space one, but the one for weaving.

on this a bit later. Finally, we're alienated from our humanity because much of what we do at work firstly has little or no relation to anything characteristically human, and secondly, we engage in only as a means of continuing our physical existence. Our behavior, ethical and otherwise, ought to be entirely free – universal in the Kantian sense, because we're not simply responding to instinct but producing things that we really don't need. Marx notes that we're capable of so much more than we do; we can produce astounding levels of culture, we can shape the environment to suit our needs – an observation especially present to me as I write this in Texas with the air-conditioning on; we can develop and abide by complex ethical systems, and so on. And yet, we allow ourselves to be subjugated and alienated by work, and this makes Marx sad ☹

Commodity and Division

Right at the outset, Marx tells us that workers sink to the level of a commodity – this may seem somewhat counterintuitive to us reading this now, as we tend to view the ability to sell our labor to the most competitive employer as a *good* thing, but let's stick with this, and see where he takes us. He then notes that our misery increases with the power and volume of our production; that the necessary result of competition (in the mart of commerce) is the accumulation of capital in a few hands. We might be able to accede this point a little easier – no matter how many sandwiches, sweaters, etc. we sell, we get paid the same, and are really just increasing our bosses' revenues, but not our own. From this we get a distinction that emerges, maybe slowly at first, but noticeably, and we're separated into capitalist and laborer, or perhaps more dramatically, as Marx seems to prefer it, as property owners and propertyless workers.

Where does this come from, if it's not a natural progression? Marx says that a primordial (think stone age) condition can't explain this – if we look at primitive societies or states of nature (probably Rousseauian,[155] rather than Hobbesian), there's nothing there to account for an elite group taking advantage of their laborers. I would contend, and I suspect that most anthropologists and historians might agree with me, that Marx is mistaken about this, but we'll give the guy some breathing room and see if he uses it efficiently. Rather, he says, we ought to begin from a contemporary (to him, not necessarily to us) economic fact: the devaluation of the human world increases in direct relation with the increase in value of the world of things. What he's describing here is called an inverse or reciprocal proportionality, and it essentially states that as one goes up, the other must go down. In this case, what's going down is the value we place on ourselves, and by extension, each other, while what's going up is the value we place on our material goods – our stuff. In other words, the more we place our value considerations on what we've got, the less we'll focus on who we are and how we ought to behave.

Following this line of argument, no matter what line of work we're in, service we might provide, or what sort of object we produce, the product at the end of our labor now stands

---

[155] Jean-Jacques Rousseau had posited a state of nature more or less the opposite of Hobbes' (to whom he was responding, essentially), in which our "uncorrupted morals" prevail and we're all really nice to one another; this is where we get the idea of the "noble savage" popular in the 19th century.

opposed to us, on Marx's account, as an alien being, as a power independent of us as the producer. The product has become the objectification of our labor, that is, our activity has been transformed into an object, the making of which is actually a sort of impairment[156] to us. We end up feeling a loss rather than a satisfaction, if for no other reason than for all the things we'd really have rather been doing during the hours we spent at work – the bumper stickers, "I'd rather be… fishing, golfing, etc." would seem to bear out the truth of this pretty well. He adds that we're really in something of a servitude to the object itself – we *have* to work, because we're the guy that produces that product, performs that service, and so on, and without us, it simply won't get done, so there's a social pressure that results as well.

Labor and Alienation Revisited

Marx tells us, quite correctly, that labor itself becomes an object which the laborers can acquire only by the greatest effort, and with unpredictable interruptions. It's not hard to find a job – really – you can find a job doing *something* pretty darn easily; what's difficult is finding a job that you're willing to do, and even more difficult, finding a job that you are likely to enjoy doing. For instance, I absolutely love the job I currently hold, but I've had a string of really awful jobs on the way to this one;[157] as Mike Myers' character says in Wayne's World, "I have an extensive collection of nametags and hair nets." And, once we get a job, it's sometimes hard to hold on to that job for as long as we might like – that's the part about "unpredictable interruptions" – sometimes we're fired, let go, laid off, or, as it's euphemistically called these days, "reduced in force." I've been all of these, and it's not pleasant, but it certainly is inherent to the sort of system that Marx is describing and responding to.

Eventually, we become a slave of whatever object we're producing. We receive an object of work from our employer, that is, we receive work, but what they're really giving us is a means of subsistence. The product we produce or service we perform, i.e., the object of our labor, enables us to exist, first as a worker, and only secondly, as a physical subject. Think about this for just a moment, and we generally have to concede that Marx has a good point here – we are first and foremost valued (and value others) for the product or service produced or provided, and only secondarily as unique individuals, and here is where we see the application of Ethics in its most direct, though still only implicit way, as far as Marx discusses it. The high point of our enslavement (note the change in terminology) is that we can only maintain ourselves as physical subjects so far as we are also workers – we feed, cloth, shelter, etc. ourselves with the money we're paid – and it is only as physical subjects that we're able to work in the first place. So it's essentially a cycle from which is there is no, or very little, possibility of escape.

---

[156] As per the usual, it's better in Latin, and Marx uses the word "vitiation," which now implies that something has been rendered less good or somehow less effective, and comes from the Latin word *vitiare*, which implies more or less the same thing.

[157] My very first *real* job was shoveling sacks of manure for a landscape company; you know how people who work in fast food restaurants smell like fryer grease? Guess what you smell like when you shovel sacks of @#$% all day – I didn't date.

To really hammer home the point, because at this point, he is really on a roll, Marx gives us a list of exactly what happens to the worker, in the same vein as Hobbes' list of what we must do without in times of war or in a state of nature. The more the worker produces, the less he has to consume – this one hits home with me when I'm reading or writing at home and suddenly it's nine hours later and I haven't eaten so much as a wheat thin all day. The more value he creates the more worthless he becomes – I can't help but think of Lewis Carroll's mad hatter here.[158] The more refined his product, the more crude and misshapen the worker – gone perhaps are the days of blacksmiths' hyper-developed hammering arms, but I can't help but think we're not entirely out of the woods as I sit here developing carpal tunnel syndrome. The more the work manifests intelligence, the more the worker declines in intelligence and becomes a slave of nature – I'm reminded of this every time I have to do long division (which granted, isn't all *that* often) but find myself without my smartphone or computer access.

Continuing on, after much beating of dead horses (he makes what are essentially the same points as I've given above two more times in various ways), Marx makes some further observations that are right on the money today, despite his having made and written them seventeen decades ago. He notes that we really don't fulfill ourselves at work,[159] but deny ourselves – we can easily think of a whole laundry list of other things we'd rather be doing, possibly even including our laundry, instead of being at work. We have a feeling of misery rather than wellbeing, don't freely develop our mental and physical energies, but leave work feeling physically exhausted and mentally debased. No matter how much you love your job, you know you've had moments when all you want to do upon arriving at home is plop down on the couch and binge-watch your favorite television show while eating takeout. As workers we feel ourselves at home only during our leisure time, whereas at work we feel homeless; for evidence of this, walk down any row of cubicles to see how their occupants have attempted (and most likely failed) to make them feel more "homey." Our work isn't voluntary, but imposed, forced labor. Don't believe Marx on this point? Stop working some time while you're at work, and see how long it takes for your boss to tell you to get back to work; my guess is, you won't be waiting for very long. Our work isn't the satisfaction of a need, but only a means for satisfying other needs – recall the earlier point about how we work to feed, cloth, and shelter ourselves, but let's also recall that no little kids dream of being busboys and tax attorneys, or only the weird ones do. The final proof offered up by Marx that labor is alien to us is clearly shown by the fact that as soon as there is no physical or other compulsion to work it is avoided like the plague – I know a guy (it's not me) who knows more or less to the hour how long he has to retirement.

---

[158] Okay, I can't resist another obscure historical digression here: felt (you know, the craftsy stuff) originated when the Mongols would shear their animals' winter coats and place them under their saddles when out riding (which was most of the time) – the combination of the friction of the saddle, the heat, and the sweat of the horse, would "felt" all of it together, and it could then be used to cover their yurts and so on. Update that to Georgian and Victorian era, when beaver fur hats were all the rage in men's fashion; not having a bunch of Mongols handy, the hatters would rub mercury into the fur in order to felt it, a bunch of which must have been absorbed into their skin, making them quite literally as mad as hatters. Neat, huh? ☺

[159] I almost feel bad including this, since I absolutely LOVE what I do, but again – I had to get through a lot of really terrible jobs to land this one, so there's that…

Marx describes the character of work as being external to us, if for no other reason than because it is (rarely) our own work, but work for someone else, beyond considerations of our product or service, the work we do doesn't belong to us but to another person. He says that we feel ourselves to be freely active only in our animal functions – eating, drinking, and procreating, and chances are we're not doing that last one at work. But even if we consider the other comparatively harmless two, I know I've had plenty of jobs when I'm told when I can eat, how long I have, etc., and sometimes it's been shortly after I arrived at work for a long shift, that I had to eat almost right away for the sake of the schedule. Our personal adornment is another area, and one we probably test to the limits if we've got a uniformed job – there's only so much you can do in terms of personalizing certain outfits, and Marx would point to all of them not as evidence of our freedom at work, but as microcosmic and somewhat pathetic rebellions in the face of our enslavement.

Species Life

Not only has our labor alienated us from nature, says Marx, but it's also alienated us from ourselves, from our own active function, from our life activity, so it's alienated us from our own species, and has made species life into a means of individual life. We're through with work for the week, we're looking forward to the weekend, decide to get together with some friends, chances are good they'll be friends from work. Think about it this way – cops hang out with cops, firemen hang out with firemen, nurses with nurses, etc. – we're so tied-in to what we do at work, that when we get off of work, we only feel we can communicate effectively and meaningfully with others who do our same job. Even when this isn't the case, and we just go on home from work instead of stopping off somewhere to hang out with your coworkers, you get home and what do you talk about with your significant other over dinner? Yup – work. So not only are we alienated from ourselves and from others, we end up alienated from human life itself.

Private Property and Sensation

Up until now, Marx has made some pretty good observations, and we're probably mostly inclined to agree with his assessments of the problems with capitalism. In other words, it's high-time he loses us completely by revealing his solution to all the problems we face in and under this system – here's the Marx we're used to seeing and reading. The basis for his claim is probably pretty accurate – that private property has made us so stupid and partial (his adjectives) that an object is only ours when we possess it, when it exists for us as capital, or when it is directly eaten, drunk, worn, inhabited, or otherwise utilized by us in some way. What this means is that possession itself is now a means of life – we are our stuff – we are what we wear, where we live, what we drive, and so on, to such an extent that we may even have a difficult time thinking of or expressing ourselves in other terms.

Taking a position that will certainly resonate with Mill's notion of higher and lower pleasures a few decades later, Marx observes that all the physical and intellectual senses have been replaced by the simple alienation of all these senses; the sense of *having*. His solution to this is that we must be reduced to an absolute poverty, i.e., have all our possessions taken away from us in order to revive our lost inner wealth. On Marx's account, then, the suppression of private property is therefore the complete emancipation of all the human qualities and senses – and here is where he more or less loses all but the most ascetical reader. Fortunately, we don't necessarily have to carry out his advice to the extreme he would probably have us do in order to note that, while his solution is extreme (though perhaps no more so than would be done in his name in the years following his death), it does call us to rehumanize our senses and appreciate the world, ourselves, and each other on a level distracted neither by our labors nor by our possessions.

Final Thoughts on Marx

I had thought about titling this short section something along the lines of, "is Marx the bad guy we probably assume he is?" but that's both verbose and loaded, and I'd rather avoid both. It's important for us to remember that it's not really Marx's philosophy that we generally take issue with, but rather what was done with his philosophy following his death. We may very well disagree with Marx in the same way that we may disagree with Bentham or even Plato, but we tend not to associate either of them, or the others we've discussed, with characters like Josef Stalin, and so we get easily distracted and go in with preconceived notions which generally though unavoidable, aren't particularly useful in the study of Ethics. Our very next thinker will suffer at our hands from a similar, though less overt stigma, and as always, it remains important for us to consider each of these men in their proper context, without adding to their words what we expect to hear them tell us.

Interlude: Meta-Ethics

Nietzsche is pretty much the only meta-ethicist we're particularly interested in discussing in this book, and I hope the reason why will become apparent momentarily. Briefly, it can be rather daunting, make your head hurt, and just generally leave you more confused than you were to begin with, not always with a whole lot to show for your troubles. In the original Greek, *meta* just means "after" like *post-* would in Latin; leave it to philosophers to needlessly complicate things – for us it means "after" or "beyond" in the sense of transcending whatever it modifies. So meta-ethics, specifically the part of it we call value theory, has to do with how (literally how we talk about, as in what words we use), why, and to what extent we place value on things, usually through those familiar but tricky adjectives, good, bad, and evil (in addition to others, of course, but these are the biggies). So basically, meta-ethics is talking about how we talk about Ethics; are your minds blown yet? No – good, then we'll proceed.

I asked you before, nearer the introduction, but I'm asking you again – think for a moment about how you might explain the term "bad" to someone if you were charged with doing so; what would you say? If your initial notion is to define "bad" as "not good," have no fear – you're certainly not alone, but that's just not a particularly satisfying answer, especially not in an academic setting. The trouble is, while we all know, or at least can identify, bad things, we have a really tough time articulating exactly what it is that makes them bad. Let's say I bring home a puppy from the shelter, having just adopted him, having gotten the bowls, puppy chow, water, strewn newspapers on the floor, etc., and all of a sudden, the puppy decides to relieve himself on the brand new rug. I'm not going to call him an "evil" puppy for having done so, though I might want to indicate to him that this behavior is "bad" before he's full-grown, especially if he's a larger breed. We know this, but again, we have a tough time saying what exactly it is that warrants and merits the jump from bad to evil. I would say it can be approached like this – good people occasionally do bad things; good people are not, however, frequently in the habit of doing evil things – so while "bad" seems to indicate something about an occurrence, "evil" appears to be more indicative of our overall character, or as Kierkegaard put it, our personality is consolidated. With these general understandings in place, we're more or less ready to proceed with Nietzsche.

Chapter 18: Nietzsche

If Marx is the guy who tells us unpleasant truths about our economy that we nonetheless probably need to hear, then Nietzsche is the guy who does the same thing for our morals, and in so doing, on the one hand, isn't nearly so uncomfortable for us to hear, but on the other hand, infinitely more-so because he connects to a culture that we're unavoidably caught up in and inescapably part of. He is the first of our thinkers to make it into the twentieth century, even if just barely, and is in many ways the culmination of our modern era thought, especially for his marked departure from the classical and medieval era perspective. He is also our first meta-ethicist, who like Kierkegaard and Marx, doesn't give us an ethical plan of action to follow per se, but is more interested in the terms we use to describe, assess, and evaluate ethical situations, proposal, actions, and so on. In this sense, his approach can be applied to and quite telling of all the philosophers who came before and will follow him in that he's interested not in their theories, but in the language they use to express them.

The difficulty when encountering Nietzsche in his primary writings (which you're being relieved of, unless you decide to go and read him on your own, and I would encourage you to do so) is that he generally writes under two assumptions, one of which he shares with his fellow existentialist, Kierkegaard, and that's that you've read everything he's read. Chances are you haven't – don't feel bad, few today have, and I'm here to help! He also seems to write under the assumption that you've likewise read everything he's written, more or less in chronological order, and that you're therefore able to follow his point even when he's not particularly clear about it, or when understanding that point is predicated on the notion that you'll of course get references to his earlier works. Again – I'm here to help, and together, we ought to be able to put together a fairly coherent notion of Nietzsche's approach and general thoughts on Ethics.

Daybreak

The Dawn, translated into English as *Daybreak* is where Nietzsche really kicks off his self-described "campaign against morality," and it is probably his harshest work in terms of balancing criticism with analyses, in other words, there's a lot of the former, without much of the latter. It's here that he refers to himself as an immoralist, which, unlike the amoralist position hinted at or espoused by Hume, takes an almost satirical or deprecatory approach to morals – mocking them, rather than ignoring them completely, and expressing a preference for those actions deemed immoral – just to irk the squares. This is also where he initiates his critique of the two prominent moral schemes of his day, Kantianism and utilitarianism, which (surprise, surprise) he considers to be in error - more on his explicit problems with both of these in just a bit...

Ecce Homo

In *Ecce Homo*,[160] Nietzsche presents the idea he'll develop more fully in our later texts, the notion of a moral system based on a dichotomy of good and evil being a "calamitous error," and the circumstances from which they developed to be likewise grievously in error. He expresses here a wish that he'll carry out later, and that we'll look at in much more detail; a reevaluation of the Judeo-Christian Ethics that have so shaped (and according to him, corrupted and weakened) our world. Instead, he would like to see us bring about a new, more naturalistic Ethics – one that finds value through uncontrived means, and which connote to our vital impulses rather than the social pressures we find ourselves under/within. Both these points should sound familiar, as the former was essentially what Hume had argued for – a natural, not artificial, source of morals, and the latter has certain Hobbesian overtones to it, specifically with references to our vital motions and so on.

Beyond Good and Evil

We're going to be spending the bulk of our time with *Beyond Good and Evil*, because this and *The Genealogy of Morals* are where Nietzsche does the bulk of his work in morality, and where we get the best sense of his overall approach to thinking about Ethics. Specifically, he's not an ethicist, but a meta-ethicist, and his writing reflects this. Like Kierkegaard and Marx, he's not going to give us a moral theory, tell us how we can become moral, or even give us a notion of what moral is, but rather, will examine the language we use in morality, across all theories, and what we really mean when we employ the terms we use without (probably) giving them much thought. So the question then becomes not so much which theory we ought to ascribe to in order to be ethical individuals, but one of what these different theories mean or are referring to when they describe something as good, bad, or evil. Here's where Nietzsche is going to really go to work...

The title of the work, and its subtitle, "Prelude to a Philosophy of the Future" is fairly telling, at least as I interpret it. Nietzsche seems to be wondering aloud, and inviting us to do likewise, "where do we go after we understand the origins of these terms?" The implication is that he will get us to a point where we are beyond them, or at least the ethical systems in which they appear, and we'll then be properly poised to move forward...into the future, ideally toward and into an Ethics that doesn't rely on evil or some of the other features of modern morality he attributes to our misguided past and present. What exactly would that "new" ethical system look like? He doesn't specify, but we can extrapolate that it's perhaps not as new as he might have us believe – more on this when we get to it. To get there though, Nietzsche is first going to subject modern morality to a destructive critique – sort of like the philosophical analysis we've seen, where arguments are broken down into their constitutive arguments, but without the synthesis part where it's put back together.

---

[160] Published posthumously, the title is a reference to John 19:5 (Vulgate), where Pontius Pilate holds Christ before the crowds and says, "Behold the Man."

The book itself is broken into nearly three hundred numbered sections, followed by Nietzsche's attempt at lyric poetry which he entitles "From High Mountains;" I don't recommend it, though it admittedly may have lost something in translation. His approach is a genealogical one – he sets out to, more or less, create a theoretical ancestry of our modern notions of "good," "bad," and "evil." In a sense too, this is an evolutionary approach,[161] not of a species, but of the terms themselves – from how they began, to what they are now. Now, he's speculating, but he's speculating with a fair amount of background – it's more than a mere educated guess on his part, not least because this is quite literally what he does for a living. Philosophy was more of a hobby for Nietzsche than a profession; professionally, he was a philologist, and taught the same. Before you go running to Google, philology as a study is the study of language in written historical documents – sort of a triathlon of literary studies, history, and linguistics – and his focus was specifically on those in Greek, Latin, and Sanskrit, so he makes several references to, or at least use of, all three.

The Master Morality

Nietzsche begins the portion that is of concern to us with a bit of storytelling, like an ethical Aesop, but with a story relating how "good" and "bad" first got their meaning. So everyone get a seat on the rug, and get ready for story time with Uncle Friedrich... Originally, there were two kinds of people – the noble, powerful, superior, and high-minded, and the low, low-minded, and plebeian. The former (the masters) held an unquestioning hold over the latter (the slaves) – they had a feeling of ruling and superiority that was justified by the fact that they *did* rule and they *were* superior. He calls this feeling of superiority a pathos of distance, in other words, and to put it much less delicately, the master think of themselves as *so* much better than the slaves that they can't bring themselves to think about how much it would suck to have their roles reverses – they're *that* different. He thinks it's through this pathos of distance that "good" and "bad" first get their meaning, "good" being everything the masters themselves are – their characteristics, attitudes, etc., and "bad" being everything the slaves are.

So Nietzsche, in his speculative ancestry of our morality, is saying that if we were to go all the way back, to the very beginnings of morality, we would find as the only option available the master morality. He associates this with the literal masters of the ancient world, and most closely with the heroes as found in Homeric Greece – Achilles, Odysseus, Ajax, Hector, and so on. In this sense, "good" is everything life-affirming, i.e., whatever the heroes themselves are – healthy, strong, wealthy, powerful; while "bad" is determined according to the sorts of traits associated with slaves in the ancient world. It's important that we note that at this point, there's no mention being made of "evil," and it's not that it's being ignored, but rather, that it simply hasn't been *invented* yet – that's coming next.

---

[161] Darwin's *Origin of Species* had been published when Nietzsche was fifteen, and its implications and approach certainly don't seem to have been lost on him.

The Slave Morality

The master morality, as an original existence (and really, the only option) was necessarily active; the slave morality, in contrast, comes about as a reaction to the master morality, and this is when the term "evil" gets invented. Now "good" becomes associated with all those particularly Christian values (think the Beatitudes) like charity, piety, meekness, submission, restraint, etc. But here's where it gets really interesting; now everything that the masters had considered to be "good" becomes "bad," but not just "bad," but evil. Why make the switch? Because it helps the slaves to overcome their own sense of inferiority as compared to their masters. How do they do this? They invent the term "evil," and recast their various weaknesses as being a matter of choice on their part, e.g., they're not "weak," they're "meek." They then do the same thing by renaming the masters' characteristics in their all-new, now "evil" versions, calling them things like cruel, selfish, aggressive, worldly, and so on.

The master morality had originated in the example and pattern of the original and actual masters of the ancient world, the powerful heroic characters that ruled the Greek world with which Nietzsche was professionally and personally dedicated to, in the era before the democracy we now so like to associate with the Greeks, thrived. The slave morality came about later, with the literal slaves, who through their own ineptitude or infirmities ended up powerless and deprived of the lifestyle enjoyed by the masters. He looks at these two groups, and laments that we have fallen so far from the golden age of the heroic Greeks; that we have allowed the slave morality to overcome us, direct our opinions, and change the way the world views its Ethics.

Ressentiment

This change Nietzsche says is born out of the *ressentiment* the slaves feel toward their masters, and yes, although he uses the "fancy" French term, he just means resentment as we might think of it. But how should we think of it? Think of it sort of like envy – it's "I hate you," but not in the everyday sense (and hopefully you *don't* hate people every day), it's "I hate you because I want to *be* you." It's the nerd who secretly pines to be a defensive lineman, the jock who wants to impress the literature major, and so on. Back to Nietzsche as the ethical Aesop, but this time taking a page from the real Aesop, it's the fox and the sour grapes – when we can't attain something, we justify to ourselves that it wasn't worth having in the first place, that we can do much better without it, and so on. The key move in doing this is inventing the term "evil" (at least in this case) and then applying it to everything the other side has deemed to be "good." To revisit our discussion of Marx, this is the proletariat rising up against the bourgeoisie, then making the values of the laboring class out to be "good," while the characteristics of the capitalists get labeled as "evil."

Exceptional People and the Masses

If you haven't felt even slightly put-off or offended by Nietzsche yet, have no fear – he's about to cover that base. Now remember, he was writing this in the late nineteenth century, so things have probably gotten worse (on his account) rather than better since then. He sees Europe, mainly due to its Christianity, as existing in a hypocritical state due to the tension between the master and slave moralities, and the inherent contradictions render them "motley."[162] In his view, modern moral thought is mistakenly and weakly egalitarian – we vocally affirm the equal worth of every person, even if we really don't believe it personally, and we express a concern for the wellbeing of everyone, even if we don't particularly care, so long as *our* needs are taken care of. This modern egalitarian morality is (you guessed it) really just the slave morality masquerading in the form of democracy and Christianity, the two dominant institutions of Western culture.

But wait – what's wrong with democracy? Take a moment, put down the book, and go look at the website PeopleofWalmart.com; then reflect for a few moments that even if those folks don't vote, they're at least eligible to. Nietzsche reasons that it should concern us more than a bit that such people are making decisions that impact us directly and importantly. So who ought to make the decisions if not them? Why, exceptional people of course! Nietzsche wants exceptional people to embrace their uniqueness, despite any protests by the less fortunate, to be bigger, faster, stronger, smarter, and so on, without trying to place limits on their own flourishing, which you'll recall is one of the numerous translations of Aristotle's *eudaimonia*. In other words, if you're naturally better in some way, you ought to be allowed to be better – even if it makes others feel somehow lesser by extension and comparison.

Morality isn't bad according to Nietzsche, it's good for the masses, and ought to be left to them, while exceptional people are allowed to follow their own "inner law" based in their personal excellences (remember *arête*?). We can see a bit of this in celebrity trials, where it seems they get special treatment as compared to the rest of us, which would seem to be a little bit of what he's promoting here. But on the other hand, we give everyone participation ribbons these days instead of just the winners getting trophies, and we tell Jimmy not to run so fast because it hurts Timmy's feelings, who is slower, so perhaps Nietzsche's criticisms aren't all that far off the mark. Here' the inevitable moment when we realize Nietzsche's a bit of an asshole, and we worry that if we're agreeing with him or even only seeing his point, we might just be assholes too. Don't dwell on that too much, but don't let it go, either.

---

[162] Which is why Nietzsche now makes me think of Tommy Lee and Nikki Sixx.

Problems with Christians, and Problems with Kant

Remember, he's not attacking morality itself; he's attacking the Judeo-Christian morality because he considers it to be nihilistic,[163] being a thinly-disguised slave morality based in resentment. The master morality, you'll recall is aristocratic and noble, and therefore independent – it seeks no confirmation from the outside that it's doing the right thing because of course it is! Today, however, the master morality simply appears as "bad conscience" – if someone isn't exactly bashful about being bigger, faster, stronger, smarter, etc., instead of praising their flourishing, we dismiss them simply as arrogant, or think of them as being a show-off. Nietzsche cautions that we shouldn't be quick so quick to dismiss them like this, but recall that their morality has its basis in personal excellences – of the sort that Aristotle indicated we all ought to be habituating ourselves in in order to become virtuous and noble, or in other words, exactly what has been deemed aristocratic.

The problem Nietzsche seems to identify with Judeo-Christian values is the same as the one he identifies with Kantian deontological approaches to Ethics, and that's that they're bourgeois. In other words, they have the "luxury" of thinking about ethical concerns in a certain way, divorced from the reality faced by the common person, at least, that's the approach he seems to be taking. He specifically goes after Kant and his categorical imperative (presumably both iterations) as being nihilistic, and in a certain sense, he's got a point; universal principles of the sort Kant encourages, don't take into account the differences between individuals. And what about love, in the specifically Christian sense? We're to love our neighbors as ourselves, but do we really? I love my wife, I love my children, I love my family, and in an extended Christian sense, I love the homeless guy on the street, but I'm less likely to give him a kidney if he needs one; Nietzsche asks if this can really be called "love" with all the qualifications we place on our various loves.

We may very well be asking at this point that if he doesn't like any of the options available to him at the time – even utilitarianism, at which he levels the same charge as against the Judeo-Christians and the Kantians, that it doesn't account for individuals in its calculations, which is accurate, if we only consider the greatest happiness for the greatest number. So what does he prefer? Nietzsche tells us that in our attempt to establish universal principles that apply necessarily, we've ignored a much older philosophy that had better credentials to begin with – Virtue Ethics! In other words, Aristotle had presented to us a nearly ideal system of Ethics (in Nietzsche's biased estimation), and if it wasn't broken, why did we insist on trying to fix it? He wants an ethical system that, like Aristotle's, doesn't focus on the masses, but rather on the individual's character, asking ourselves, "what sort of person ought I to be?"

---

[163] From the Latin *nihil*, a nihilist is someone who believes in nothing.

Transvaluation

Okay, so back to the slave revolt, the rise of *ressentiment*, and all the rest. Next, something a little weird happens. A few generations into the slave morality, the descendants of the slaves start to (understandably) resent being so powerless and being thought of as "bad" through no apparent fault of their own, and their resulting hatred of the masters leads to a "radical transvaluation of their values," according to Nietzsche. So let's look at his choice of words, which unless I'm mistaken, he coins himself; "trans" as a prefix simply implies that something is going across something else, as in Transylvania, across the forest, or transsexual, across the sexes. Valuation should be fairly apparent – it's the values held by one group or other. Bearing this in mind, then, a transvaluation is when values are flip-flopped, exchanged, flipped, swapped, etc. That is to say "good" and "bad" now change places in such a way that "good" now describes the attributes of the slaves, while "bad" designates the qualities of the masters.

Going all the way back to our earliest discussion, of Socrates' *Euthyphro*, and its focus on the pious and impious, we have the slaves now occupying the former and the masters the latter. This is only possible when the *ressentiment*[164] of the slaves for the masters has increased to such an extent that the only way they settle on to compensate is in imagining a brand new moral code. The results are more psychological than practical, as Nietzsche sees this mainly serving as a way for the slaves to feel better about themselves, while simultaneously casting their superiors as not just bad, but evil. That makes sense – it's an understandable, and perhaps even natural response to the situation they find themselves in, but what happens next is even weirder…

For what happens next, we're probably at about the same place in our speculative history – maybe just a few generations into the slave morality, following its creation/invention as a reaction to the master morality. Once the slave morality is firmly established, the descendants of the privileged master class begin to doubt their own legitimacy. Slowly, at first, the start to buy into the slave morality, coming to accept and embrace the notion that their position of power and superiority might actually be a mortal sin that they will in due course be punished for. On Nietzsche's account, this sense of guilt is invented (just like evil) as a way for the inferior slaves to feel better about themselves. In blaming the masters for their suffering, the slaves experience a sort of catharsis, their own anger purged as they enjoy the suffering of the privileged, who are now being punished for the wrong they have done – think of it as being like schadenfreude, except they're probably *not* friends. Doing their part to perpetuate this notion, the masters themselves suffer more and more as they buy into the slave morality, feeling guilty for having things that are now condemned – wealth, influence, power, privilege, and so on.

---

[164] I'm just going to use "resentment" from here on out, okay? The French just seems needlessly pretentious to me, and besides – you get the idea absent the extra "S."

On the Genealogy of Morals

Written a year following *Beyond Good and Evil*, and something of a sequel to it, *On the Genealogy of Morals* is very appropriately subtitled *A Polemic*, and that's exactly what it is. Nietzsche had presaged this later work in the earlier one, and a lot of the same themes will be returning, some more refined, others the same, though more strongly and vehemently expressed than before. This is arguably the most straightforward of his books, by extension the least aphoristic in style, and is thought by many (myself included) to be his masterwork, and the best his philosophical expression would get before the syphilis[165] really started to affect his thought and writing. The structure of the book is quite different from its predecessor, consisting of a preface followed by three interrelated essays that trace and relate episodes in the evolution of the moral concepts under consideration. I like it to the fantastic television miniseries that were so popular in the 1980s, but instead of learning about Drogheda or Centennial,[166] we're learning about the master and slave moralities – specifically as the latter appears in Judaism and Christianity.

The Preface, Poor Paul Ree, and Tartuffery

You might say Nietzsche had been mulling over, okay – stewing is probably more accurate – the origins of our "moral prejudices" for quite a while – at least nine years by this point, since he had first (that I'm aware of) mentioned them in passing in his 1878 Human, All Too Human. He seems to have mentioned it then in response to his friend (and I use the term loosely here), Paul Ree's book, *The Origin of Moral Sensations*, published the year before. Poor Paul Ree – seriously – how'd you like to be remembered in history as having basically been called an idiot by your more famous friend who did Philosophy as a hobby better than you did as a profession? As you can tell from the title, Ree had applied a genealogical approach to moral terms, but specifically toward altruism, in his attempt to explain its origins in humanity, and why we consider it moral. Ree's conclusion was that altruism has an innate human drive that had been selected for (ala Darwin) over the centuries.

Remember those assumptions I mentioned Nietzsche makes – that you've both read everything he's read, and everything he's written? Well, a reference he makes here (and elsewhere) reinforces that. He's discussing the need for a critique of moral values, which we'll discuss in more detail momentarily, but refers to the whole project of morality as being an instance of "tartuffery." Now, *of course* you've read Moliere's 1669 play, *Tartuffe* –

---

[165] Oh yeah – hadn't I mentioned that? Someone braved that moustache, apparently.

[166] Okay, so I'm a bit obsessed with Richard Chamberlain's television miniseries career; if you haven't seen them, check out (in this order): Shogun, Centennial, and the Thorn Birds – you'll be glad you did.

right?[167] Nietzsche uses the term frequently in his works, but doesn't just mean a hypocritical pretender to religious piety at the play implies, but hypocrisy of any kind. So anyway, his point is that a critique of moral values is in order – that the value of the values themselves must be called into question. Here's an interesting observation: we haven't really seen this done yet. Plato asked us to consider which category of good things Justice would be properly placed into, but we've more or less left it alone since then.

Even when Aristotle gave us his laundry list of the various virtues, their value was more or less understood to be implied and generally accepted as good, but was never really examined with regard to, "just how valuable are the values themselves?" To this end, Nietzsche would have us consider how we might have come to arrive at our valuations of terms within Ethics, and we are best-suited to do so by constructing a history of morality to the best of our knowledge an ability, rather than a hypothetical account as Ree had tried (and failed, on Nietzsche's account) to do. He accuses Ree and others of being "English psychologists" – apparently a "sick burn" in his day, but really, he's just accusing them of having utilitarian leanings in their ethical thought, referring to their intellectual disposition, rather than their nationality (Ree was a German). More on this as we get into the first treatise…

The First Treatise

Nietzsche opens the first treatise after the preface of *On the Genealogy of Morals* by rehashing a few of the main ideas he set up in *Beyond Good and Evil*, but also by drawing our attention to the importance of understanding which morality someone might be coming from, with whom we're discussing "good" things. Depending on that person's moral orientation, they could have a completely different understanding of what makes a thing, an action, a policy, and so on "good." The noble mode of valuation, who up to this point he's referred to as the master morality, calls "good" what it itself stands for – everything that is powerful and life-affirming. The servile mode of valuation, up to this point called the slave morality, calls the same things "evil" which the noble calls "good." Remember, this good/evil valuation has developed out of the reactionary resentment of the weak in the face of the powerful, by whom they feel oppressed and whom they envy.

Indicting the English Psychologists

For our purposes, just think of Nietzsche's "English psychologists" as utilitarians,[168] and that's exactly why he has problems with them – because as a group he sees them as lacking historical sense in their attempts to support their theories with what he views as faulty attempts at genealogy. Just so we're all on the same page, altruistic acts are the "random

---

[167] You really should find and read a copy of *Tartuffe* – it's excellent. There's even a few stage/movie adaptations if you're not much of a reader (of drama). Tartuffe is a lovable scoundrel who befriends the wealthy Orgon, and then attempts to seduce both his new friend's wife and daughter, all the while pretending to be a pious man whose faith convinces Orgon and his family to succumb to his influence, but he's undone when his womanizing ways make it clear that his piety is a charade.

[168] In the patrimony of Bentham and Mill.

acts of kindness" to which the bumper stickers refer, and which are done purely for their own good, with no expectation of reward or return. Ree and company had attempted to explain altruism by ascribing to it a utility – a usefulness – that they claim is forgotten as altruistic actions become the norm for human behavior, and as the beneficiaries of altruistic acts come to label them as "good." But Nietzsche observes that the valuation "good" didn't originate with the beneficiaries of altruistic actions, but with *the* good, that is, the powerful masters themselves, as a means by which to describe their *own* actions. But he's not content to let it go here, and further argues that it's absurd, psychologically and practically, to argue that altruistic actions derive their merit from a utility that has been somehow forgotten – if it was so useful, then what was the incentive to forget it? He maintains instead that value judgments gain currency by being increasingly burned into the consciousness – something we're not likely to forget.

Redress and Revenge

One of the problems Nietzsche cites with the slave morality is how it addresses problems with the master morality, or with anyone, for that matter. He notes that in their feeling of resentment, they (the slaves) don't seek direct redress for grievances by taking their revenge through action, as the masters would, but instead by setting up an imaginary revenge, "surreptitiously exacted." In other words, if someone of the master morality has a problem with someone else, it will be dealt with directly – by confronting them with it, discussing it, possibly even deciding it through physical altercation, if it comes to that, but there will never be any question of it being avoided or otherwise ignored. The slave morality on the other hand, has its adherents sneaking around (hence the "surreptitious"), setting up an elaborate but wholly imaginary situation in which they themselves are the victors over the hapless masters, who all this time have no notion at all of their having been vanquished – since it was all in the heads of the slaves all along.

Nietzsche describes the slave mentality as needing enemies in order to sustain itself – not unlike the revolutionaries in Marxism, which, even on Engels' account, think of themselves as revolutionaries long after the revolution itself is over. One might rightly be inclined to think then that like the Marxist variety, the slaves will most likely, having successfully revolted against one set of masters, set their sights on another set to then revolt against, preying on their own group if nothing else presents itself. Meanwhile the noble morality hardly takes enemies seriously to begin with, and forgets about them instantly once having dealt with them. Ultimately, Nietzsche tells us, the weak deceive themselves into thinking that the meek are blessed and will inherit the earth, ultimately vanquishing the strong, despite their clear temporal superiority. So what do they do in order to console themselves in the meantime? They invent the term "evil" to apply to the strong and to everything that proceeds from strength, which we'll recall is precisely what the noble, aristocratic valuation had called "good" to begin with.

One might wonder what the master morality is doing during all of this – amidst the imaginary revenge, surreptitiously exacted, the being deemed "evil," and so on – surely they're plotting some elaborate revenge that will be directly and finally exacted in order to keep the weak in their places, right? Nope – not remotely. While the weak are busy inventing the term "evil" to apply to the noble, the noble refer to the weak only as "bad," although not "bad" in the sense of "evil," but "bad" in the sense of "worthless" and "low-born." Nietzsche specifically cites the Greek terms κακοσ and δειλοσ, respectively, for these; Spanish speakers will recognize the former of these, as it's evolved from Greek through Latin to a common word for excrement – and that should tell you everything you need to know about how the noble view the weak, or how he thinks they ought to, or would at least be entitled to.

Fascism

It's also in the first treatise that Nietzsche employs one of his most controversial ideas, that of the blond beast, an image he had previously conjured in *Thus Spake Zarathustra* to represent the lion, but that has obvious negative connotations derived from what he mentions right after it. The blond beast would have been fine on its own (probably), but he follows it up with a reference to Sanskrit word *arya*, which means noble, and from which our modern word Aryan is derived. Now, we can think about this word in two distinct ways, both interesting from a sociological perspective, but one somewhat more provocative than the other. The oldest sense refers to the Indo-European people who invaded and conquered the civilizations at Harappa and Mohenjo-Daro, subjugating the native Dravidians and giving rise to what today is known as Hinduism, as well as the caste system within it. In that sense it may cause some slight offense, or at least discomfort, but not nearly as much as it does in its more recent, derived sense – that of White superiority movements, many of which refer to themselves with this term, the ultimate irony being that the ancient Aryans probably more closely resembled Iranians. So if you know any neo-Nazi sorts, you might remind them of this fact – and then run. Now, obviously Hitler and company are going to pick up on and have a field day with these concepts in Nietzsche, but it's important for us to separate his philosophy from what's been done with it since him, just as we did with Marx. But the point should also be acceded that he is espousing something like fascism, named for the fasces – the battle axe strengthened by the bundle of sticks, sometimes seen in heraldry – and like Marxism, this is most frequently, and unfortunately, known to us through its radical expressions that seem to diverge from the original intention.

The Lambs and the Eagles

At this point, we may very well feel horrified by what we're reading, all the more-so if we view Nietzsche in any way sympathetically; so what are we to make of all this, and how can we possibly understand this as objectively as possible? He tells us that it can be salvaged – we need look no further than the natural world around us, wherein it would be a mistake to hold beasts of prey to be "evil" for doing what they do. If a hungry bear makes his way down out of the mountains and mauls a camper, it's not because the bear was "evil" in any meaningful sense of the word; all we can say with any degree of certainty and sense is that the bear was behaving precisely as we might and should expect him to, knowing that his actions stem from his inherent strength. The strong, Nietzsche tells us, shouldn't be blamed for their "thirst for enemies, and resistances, and triumphs," and that by extension it would be a mistake to resent the strong for their actions, because just as in the case of the bear, there is no metaphysical subject to blame. Only the weak, he says, need the illusion of the subject to hold their actions together as a unity and place blame on those stronger than them, but they have no right to make the bird of prey accountable for what he is.

Carrying forward the bird of prey analogy, Nietzsche gives the example of the lambs and the eagles as exemplary natural world manifestations of the slave and master moralities, respectively. The lambs may not particularly appreciate that the eagles take off with one of them occasionally, but it would be more than a bit absurd for them to blame the eagles for acting this way. He tells us it would be equally ridiculous for the eagles to blame the lambs for what *they* do – sitting there stupidly, just waiting to be eaten! To place demands on strength such that it not express itself strongly, that it not be a will to overcome, overthrow, dominate, and have that thirst for enemies and resistances, and triumphs, would make as little sense as to demand of weakness that it should instead express itself as strength.[169]

The obvious question then should be, if this is true for the rest of animate nature, then why should humanity be considered any differently? According to Nietzsche, the strong and superior can't resist being what they are any more than the weak and inferior can resist being what they are, proving directly (on Nietzsche's account) that there is (our ought not to be) any distinction between strength and the *expression* of strength (and the same for weakness). He says, "the doing itself is everything" – very likely yet another take on something we've seen over and over at this point – "actions speak louder than words." The main problem he identifies with the slave morality is that it seems to have convinced itself of the exact opposite of this; that somehow they seem to believe that the strong could freely choose to be weak. But if being strong is just doing strong things, and being weak is just doing weak things, then the thought of trying to temper or tame the strength would just result it in becoming gradually weaker. Likewise, somehow beefing-up weakness would gradually result in it becoming stronger – an undeniably Darwinian perspective, if a grimly unkind one.

Historical Evidence

If you're feeling bad upon your realization that you've bought into the slave morality, don't allow yourself to get too down in the mouth – Nietzsche essentially says you can't help it, because the modern age is inescapably the result of two millennia of the slave morality, suffering a double-whammy at the hands of democracy and Christianity. Does that mean all hope is lost for the master morality and those who might otherwise aspire to ascribe to it? Not in the least. It has been sublimated,[170] but has never completely disappeared. As we discussed earlier, today it appears only as "bad conscience" – as the arrogant posturing of

---

[169] In other writings he refers to this as the "Will to Power;" an adaptation of Schopenhauer's "Will to Survive," the notion is that we desire power for power's own sake, even when we don't intend to use it instrumentally for some further good.

[170] Okay, so the liminal world is that in which we live, and that of which we're aware; the subliminal (the one the advertisers capitalize and prey upon) is the one that has been quite literally pushed below the liminal state – it's still there, it's even identifiable if you're looking for it, but it's almost subconscious in its appeal to us.

those who are bigger, faster, stronger, smarter, and the like, in the face of the common masses. Need further proof? Here's how you see it: *You* got the job – that's right – you beat out all the competition, you had the experience, you knew the right people, you had the best resume, and so on. But here's the catch – you can't be proud of your achievement, or if you are, you had better rein it in – a lot, lest you butt-hurt the others you beat out for the job. You're encouraged instead to be humble so as not to appear to be a show-off, and this is the war that Nietzsche tells us is (quietly) raging between pride and humility.

The war being fought between pride and humility could also be thought of as a war between excellence and mediocrity, and just as before when we compared an Ethics based in excellence versus one based in self-denial, which do you suppose you're going to want – really? Nietzsche is quick to remind us, however, that masterly strength and virtue never truly disagree. This makes sense, or at least is in keeping with what we've been told so far – our virtues, based in *arête*, moral excellence, goodness, etc., is that which the masters would have habituated themselves in and then self-identified as "good," so it stands to reason that it would be in keeping with a noble morality. The master morality he sees as having been driven underground, or having sublimated itself into other outlets, and he gives the example of the Renaissance popes as prototypical of this – a quick study of Rodrigo Borgia, aka Alexander VI illustrates nicely the most powerful man in the (then) world, disguised as the humble Vicar of Christ – the television series' attempts to point this out to a popular audience all make sense now.

We might be tempted to think at this point, okay – I know we said this was going to be a speculative history, but he's taking this one a bit far, right? Well, maybe not quite so far as we might be inclined to think, and so Nietzsche walks us through some historical events where we might have witnessed the master morality, slave revolt, and resulting ebbs and flows of both throughout the history of Western civilization – it's actually pretty cool to see it all play out like this. We start with the Roman Empire – the masters, by anyone's estimation – at least until they allow themselves to be weakened through the slave revolt that occurs as they're Christianized, but we're getting ahead of ourselves. Judea represents the slave morality, overcome by the masters when Rome destroyed the second Temple in 70AD during the Siege of Jerusalem. Fast-forward quite a bit and the black plague wipes out about a third of Europe's population, allowing the master morality to once again take the lead, as the exceptional people thrive in a period we've come to call the Renaissance. Then Martin Luther and company turn the tables yet again, allowing the slave morality to gain the upper hand (which coincides with those naughty Renaissance popes, conveniently enough). And according to Nietzsche, the final nail in the coffin of a public master morality was the French Revolution, wherein *ressentiment* was allowed to triumph as the rabble overcame the aristocracy.

Interlude: The Contemporary Era

While it really doesn't deserve a chapter all to itself, since we're only going to be discussing two "contemporary" ethicists, it is something different, and a break from the Modern Era, so we'll chalk it up to an "interlude," and call it good. So what exactly do we mean by "contemporary?" For our purposes, it's the period of history now in living memory – that is, how far back most living people have a reasonable memory of or that a first-person account could be readily obtained for by someone out and about, or between thirty and seventy years or so. Needless to say, this is changing constantly, so someone reading this book several years and several editions from now[171] may very well label the two philosophers we're about to discuss, as well as the era(s) they fall within as something different entirely. But for us, seeing as this is being written in the mid-2010's, it's fair to say that it stretches back to the post WWII era, through the Cold War, and well into the internet age. And now, without further ado, let's see what Jean-Paul Sartre and John Rawls have to contribute to our morality project...

---

[171] Hey – a guy can dream, can't he?!

Chapter 19: Sartre

I'm going to admit a bit of bias here – I absolutely LOVE reading Sartre's philosophical writings – why? Because he just writes so darn well, and, perhaps more importantly, because with few exceptions, the bulk of his work *isn't* in the form of dusty philosophical treatises, but in works of really good literature. My favorite play of his (he also wrote novels and short stories) is *Huis Clos*, usually translated as *No Exit*, the classic work wherein we're told that, "hell is other people," something we have an even easier time believing when we're stuck in traffic or a meeting. Anyway, I find him to be infinitely readable, so along with a handful of the others that I've encouraged you to add to your bucket list, Sartre really deserves a place there as well – you won't regret it. He didn't get the opportunity to turn down the Nobel Prize for Literature for nothing!

Sartre has the benefit of writing retrospectively, as an existentialist, not only self-identifying as such, but looking back over the history of the movement, all the way to Soren Kierkegaard. As such, he's able to take a few liberties in crafting his own definitions, which, because he's just cool like that, work equally well with what we've already covered in our previous two, Kierkegaard and Nietzsche. So as our third and final existentialist, he starts off by telling us that existentialism is easy to define,[172] but that we then run into problems as soon as we try to understand what the definition means.[173] Here's his definition, and it is indeed simply: "existence precedes essence." Well, he's right – that doesn't seem all that tough – it's three words, seven syllables, and not all that daunting on the face of things; let's break it down, word-for-word, and see where that gets us. *Existence*, as previously defined, isn't all that tricky – it implies that something exists, it's an ontologically[174] valid something, etc. *Precedes* is exactly what it means in any context – comes before either temporally or logically (in this case, it's both). Essence is perhaps a bit trickier, and I hate to do it, but we might think of this as that "certain *je ne sais quoi*" or the *sine qua non* you sometimes hear about; in other words, it's the certain something that makes something what it is – essentially – literally essentially.

As it turns out, he seems to have been right – we can make our way through the definition in pretty short order, only to be left wondering just what in the hell it means. Well, what it means is this: you have to exist before you can be said to have anything that really defines you. What he's attempting (and I think, succeeding) at making the argument for here is this: there is no fixed human essence in which we all participate, no fixed ideal of humanity to which we should all aspire, in short, the philosophers who thus far have pondered the "nature of human nature," have all, on Sartre's account, more or less been wasting their time, as there isn't any such thing. This may not seem all that bad on the face of it, but what

---

[172] That gust of wind you may have just felt was probably the collective sigh of relief breathed by freshman seminar students.

[173] Perhaps they spoke too soon...

[174] From the Greek, *ons, ontos* – that which is; for us, that which <u>exists</u>.

that means by extension is that there's nothing to provide us with a set of objective values, nothing to guide our actions, and nothing to give meaning to our lives. It's suddenly becoming much clearer why existentialism sometimes gets the reputation of being bleak and melancholy. The upshot of all this is that we're individuals in the truest sense of the word as Sartre sees us, so we're free but also tasked with the difficulty of choosing our values and what we are.

What each of us is and what we become depends on our individual decisions and actions, so as we're going along living our lives, we're creating ourselves and simultaneously creating a set of values. So what results is that Sartre maintains something of a balance – we're radically free to do anything and everything we want or could think of, but we're also radically responsible for anything and everything we do – the praise or blame lays solely and squarely on us. This is another one of those moments that provides a startlingly accurate, "what are *my* Ethics?" type tests; if you find the idea of fairly *extreme* personal responsibility for better or for worse to be a good thing, then your personal ethics are probably existential. On the other hand, if this sort of finality irks you, or you find yourself longing to attribute it to circumstances or other outside influence, well, then this might not be your particular cup of tea. The overall idea, whether we base our personal moral philosophy on it or not, is that what we see actively taking place here is a unique for of individual self-creativity of a sort reserved exclusively to humans – think of it as Aristotle, cynically updated for Sartre's day and age.

Existentialism: Christian and Atheist

As I mentioned a bit ago, Sartre is writing somewhat retrospectively, putting himself and Kierkegaard both in the category of existentialists, though on opposite sides of the aisle, as it were, just as existentialism itself is split – between Christians on the one hand, and atheists on the other. I mentioned in one of Kierkegaard's footnotes that I consider Sartre to be a reluctant atheist, and I promise – I'll explain why shortly, but he maintains that religion notwithstanding, both camps have something in common – they both agree that subjectivity must be the starting point for any sort of meaningful philosophical understanding. For Sartre, this subjectivity is expressed in his dictum, "existence precedes essence," which we've already been through, but which hopefully is starting to make a bit more sense as he intends it. We might also think of his atheism as a principled, carefully-reasoned atheism, because it legitimately is both – his next steps are going to present his arguments for the non-existence of God, which will show him to be more than a little disappointed by his own conclusion, rather than vindicated as we might expect.

The Paper Cutter

In yet another digressive foray into literature and history, think back just a moment to when you had (or chose) to read *The Great Gatsby* in high school, specifically the part where Nick and Jordan encounter "Owl Eyes" in Gatsby's library.[175] Now, when we think of

---

[175] Is it all coming back to you now? If not, the scene is also remarkably well-done in the most recent Baz Luhrman film adaptation starring Leonardo DiCaprio as Gatsby.

a paper cutter, we probably envision the office supply contraption with a small gridded table and a machete-like blade that pivots along one edge – this isn't at all what Sartre means when he uses the term; he thinks of something like what we would call a letter opener. Now, a bit of explanation is required here, and this is where we get back to Gatsby – you may recall in that scene that Owl Eyes remarks with surprise that the books haven't even been cut yet. Books used to be printed in such a way that you would have to cut along the edge of every other page in order to keep reading; a modern holdover from this are the now "fancy" deckle-edge some publishers like to use to give their hardcover editions an extra bit of panache.

So, what does any of this have to do in the least with Ethics? We're getting there. Sartre's point is that inspiration comes from a concept; you've heard this notion before, but phrased differently, as "necessity is the mother of invention." In other words, we identify a need, e.g., it's hotter than Hades in Texas in August, and we invent something to compensate for it or otherwise meet the need, i.e., air conditioning. It's the same with the paper cutter – we don't make something like that and only then sit around pondering what we might do with it – we had a need, and it was fulfilled, and he maintains we're not all that different in our humanity. We think of objects produced in a certain way, objects which have specific uses, and we can't think of these objects as being produced prior to their use being imagined or necessitated. Sartre says that our technical view of the world is such that we can say, in addition to existence preceding essence, that *production* precedes existence.

God Enters the Picture, or rather, doesn't

Sartre rightly points out that in just about every religious doctrine, with the exceptions of many of the Eastern traditions, and, like Augustine, he's probably working in the confines of ethical monotheism, we generally find the accepted notion that when God creates, He knows exactly what He's creating. In this specifically religious sense, then, the individual man (again in the sense of *anthropos*) is the realization of a certain concept in the Divine intelligence. He's referring here to the familiar concept found in *Genesis* 1:27 – the belief that we're all made in God's own image, though what aspects of us are entailed in this aren't specified.[176] The problem we run into then is that this doesn't exactly jive with the dictum that existence precedes essence; essence, on an ethical monotheistic account, is the soul – as created by God. In other words, for Sartre to be right, the Genesis account has to be wrong, or vice-versa, at the very least one or the other could be accused of being awkwardly worded. To get to the bottom of it, let's pick through a bit more of what Sartre means...

So, the question then becomes one of what we mean when we say that existence precedes essence, and recall, that's where Sartre initially warned us the difficulties would arise. It means first of all that we exist, we turn up, we appear on the scene, and then and only then do we defines ourselves by our choices and commitments. This is precisely why existentialism maintains humanity is so difficult to define, in fact – indefinable, it is because

---

[176] For instance, it doesn't specify whether we're made literally or metaphorically in God's own image; whether our bodies, minds, spirits, etc. are like God's is unclear.

at first we are nothing. Only afterwards will we be something, and whatever it is we become, we will have made ourselves that thing. Where's he going with all this? The conclusion he maintains these premises are leading toward is that there is no human nature simply because there is no God to conceive of it. So not only are we what we conceive ourselves to be, but we are also only what we will ourselves to be after our initial thrust toward existence.

The Self-made Man

Man (as a species) is nothing else but what he makes of himself – this is Sartre's first principle of existentialism. We first exist, we first of all are the beings who hurl ourselves toward a future and our conscious of imagining ourselves as *being* the future. This is why we have such a difficult time of imagining a future without us in it, and even if we think we manage, we still see it as if we've been made to expect to – as if we're off to the side or slightly above, observing it all mutely omniscient, but entirely imaginary. We can't think of a future without us in it except in the abstract notion that things will (probably) continue once we're no longer here, but that's about it.

It all comes down, Sartre maintains, to what our plans are. We will be what we have planned to be; not necessarily what we want to be, or even what we need to be, but only what we've planned to be. We can't all be the astronauts we dreamed of being, and certainly a few of us need to work in maintenance, but we are ultimately, whatever we've planned and taken steps toward being and becoming. In planning, we made a series of choices, and in choosing our path we involved our will. By "will," on Sartre's account, we mean the conscious decisions we make, each of which is subsequent to what we have already made of ourselves. All our desires, he says, are really only the manifestation of an earlier, more spontaneous choice which we call our "will." So if existence really does precede essence, then we are fully and solely responsible for what we are.

Existential Ethics

This may seem all well and good, but the question ought to be coming to us right about now, "okay, so what does anything of this have to do with Ethics?" After existentialism has made its first move, making us all aware of what we are and making the full responsibility of our existence rest of us, then the ethical implications begin. Why? Because we don't only mean by this that we are responsible for our own individuality, but that we are additionally responsible for all people. Does this mean that like Kant our Ethics are contingent wholly on our rationality, and we can't really choose them except to follow along with that which is universalizable and necessary? No, but it does mean that subjectivism now takes center stage in our considerations. We, and our morals, are what we choose and make them, and we find it impossible to transcend this radical subjectivity. No matter how Kantian we might personally desire to be, we can't leave behind those aspects of ourselves that are distinctly and uniquely ours, as part of the background of the person we've created – ourselves.

In creating the person we want to be, every single one of our actions at the same time creates an image of humanity as we think it ought to be. Put simply, in everything we do, we're acting in such a way that we might consider reasonable for anyone and everyone else to act the same way. Gosh, that sounds awfully familiar – at least it ought to – it's basically a less stringent phrasing of the first iteration of Kant's categorical imperative. For Sartre, to choose this or that is to affirm at the same time the value of what we choose, because we can never choose evil. Wait a minute, now *that* sounds like Kierkegaard and the business about the crossroads. He says further that we always choose the good, and nothing can be good for us without being good for all. In other words, we choose what we *think* will be the right course of action – even if it results in bad outcomes, we can say that we chose with only the best of intentions.

And so we proceed, asking ourselves, "what would happen if everybody looked at things that way?" a position we can't escape without lying to ourselves, again echoing Kant, if tempered a bit. For instance if we lie and make excuses for ourselves, reasoning that not everyone acts like that, then Sartre notes that we already have an uneasy conscience because the act of lying itself implies that we've conferred a universal value on the lie. When we find ourselves in transgressions of this sort of duty toward ourselves and others, we risk that famous existential anguish, the realization that we have a direct responsibility for other people whom we involve in our life sometimes being too much for us.

The Reluctant Atheist

At long-last, why I call Sartre a reluctant atheist – it's based in his own words. He says the existentialist (presumably himself) thinks it is very distressing that God does not exist because all possibility of finding values in a heaven of ideas disappears along with Him. On Sartre's account there can no longer be an *a priori*[177] Good, since there is not an infinite and perfect consciousness to conceive of it. Outside of a religious context, nowhere is it written that the Good exists, that we must be honest, that we must not lie, and, Sartre posits, the fact is we are on a plane where there are only men. This is why I call him a reluctant atheist – it seems he'd greatly prefer to believe in God and in so doing find a readymade example of the sort of behavior that he and the rest of us ought properly to aspire to live up to. He quotes Dostoyevsky (incorrectly) as having said that "if God didn't exist, everything would be possible," and says that this is the very starting point of existentialism. Sartre goes further than the dreary Russian writer, though – not only would everything be possible if God does not exist – everything would be permissible.

As a result, we are forlorn, because neither within ourselves nor without, in God, do we find anything to cling to. When we lose everything else, or even perceive ourselves as having lost everything, we turn to God, but if God is not there... and that is precisely Sartre's point. We can't start making excuses for ourselves because there is no determinism to guide our actions for us or on which to blame them – we are alone, with no excuses. We are free, and in a very real sense we *are* freedom; we are no longer merely Aristotle's rational animals, this notion is closer to Kant's human enlightenment as freedom – our freedom is what

---

[177] Remember? It means prior to or before experience.

defines us on a species level. We are, in this sense, condemned to be free – condemned because we didn't create ourselves – not a single one of us asked to be here, to be born – and yet, in other respects we are free because once we are thrown into the world, we are responsible for everything we do.

Existential Ethics Revisited

Where has Sartre left us with regard to our Ethics if everything we thought we could depend on was all just a misguided misunderstanding? He says we find ourselves wavering between two kinds of ethics – one of sympathy and personal devotion, i.e., Humean consequentialism, and a broader ethics, but whose efficacy is more dubious, i.e., Kantian deontology. And how are we best to choose between them? Christian doctrine can't help us choose, ostensibly since neither really goes along with turning the other cheek and loving our neighbors as ourselves. We can't decide *a priori* either, because then we're back at Kant's crossroads, caught between the maxim we set for ourselves and the situation that tests the maxim. Finally, he tells us that no book of Ethics can tell us what to do – sorry, not even this one. ☹

If values are vague, and if they are always and inevitably too broad for the concrete and specific case that we're considering, then the only left for us is to trust our instincts, which seems to be a simultaneous reject of Kant and embrace of Hume, but not so fast, says Sartre. He reminds us that the only way to determine the value of affection is to perform an act that confirms and defines is, but since we require the affection in question to justify our act, we find ourselves caught in a vicious cycle. In other, more direct words, we won't know whether or not we've made the correct decision until we've already made it – once we've made our choice and committed ourselves to it. Unfortunately, especially for our purposes, Sartre points out that no general ethics can show us what we ought to do, because there are no omens in the world, and even if there were, their interpretation would be left entirely up to us. For the existentialist there really is no love, no genius, there is nothing – at least not as concepts or ideals to be sought or worked toward outside or independent of the self.

At the end of the day, we're involved in life, we leave our impress on it,[178] and outside of that, there is nothing. On Sartre's account, all we are is a series of undertakings, of which we are the sum, the organization, the ensemble of the relationships which make up these undertakings – a remarkably Lockean[179] take on things. We didn't have time to discuss John Locke (though Hume was a Lockean of sorts), but he viewed our personalities in a similar way – we're a series of experiences – those things we've done and that have been done to us. So we had better be very careful both of what we do and what we allow to be done to us – if Sartre's correct, that's all that will remain of us.

---

[178] Think back to Kierkegaard's *character indeliblis.*

[179] You're used to this by now – it refers to Philosophy having to do with John Locke.

Man, Freedom, and God

If it's all so bleak and hopeless, why do we keep going day after day? Sartre says we ought all to be accused not of our pessimism in realizing every day is one closer to death, but of our optimistic toughness as we keep on keeping on. When for instance we discuss a certain vicious character trait (Sartre chooses cowardice), the existentialist says that the coward is responsible for their behavior – they have willed themselves to be cowardly, but this makes us uncomfortable. We would much rather think or say that the coward was simply born that way, without any chance or hope of improvement or change. Progress, Sartre says, may be betterment, but man is always the same – the situation confronting us varies, but the choices we make always remain a choice made within the context of a given situation.

Ultimately it comes down to a question of our freedom – we want freedom for freedom's sake (not unlike Nietzsche's will to power), and we want this freedom in every particular circumstance we encounter. But here's the catch: in wanting freedom, we come to discover that ours depends entirely on the freedom of others, and that theirs depends on ours. Furthermore, Sartre tells us we can take freedom as our goal only if we take that of others as our goal also. The ultimate outcome is that we come to realize that we are beings in which existence precedes essences, free beings who in various circumstances want only our own freedom, we recognize that at the same time we want only the freedom of others.

Ending at that which makes him as our third and final existentialist so different from Soren Kierkegaard, our first, we must again consider God, and specifically His role or lack thereof in Sartre's understanding of our Ethics. He says if we've discarded God the Father there has to be someone who can invent values for us, and he seems to indicate that for each of us that is only ourselves. Before we come alive, life is nothing,[180] and so it is up to each of us to give our lives meaning, and value is nothing else but the meaning(s) that we choose. In this way alone according to Sartre, does there exist the possibility of creating a human community, because there is no universe other than a human universe, and this is the universe of human subjectivity.

---

[180] This is sort of an existential take on an idea advance by Bishop George Berkeley – a radical sort of empiricism where the world quite literally doesn't exist until we get here to experience it.

Chapter 20: Rawls

It's really a bit of a tragedy to end this with Rawls – not because he's bad necessarily, but because he's just rather dull compared to some of our more colorful philosophers. So why include him at all? Well, a couple reasons; he plays an important role in refocusing moral philosophy for one, and second, as our final thinker chronologically he combines several of the theories we've covered in a slightly different/updated form. That's not to say that he's either the culmination of or the final word in Ethics – far from it, and he's certainly got his fair share of critics, but he's worth a look, just the same. Think of Rawls as a bit of an Ethics salad bar – he mixes a handful of the concepts we're now familiar with together with a few new additions of his own, and comes up with a theory that while ever so slightly less "in a perfect world" than Kant's is still a bit tricky to apply practically. Let's a take a look, and see what he has to offer us...

As mentioned earlier, from about the 1860s until the 1970s, utilitarianism was the dominant moral theory in the English-speaking world, i.e., from the time of John Stuart Mill and his publication of *Utilitarianism*, until the time of John Rawls and his publication of *A Theory of Justice*. The 1973 book put forth not the first, certainly not the only, but perhaps the best alternative to Millian utilitarianism that had come up in that nine-decade interval. The book itself presents a systematic examination of social justice from the perspective of political philosophy in such a way that it calls on both deontological notions (ala Kant) and social contract theory (ala Hobbes). While still somewhat abstract in scope and approach, the questions addressed are perhaps a bit more directly applicable than we've seen so far, focusing on cataloging our basic rights and freedoms, clarifying notions of equal opportunity, and a somewhat newer notion of distributive justice that will be Rawls' lasting contribution.

The publication of his book serves to put the spotlight of philosophical interest not only on Rawls himself, but more importantly, back on normative theory and the substantive moral questions it addresses. Nietzsche had distracted the project with meta-Ethical questions for about 80 years at this point, and along comes Rawls to get us back on track with normative theories that we can directly apply, and in doing so, whether you agree with him or not, it must be admitted that he revitalized moral philosophy and defined the terms of debate in contemporary Ethics. Today, it's read right alongside Plato's *Republic*, Aristotle's *Politics*, Hobbes' *Leviathan*, as well as Kant, Mill, Marx, and others. So even though we won't be looking at it quite as in-depth as a few of the others, and we'll be going through it rather quickly,[181] it's still worth our (momentary) consideration.

---

[181] Mostly because he makes two main points then proceeds to repeat them for a few hundred pages...

The Social Contract

We've seen the social contract before – overtly with Hobbes and implicitly with Kant; Rawls is going to have a significantly different take on this, but one that revives a tradition within morality that had been pushed out of the spotlight by Mill & Co. Recall Hobbes' was a very literal social contract, in which you and I agree not to kill each other, then we meet some other folks and agree not to kill them, and on and on we go as we extend both our society and our contracts within it by agreeing to certain standards of behavior. Kant never comes right out and says that's what he's doing, but implicit in the idea of universalizability is the notion of a contract with those whom we can reasonably expect to follow the same maxims we establish for ourselves; in this sense we see more or less the same thing in Sartre as well. Rawls, rather than trying to develop a theory of legitimate government (as had his predecessors) envisions the social contract model as a fair agreement between free and equal people to develop the essential values of a just society.

Justice as Fairness

Rawls calls his theory "justice as fairness," and there's some implications there that we really ought to get out of the way before we proceed much further with his line of thought. First and most obviously, we have the continuation of our dynamic discussion of justice which we began in Plato and have seen at regular intervals since then, with definitions and understandings as varied as the philosophers who offered them. Secondly, we're confronted by the notion as fairness, the obvious problem being our having been told since childhood that, "life isn't fair," and we're then left to reconcile the dictum/reality with the theory. Can it be done? Well, yes and no. As it will turn out, Rawls' notion of fairness actually leaves room for a bit of unfairness (I know how that sounds, just trust me) and lends itself well to being our most recent and conveniently final notion of justice.

Before we actually get into the two principles that comprise his justice as fairness theory, it's important to understand where he's coming from, and we can probably best do that by examining what I consider to be Rawls' summative quotation, taken from *A Theory of Justice*: "Each person possesses an inviolability founded on justice that even the welfare of society as a whole cannot override." Alright, so it sounds impressive, but what does it mean? Well, let's break it down piece by piece and see. An inviolability is exactly what it sounds like – an ability to be violated that has been negated – in other words, they can't be violated. And why can't they be violated? Simple – justice requires that they not be. What's more, the second half of the quotation is his direct salvo fired against the utilitarians, who would nominally sacrifice a few (at least one) for the good of the many, i.e., to achieve the welfare of society. So we know right from the outset that this theory is going to speak to individual rights as being insuperable, even in the face of a perceived greater good for the society in which the individual lives, and that justice will be our paramount concern.

The First Principle

The justice as fairness theory is presented as two principles (generally called "P1" and "P2"), the second of which is broken down into two parts. In order to make sense of them, we'll take a look at how Rawls phrases them, and then try to get an idea of what he's talking about. For right now, we'll just go over these briefly, with an eye to revisiting them a bit later, after some other ideas have been introduced. The first principle, aka "P1" is presented as follows: each person has an equal right to a fully adequate scheme of equal basic liberties that is compatible with the same scheme of liberties for all. It's really not as convoluted a concept as he makes it out to be, but hey – that's Harvard philosophers for you. The scheme in this sense is just an arrangement, pure and simple; in this case one in which rights and liberties are at issue. Regarding rights and liberties, no – they're *not* the same thing (at least not in this instance). Rights are those things we can reasonably expect from our society, our government, our neighbors, and ourselves, whereas liberties are probably best thought of in this context simply as the absence of obstacles or other impediments. Basic rights implies those reasonable expectations that are quite literally at the base – in the same sense as Kant's groundwork/foundation – what we must have at a bare minimum. Along the same line is the "adequate" aspect of the principle which, just like it sounds like, means "good enough," "sufficient," or "satisfactory," but by no means does it include or entail everything we'd like to have in a given situation. So Rawls is saying we need to have an arrangement in which everyone can have the same essential expectations (more on which these are later) and freedom from impediments that everyone else has, as part of a system where everyone likewise has at least the bare minimum of what they need. Wow – even simplified that still seems fairly convoluted.

The Second Principle

The second principle, remember is broken into two parts, and the premise-establishing statement for them reads as follows: "Social and economic inequalities are to satisfy two conditions: they are..." Let's pause right here for a moment – I really dig this about Rawls, and have to give him credit where it's due; why? Because unlike Marx, who tells us we can eventually overcome social inequalities following a revolution, and unlike Nietzsche, who reminds us that we'll always have a gradation of social ranks, but is sort of a jerk about it, Rawls seems to address this in a calm but commonsense way that I really appreciate. We have social and economic inequalities – it's just a fact of life, and we're always going to have them; Nietzsche seems to be telling Marx, "revolt all you like, Karl – we're just going to have a redistribution of inequalities, but never an elimination of them," and that seems accurate here as well. Taking this into account in a very realistic manner, Rawls seems to be saying, "alright, if we've got to have inequalities, what can we do to make sure they're as fairly distributed as possible?" That being established, we can move on to the two conditions he'll place on inequalities to make sure they're as fairly distributed as possible.

Facing the perennial reality of inequalities, Rawls' first condition of the second principle[182] he places on them is that they must be "attached to positions open to all under conditions of fair equal opportunity." We're used to seeing employers (and just about everybody else, nowadays) providing a lengthy (and growing) list of those against whom they officially don't discriminate when hiring; think of this as roughly the same sort of list, but instead of getting a benefit (e.g., a job or benefits, in this case, you have an equal opportunity to get a *negative* impact in your life – an inequality. Think of this as a principle of equal liberty[183] – we (or at least we *ought*) to have an equal freedom from obstacles in our path when we stand to encounter good or bad, i.e., benefits or inequalities. It also serves to establish the equal basic liberties we can expect our fellow citizens and our government to uphold and enforce on our behalf, and those that can be expected of us. They are freedom of conscience, we may think whatever we like; freedom of association, we may hang out with whomever we like; freedom of expression, we may express ourselves in any way we like (provided it doesn't infringe on the rights or liberties of others); and finally, freedom of democracy, we may vote how or for whomever we like. And this last one is legitimately that – not a Hobson's choice like Stalin's "vote for any candidate you like, but I'm the only one on the ballot" or Ford's "they can have any color they like, so long as it's black!"

The second condition placed on "permissible inequalities" is that they must be to the greatest benefit of the least advantaged members of society. Now, this should not be mistaken for trickle-down economics, nor for Marxism – we're not taking anything away from the most privileged or the bourgeoisie in order to bring them down to the level of the lower class/proletariat, as this is sometimes misinterpreted as promoting. Rather, we're bringing that less-privileged group up, so at least their opportunities are on par with the more-privileged. If folks are so dead-set on comparing this to economic theorems, the Laffer curve is probably their best option, though in this case, rather than taxing at 0% or 100%, think of it as providing opportunity neither at the top nor the bottom of the spectrum, but putting everyone on equal footing and a level playing field, squarely in the middle of the arrangement. The official name for this second part of the second principle is the "difference principle," and the real notions is that inequalities are fair (sounds like an oxymoron, but isn't) when the least well-off, whoever they may be, are better off than they would be under alternative social arrangements. At first blush, that really doesn't sound all that bad, seems like a good idea, etc., but there's a few problems potentially lurking under the surface that we should at least address, even if we don't have time to really "solve" them here.

The "well-off" part is particularly tricky. Just who's to say who's what degree of well-off, and in what respect? Say for instance we have someone flying at the highest heights of the financial stratosphere, but dumb as a sack of hammers; or an erudite young scholar who finds himself impecunious to an extent that church mice would look down upon – what about them? On the one hand they're extremely well-off, but on the other hand, they're severely impoverished; one of the drawbacks of Rawls' theory (in my own humble opinion) is that it fails to address just which sense of well-off we are or ought to be concerned with,

---

[182] A flowchart would probably be helpful at this point...

[183] It's sometimes also referred to as the "liberty" principle, but it refers to the same thing either way.

and what to do with the counterbalancing factors, if any. Another concern deals with the "better off" aspect of the principle – just how much better off must we help them be? Let's say you're literally penniless, and I come along, and in my great generosity that will be recorded in story and song, and I give you a penny (a nice, new, shiny one!); technically you're better off, but not substantively so. If the theory doesn't specify to what extent or how much better off you must be, how can we realistically and reliably apply it? Sure, common sense probably prevails here, but these are questions we ought to consider when deciding how applicable the theory might be.

The Original Position

Rawls rationalizes the principles he presents by arguing that they're what ought to result from the hypothetical rational choices made by a group of free and equal people. "Hypothetical" should tell us firstly that he's not a hard and fast Kantian, slavishly avoiding such constructions, and secondly that it's a "for instance" rather than an actual thing they're going to do; think of it as "imagine a situation in which X were the case..." It's "rational" in that we're not being subjected to an emotional appeal like on the commercials, where just a dollar a month will feed little so-and-so in a third world country; rather, it *must* present rational premises that lead to a rational conclusion. "Choice" tells us that there are options to be decided between, and we're not stuck with whatever benefits the majority, whatever duty dictates be done without concern to consequences, of whatever would be exemplify certain virtues, etc. The people are free in the sense that they're not under and coercion and enjoy the basic liberties discussed earlier; and they're equal in that no one opinion or vote will count for any more than any other. This whole arrangement is what he refers to as the "original position."

The Veil of Ignorance

In order to make sure that everyone in the original position actually follows the rules set forth (i.e., the requirements just described), Rawls adds the additional stipulation that the free and equal folks who are party to this decision making process do so from behind a "veil of ignorance." Behind the veil of ignorance, which again, remember is only a hypothetical veil, people are deprived of all particular information about themselves and their social position; you don't know if you're male or female, what your race or religion is, if you're gay or straight, disabled or not, etc. This is all in order to ensure (as best as possible) that they will choose under free and fair conditions that aren't biased for or against anyone. Say for instance you're deciding a policy that will benefit everyone, except a small fringe group, and you make it as obscure as you can think of, just to make it as remote and unlikely as possible; and then you end up being part of that group yourself – uh-oh. The veil of ignorance is largely designed to make sure that no one group will be either targeted or benefitted over and above members of any other group.

Fair Conditions and Practical Application

According to the theory, a choice made under hypothetically fair conditions will result in fair principles being chosen, and the society that allows itself to be guided in this way and by these principles could be called a fair society and would be considered to treat its citizens fairly – all of which could be substituted with "just" and "justly" just as easily. It may be hard to think of a time when something like this has actually been tried and succeeded, and I can only think of one instance in which this has actually been done, now an example over two decades old – the 1990 Americans with Disabilities Act (ADA). If you or someone you know is or ever has been wheelchair-bound, on crutches, or otherwise inhibited with regard to your ease of getting around and faced a flight of stairs, a high stoop, or similar impediment, then you know just why we have this particular Act in place. If you haven't been or aren't in any of these situations you can still imagine what it would be like to be (sounds a bit like Hume) or see the need to legislate as if we could at any point find ourselves in such a position, so the theory is practically applicable, if only once in a while that we're able to easily observe.

What we're seeing here isn't completely unique nor particularly new – it's really just an updated take on the social contract tradition that's been with us since the beginning of the Early Modern Era (and theoretically since long before). We recall from Hobbes that all the social contract theory really is is an account of what rational individuals would agree to in a state of nature in terms of establishing a legitimate government and the political authority by which it would be administered. Recall also that this is always only ever hypothetical - a thought experiment to help us decide what we might do in the absence of extant political structures and when individuals find themselves as free and equal fitting their own abilities. Rawls takes this same notion, and adapts it to the question of social justice in such as ways that we arrive at the principles we'll follow not based on avoiding war or obeying obligations, but by following the plan of action that is impartial to all.

He's able to do this because he gives credit to humanity as being both rational and reasonable, two ideas that we might have up to this point considered practically synonymous, but they differ in important respects. We're still rational under the Rawlsian[184] scheme in the way that Aristotle had said we are – that is, we have the capacity to problem solve, think abstractly, live under the rule of law, etc., but we're also able to identify and seek out paths to achieve our goals. And we're reasonable to the extent that if we have goals and others have goals as well, we're able (if not always willing) to help them achieve theirs alongside our own, provided there's no other conflict(s) of interest. In other words, we can and do work cooperatively by establishing and then following mutually acceptable principles that regulate our social interactions. In this sense Rawls has quite a bit to offer us in terms of an approach to certain types of ethical problems, but it might be difficult to apply his methodology in more pedestrian, day-to-day moral considerations, in much the same way as it would be difficult to test *all* our actions as categorical imperatives or according to the memoriter verses. For certain things though (like the ADA), we'd be hard-pressed to think of a better approach than Rawls' at least in terms of fairness.

---

[184] You get the idea at this point, and I know it sounds silly, but yes – it's pertaining to Rawls and his philosophy, just like you might expect.

Chapter 21: Review and Wrap-Up

Wow – that was a bunch of ethicists! But have we answered the question with which we began, that is, "why take an Ethics class or read an Ethics text?" Maybe, maybe not – I certainly hope so though. Moral philosophy is currently the most active area of professional academic philosophy, especially the specializations that deal most directly with medicine and business. Sure, we still have folks who are specialists in the Scottish Enlightenment, German Aesthetic Movement, and just about anything and everything else you can think of, but most of us in teaching positions are teaching Ethics. Why? Because clearly they're needed,[185] and we have a lamentable cultural tendency to dismiss them as part of religion, and either 1) assume the religious leaders have it covered, or 2) toss the baby out with the bath water so to speak in our increasingly secular society. Now, that's not a criticism – not of society, not of religion, and not (necessarily) of academia – it just is what it is. But back to the present topic at-hand, that's what I set out to accomplish in writing this book, and hopefully I have done so – given you an idea of the basic tents of Ethics in a tolerable, if not enjoyable, way, with you now having (provided you didn't just skim the whole thing – you know who you are) a pretty well-rounded understanding of Ethics, roughly equivalent to if you'd sat through my seminar all semester.[186]

In order to wrap this whole thing up, I'd like to go over a few of the major issues being dealt with in modern academic and applied Ethics, as well as briefly gloss over a few of the figures we skipped by in the contemporary era – because you know you're wondering what/who else is out there. As part of this, we'll look at some of the questions addressed, get a bit of a refresher on normative, applied, and meta-Ethics, and see about where we end up...

Questions Addressed

First and foremost, recall moral philosophy is not something merely studied, but something *done* – we're interested in what can be realistically done with these concepts when they're practically applied to real-life contentious issues. This isn't to say that we can always solve them or pronounce on them finally establishing a reference point that will be thenceforth followed blindly, but it can give you an idea of what principles are at work, and what the implications of employing those principles might be. We want to make sure that we're not simply engaging in maximin reasoning though, either (something Rawls has been accused of) – we're not merely trying to get the most benefit out of a worst-case scenario, but rather to see if we can establish some genuinely helpful and compelling ideas to give ourselves and others a standpoint from which to engage, to judge morally, and ultimately to act.

---

[185] A quick flip through the cable channels or even the nightly news should demonstrate this.

[186] But of course without the early class time, commute, and so on...

Many if not all moral issues can be distilled down to the question of right action – just what makes a given action right (or wrong), and how we ought to interpret that action in variety of lights and situations (if indeed the situations matter, with apologies to Kant). Related to this are the requirements we place on justice, which certainly isn't made an easier given the wide variety of understandings and definitions of just what justice is to begin with. Regardless of our other interests, it should be clear at this point that if we can settle on a basic understanding of justice that we're willing to accept for ourselves and promote to others, that's going to speak volumes with regard to what we will then view as right action. Inevitably connect to this are our understanding of the virtues that make life good, especially the question, "which ones must we have or cultivate, if any at all?" No one really addressed this – not even Aristotle, so we're left with the tricky proposition of picking the virtues we ought to seek out in others, habituate ourselves to practice and become, and ultimately have no better answer than recourse to our understanding of right action, justice, and the like.

The question of whether or not there are universally valid moral principles is one that comes up frequently – especially in our increasingly globalized world – and this is predictably when things also get a little uncomfortable for most of us. For starters, we have a pretty easy time coming up with universally valid good things, but they tend to be on the shallow or sentimental side – everyone should smile, recycle, not steal, and so on. These are all well and good, but they're not particularly poignant or earth shattering, and so most are inclined to politely dismiss them. On the other end of the spectrum, it's easy to come up with universally valid (or so we would hope) bad things; those that come to mind most quickly are crimes of sexual predation and child molestation. But here's where we run into problems – both those things, heinous though we consider them to be, are perfectly acceptable in some cultures; does that mean we're right and they're wrong? We can't both be right, and we can't just "agree to disagree," either – to say that, "well, it's not *my* ethics, but it's okay for them because it's their *culture*" is simply a cop out and a rather sad attempt to avoid moral responsibility. *We* don't, for instance, approve of female circumcision, but other cultures do, and since it's often presented in the context of religious justification, we get all awkward and squeamish in corrected others with regard to their adherence to the belief and/or practice. But uncomfortable as this might make us, this is the bailiwick of modern applied Ethics.

How about the basis of moral obligation and the source(s) of our moral motivation(s)? Without delving too deeply into Descartes' mind/body problem, just how can my immaterial mind make my material body do things, and in this case, perhaps even more compelling is how can moral concepts rattling around in that immaterial mind keep my material body from doing things it might find enormously satisfying if simply left to its own devices? The question of just what hold moral obligations hold over us is a compelling one, and as you might expect, moves significantly beyond what's contained in just in the individual theories themselves, and of course a great deal of work is being done addressing just this. As for what motivates us to behave morally, that's slightly different than the basis of our obligations in that we choose them for ourselves, at least somewhat free from the constraints of duty. We've surely seen enough attacks on pure altruism (poor Paul Ree) to know it's not quite as simple as that, but we do seem motivated to behave in certain ways,

163

and that's got to be based in and on *something* – just what that is though is again the source of contention and the beginning of a lot of philosophers' work.

Refresher: Normative Ethics

Most of what we've been spending our time doing, with perhaps the work of Nietzsche being an exception, has been in the realm of normative Ethics, which, just like the name implies, establish norms of our moral behavior and judgment. This is also where we spend our time identifying which are the substantive principles and values we use to assess actions or policies, and then argue for or against them. Notions of what good, bad, evil, etc. mean are generally assumed to be understood, or at least not directly focused on as independent from the theory, and the focus instead are things like our conduct, the end(s) of our action(s), our states of character, our social structures and public policies, and so on. The four broad categories of normative theories we've covered include (in chronological order) virtue theory, utilitarianism, Kantianism, and existentialism. We could go through conduct, ends of action, and the rest, but it's going to vary so widely according to the vagaries of the different theories, that you'd be better off to look over each one, asking these questions and applying these theories.

Refresher: Applied Ethics

Welcome to the not-so-happy land of contention and hurt feelings – this is where we apply all the normative theories just discussed to social issues, actions, policies, and the like. This is where we encounter biggies like abortion, physician-assisted suicide, capital punishment, affirmative action, questions of when wars are justified, and so on. Clearly, this is several books all their own, just waiting to be written. To that end, we're not even going to mess with it here. Why? Because we ultimately end at one of two extremes; on the one end (not necessarily the lower one, except in my personal estimation) we've got ethical relativism – that's the "it's cool for them, but I don't approve of it, just the same, who am I to say their wrong or evil, and let's agree to disagree." Argh – that drives me nuts! Sorry, but at the end of the day, one of us has to be wrong – and by extension, immoral, unethical, and the whole nine yards. The other (perhaps preferable) end of the spectrum is a moral absolutism, where guns are stuck to, but few are convinced our opinions are rarely changed. There you see, is the root of our contention because one way or other, someone is going home butt-hurt from this discussion – and that's precisely why we're leaving it for another day, another book, and so on. So moving right along, we'll continue our refresher and wrapping this whole thing up...

Refresher: Meta Ethics

Meta-Ethics is generally considered the most cerebral, and by extension the most academic, but that doesn't have to mean it's necessarily also the scariest – just the most difficult for us to articulate exactly what we mean – especially in a way that we can get whomever we're talking with to agree with us. This is the part of moral discourse where we engage in a discourse about the discourse itself.[187] This is also where we agree to the terms based on which we'll make our distinctions between factual claims and value claims – exactly what they sound like, respectively, but which people especially passionate on either side of any given debate will tend to mistake for one another. Also included here is the delightfully slippery slope down which we slalom between and amongst the subtle differences of meaning of moral terms like "right" and "good" and the rest. Now when we get into this area of Ethics, we tend to get a bit more abstract than we would be likely to encounter when covering more normative content, and this is why we have done relatively little in this area. Generally you also find that philosophers working in this area are a bit less likely to (openly) commit to a specific normative theory, however, generally our meta-ethical views will inform our individual normative views (and vice-versa).

---

[187] Again, we seem to almost need a flow chart here…

Afterword

It seems abrupt to me now, having been working on writing this text for the better part of a semester and more, to leave things here, but that's about it for Ethics – at least for now. Now I can't make any guarantees, but if you've read this whole thing from front to back (you glutton for punishment, you) then you ought to have a pretty good understanding of this thing we call Ethics. Hopefully you will forevermore think of this as something done, and not something merely read or discussed. Beyond that, I hope you've enjoyed it; I know it may seem crazy compared to all the "useful" pursuits that someone could study, work in, and teach, to go into Ethics, but I have, and I love it, and I hope that at this point, if you don't share my love, you at least understand passion for it, and the fun I have sharing it with my students and readers. So thank you for reading, thank you for sharing your very precious time with my work, and thank you for being at least a bit of an Ethics nerd for having picked up this book in the first place.

Printed in Great Britain
by Amazon

13407603R00099